Parks for Profit

Parks for Profit

Leslie Bella

Harvest House

Deposited in the Bibliothèque Nationale of Québec, 3rd quarter 1987

Typography and cover: Joanna Gertler

For information, address:
Harvest House Ltd., 1200 Atwater Ave., Suite No. 1
Montreal, Canada   H3Z 1X4

Canadian Cataloguing in Publication Data
Bella, Leslie
    Parks for profit

Includes index.
Bibliography: p.
ISBN 0-88772-033-1

1. National parks and reserves—Canada—
History. 2. Parks policy—Canada. I. Title.

FC215.B44 1987   333.78'3'0971   C87-090067-6
F1011.B44 1987

Dedication

Parks for Profit *is dedicated to the idealistic men and women of Canada's two national parks movements, and to the men who worked in the national parks for less than a living wage, building many of the facilities we enjoy today. Thank you.*

Leslie Bella.

❧ Contents ❧

Preface

Canada's decision to preserve vast areas of wilderness in national parks seems to me both wonderful and strange. Wonderful, because in the twenty years I have lived in this country I have grown to love those parks. I have hiked, cross-country skied, camped, canoed and swum in them, and they are a glorious heritage. Strange, because Canada is economically dependent on the export of natural resources. Furs, fish, wheat, timber, coal, oil, gas and hydroelectric power — these staples have been crucial to Canada's economic well being. How could Canada devote so many areas with timber, coal, fish and other resource potential, to national parks?

Why did Canada, a country dependent on natural resources, decide that some of those resources should not be exploited for profit, but preserved in national parks? My research has revealed a simple answer — that most of Canada's national parks were created as another form of natural resource exploitation. Canada's scenery is itself a resource, but one that cannot be exported. If scenery cannot be exported, then the resource can only be profitably exploited if tourists are imported. The Canadian and the provincial governments, the railroads, and the smaller businesses which serve the tourists arriving by car or plane, all have promoted national parks as a stimulant to profitable tourism.

Profit, though, was not always the dominant motive. Preservation sometimes gained ascendency. Conservation groups, bureaucrats, and some politicians tried to defend national parks against the profit motive. I hope *Parks for Profit* will guide those who would save Canada's national parks from economic imperatives.

Acknowledgments

I wish to recognize the cheerful assistance of archivists and librarians with Parks Canada Documentation Centre, the Canadian Archives, the Glenbow Foundation in Calgary, the Rocky Mountain Archives in Banff, and the Universities of Alberta and Carleton. Also, I thank those people who gave me access to documents in their personal collections, or gave time to share their memories or to provide me with information.

I am grateful also for the generosity of my colleagues at the University of Alberta, who worked out ways of releasing me from teaching so this work could be completed. My university also defrayed some of the necessary research expenses.

Finally, I wish to thank my family and friends, who encouraged me to believe that the project was possible and who supported me to its completion.

This book has been published with the help of a grant from the Social Science Federation of Canada, using funds provided by the Social Sciences and Humanities Research Council of Canada.

Introduction

National parks are supposed to be about preservation. Over a hundred countries have set aside more than 1,000 such parks, covering about 2 per cent of the earth's land surface. The United States established the first at Yellowstone, and has since created many others. Ecuador tried to protect the Galapagos in a park, though without sufficient funding to supervise visitors. Almost 25 per cent of Tanzania is set aside for wildlife and nature preservation. South Africa, for all that country's other problems, has superb national parks. In Nepal visitors hike through a national park to Mount Everest.[1]

Not all parks, though, meet the standard for recognition by the United Nations.[2] A national park must be preserved close to its natural state and also provide for visitors. This implies a conflict between preservation and use.[2] In a capitalist economy national parks have to combine profit from tourism with preservation from human impact. Competing resource exploitation also has to be considered. Compromises are always necessary. In the United Kingdom, for example, agriculture continues in the national parks, which do not meet UN standards. Kenyan national parks protect wildlife by restricting tourists to their cars. In Malaysia a hydro dam is planned in an increasingly rare tropical forest already within a national park.

Canadian national parks, too, represent a compromise between the demand for profit and the need for preservation. The Canadian compromise reflects her particular political and economic situation. Many national parks were only created for profit. Parks would stimulate tourism, whether the tourists arrived by rail to use the CPR hotel in Banff in the 1890s, or drive in the 1980s to

1

camp in the Maritimes. Sometimes the Canadian government has unilaterally created parks, using the centralization inherent in parliamentary government. In other instances the division of powers between federal and provincial governments has made national park creation difficult, and preservation has been sacrificed to profit.

As a result, most Canadian national parks have not been removed from economic development, but have been the focus of that development. In the late nineteenth century the railroads wanted national parks to protect their monopoly of tourist accommodation and transportation. Parks were not allowed to prevent exploitation of other profitable resources. Mining and lumbering continued. After policies were put in place in 1930 to prevent resource exploitation in the parks, industry opposed new ones. Resource sector profits were secured by rearranging park boundaries to exclude areas with mineral or hydro potential.

In the twentieth century the automobile brought a new form of tourism. The railroads lost interest in national parks. Instead, the small business people of Canada's towns and villages advocated national parks with good roads to and through them, to attract tourists. While Canada faced the major emergencies of war and depression national parks were not a high priority. But a side effect of these emergencies was a series of make-work programs building park roads and other facilities. After the Second World War Canada's post-war economic development program included the Trans-Canada Highway, built beside the cpr line and stimulating tourism in the parks. By the 1960s the demands for commercial expansion in the national parks was inexorable. Preoccupation with economic development led most provinces to prefer parks for profit rather than preservation. They supported resource exploration and tried to avoid locking resources into national parks. Provincial parks have been created instead, where resource extraction coexists with tourism. These parks are designed to attract tourists, rather than to restrict visitors in the interests of preservation.

Two national park movements in Canada have challenged the dominance of profit over preservation. In the first from 1910 to 1930 the Alpine Club and the National Parks Association tried to stop hydroelectric development in the parks. In the second, in the 1960s and 1970s, environmental groups tried to stop urbanization in the parks. They opposed new ski developments, new hotels, twinned highways and plans for larger townsites. National parks have affected native people. They insist new national parks not be confirmed until land claims are settled. Some continue their traditional life styles, hunting and trapping in the parks. Others serve tourists, either as Parks Canada employees or as private guides.

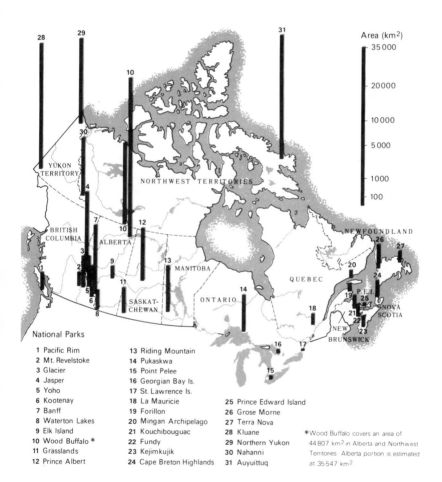

National Parks

1 Pacific Rim	13 Riding Mountain
2 Mt. Revelstoke	14 Pukaskwa
3 Glacier	15 Point Pelee
4 Jasper	16 Georgian Bay Is.
5 Yoho	17 St. Lawrence Is.
6 Kootenay	18 La Mauricie
7 Banff	19 Forillon
8 Waterton Lakes	20 Mingan Archipelago
9 Elk Island	21 Kouchibouguac
10 Wood Buffalo *	22 Fundy
11 Grasslands	23 Kejimkujik
12 Prince Albert	24 Cape Breton Highlands

25 Prince Edward Island	
26 Grose Morne	
27 Terra Nova	
28 Kluane	*Wood Buffalo covers an area of
29 Northern Yukon	44 807 km² in Alberta and Northwest
30 Nahanni	Territories. Alberta portion is estimated
31 Auyuittuq	at 35 547 km²

Area (km²)

35 000
20000
10000
5 000
1000
100

Map 1: The National Parks

Conservation groups have pressed for preservation of more Canadian landscape in new national parks. However, in Canada, public interest groups have less legitimacy and fewer opportunities than under the more pluralistic political process of the United States. As a result, the key influences towards preservation have not been pressure groups, but government itself. Ministers responsible for parks and members of Parks Canada staff have stimulated, and even at times simulated, public support of the parks.

These influences, pressing either for profit or for preservation, produced Canada's National Parks. In 1987, a century after the first park was reserved around Banff, Alberta, Canada has thirty-two national parks across all ten provinces, and in both the Yukon and the Northwest Territories (see Map 1). Each park results from a combination of forces — pressure from the railroads and the tourist industry; from resource industries and native peoples; from provincial governments and environment groups; from federal bureaucrats and (of course) politicians. The parks represent a range of solutions to the conflict between profit and preservation. Some recent northern parks, such as Northern Yukon Park, emphasize preservation, with very little provision for profit. Others, such as Gros Morne, Newfoundland and Banff were created explicitly to attract tourists. Profit was emphasized, rather than preservation. In some parks, such as Wood Buffalo and Pacific Rim, the resource lobby has been so effective that profit from natural resource exploitation was given priority over both tourism and preservation. The diversity of Canada's national park system is demonstrated in Appendix 1, describing the parks in order of their creation.

CHAPTER ONE

The
Canadian Pacific
Parks

*V*OYAGEURS OF THE HUDSON'S BAY and Northwest companies were the first to penetrate the mountains in search of profit. In the 1700s they traded with the Indians, seeking that ultimate opportunity for profit, a link to the Pacific and to oriental trade. Amongst this scattering of early explorers came missionaries, scientists and diarists who returned home to inspire people with both the grandeur and the potential profitability of the vast territories west of the Canadian Shield.

David Thompson was among the earliest white men to seek his fortune in the mountain ranges of western Canada, and to explore valleys now in national parks. On one expedition from the trading post at Rocky Mountain House, while bartering beads and tobacco, needles and fur, Thompson left his men and horses, and continued on foot until he saw "a sea of hills and peaks to the West".[1]

He could not forget this sea of mountains, and on the sixth of June, 1807, with his wife, their three small children, and a few men, returned to the Bow valley, entering what is today Banff National Park. They followed the traditional voyageur's route through Howse Pass, along the Columbia River to camp on Lake Windermere. Here Thompson built Kootenay House, the first trading post on the Columbia River. But the Piegan Indians were hostile. He sought another link between the Columbia River and the plains. In 1810 he travelled north to Brule, just east of the present boundaries of Jasper National Park. His party travelled up the Athabasca, passing the site of the present Jasper townsite and climbing beside the Whirlpool River. As they approached the pass they felt the warm Pacific winds, a relief after the bitter conditions on the eastern slopes of the Rockies. But with the milder climate came seven feet of wet heavy snow. The dogs could hardly drag the sleds.

Even under these conditions, Thompson recorded his admiration for the beauty around him: "The view now before us was an ascent of deep snow, in all appearance to the Height of Land between the Atlantic and the Pacific Oceans; it was to me an exhilarating sight. . . ."[2]

The party trudged through that snow, and then struggled down towards the Columbia River, through forests so thick that they felt like "pygmies" with their two-pound axes. One man was ill, and another deserted. The dogs were exhausted and the men resistant. At the junction of the Columbia and the Canoe rivers they rested, waiting for provisions. They built a boat, and when the ice broke up they struggled to haul it upstream, portaging past rapids and wading in icy water. By May 8 they were thankful to see the familiar scenery near the descent from Howse Pass.

While David Thompson did take time to note the scenic beauty in his diary, his travels were primarily motivated by profit. He penetrated the wilderness to develop trade and trade routes. But, by the time he arrived on the Pacific Coast on 11 July 1811, David Thompson had not only expanded the trading opportunities of the company he served. He had also visited, mapped and described in his journals the mountain scenery at the heart of what were later to become Canada's mountain national parks.

In 1824, at 39 years of age, Sir George Simpson was the new chief administrator of the Northwest Company, eager to end the ruinous rivalries threatening the fur trade. Simpson travelled the route established fifteen years earlier by Thompson, returning to the Banff area in 1841. His nickname "the little emperor" had been well earned, but because of his treatment of others rather than any luxurious lifestyle. He camped at Lake Minnewanka with no more to eat than a bit of pemmican and two partridges made into a "sort of burgoo, which served as breakfast and supper for eight hungry travellers". Sir George Simpson was on his lightning trip around the world, a real journey as exciting as the fiction of Jules Verne. His was the first "pleasure trip" into the mountains, the first made without economic motive. Simpson's written "narrative" of the expedition captured the imagination of easterners. In 1846 Sir George commissioned painter Paul Kane to commemorate his expanding empire. Kane wrote of his amazement at the "sublime and apparently endless chain of the Rocky Mountains", a sight greeted by the men "with a hearty cheer". Kane followed David Thompson's northern route through the Athabasca Pass, and wandered with his sketch pad down the Columbia valley. He returned to Edmonton in 1847, in time for Christmas, with his sketches brought to Simpson on men's shoulders.

Surveyors also sought their fortunes in the mountains. Palliser's was the first major expedition, sponsored by Britain to investigate the potential profitability of agriculture and other economic ventures in the Canadian West. All possible passes through the mountains had to be investigated, from the United States border and north to the Athabasca Pass. In 1858 Palliser's party penetrated the Kananaskis valley (now a major Alberta provincial park), hiking over to the Kootenay area (which in 1920 became Kootenay national park). Another member of the party camped at the lakes now within Waterton National Park. A third group, led by Dr. Hector, travelled into the Bow valley to the site of present day Banff, and through Vermillion Pass along a route used later for the Banff–Windermere Highway. From the Kootenay valley they followed the "Kicking Horse" river up to the pass that is now the route of the Trans-Canada Highway. They also found Bow Pass, from the Bow valley to the North Saskatchewan, but failed to reach the Howse or the Athabasca passes used by earlier explorers. They also failed to find a pass through the Selkirks, an even more impressive chain of mountains lying to the west of the Rockies.

The return of the Palliser expedition brought more excitement to eastern Canada. Their news suggested fortunes could be made in the uncharted western wilderness. Many set out, individually and in small groups, with few horses and minimal supplies, they lived off the land and prospected for minerals. They staked claims, and tried to finance them. Even before the arrival of the railroad, or the creation of the mountain national parks, there were many such men, and a few women, in the mountains. By the 1880s Silver City, half way between Banff and Lake Louise, had four working mines: the Pioneer, the Queen of the Hills, the Alberta, and a fraudulant gold mine run by two rascals called Patton and Pettigrew. The first claim had been staked by the Healy brothers, who were on their way to inspect it in 1883 when they met three other prospectors, Frank McCabe and the McCardell brothers. Shortly after this meeting the McCardell brothers and Frank McCabe discovered the hot springs at Banff, and set in motion the events that would lead to the creation of Canada's first national park.

THE RAILROAD AND THE WESTERN MOUNTAINS

By the 1880s Prime Minister Sir John A. Macdonald had become committed to his "National Dream". The West would be developed, to produce food, mineral resources and timber for central Canada. The West, in turn, would be a market for the products of industrial central Canada. His government collaborated with the CPR to build a railroad to link the country together. As the new line inched across the shield and the prairies towards the Rockies, the western mountains attracted even more people. Surveyors were looking for suitable mountain passes, and locating the rail right-of-way. Government and railroad officials sought timber for railroad ties, and coal to fuel the steam engines that would soon haul trains through the mountains. After the surveyors came the contractors and their men and horses laying the road bed, then the teams laying the rails.

More people brought more opportunities for profit. Businesses sprang up along the route of the future railroad. The workers needed to eat and drink, so food and liquor were sold. Bunkhouses and hotels were built. In Silver City workers had a choice of the Queens, the Castle Park Hotel and the Miner's Home. But, these early hotels and eating places in the Banff area were not world-class tourist facilities — far from it. They were simple and inexpensive, intended for those who spent their days building railroads, driving teams of horses and clearing the forest.

Silver City also had a general store, restaurants, rooming houses, saloons and last but not least (in the view of one visitor) gambling dens, many of which were run in the rear of some of the restaurants or saloons. The law was pretty lax, and businesses stayed open all night. Moonshiners did well, helping to make the community "one of thrilling adventure".[3] A detachment of North-West Mounted Police, including tough "Dog Face Brown", tried to prevent complete deterioration to the law of the jungle. Eventually, though, Silver City's bubble burst, as the mines failed. Businesses in Silver City disappeared as quickly as they had come. A geologist called Coleman travelled through these mountain boomtowns while evaluating mining potential in the Rockies. He arrived at Lake Louise, then called Laggan, just west of Silver City:

> It was evening, and my eyes turned from the mountains across the valley of the Bow River to the "city", temporary and hideous, where night quarters must be found. The chief hotel seemed to be the "Sumit" House (Summit?), a low-browed log building with a floor of "puncheons" — slabs split with the axe — instead of boards.
>
> When darkness fell I paid for my bed in advance, according to the cautious practice of the hostelry, and retired to the grey blankets of bunk No. 2, second tier, in the common guest chamber, trying to shut out sights and sounds from the barroom by turning my back. An hour or two later another man scrambled into the bunk, somewhat the worse for whiskey, and tucked himself into the blankets beside me. It appeared that my half dollar had paid for only half the bed.[4]

Accommodation was less than luxurious. The landscape was also losing some of its purity. Sparks from the steam engines, as well as lightning storms, had caused forest fires. In 1884, a year before the park was created at Banff, the valleys were hung over with smoke. The Spray valley, the Kananaskis valley, and the lower part of the Bow valley were all burned over.[5] In the late 1880s, when the CPR began to exploit the Banff area for tourism, the company had to touch up their picture postcards, adding green to the skimpy forest of black bristles.

Travel conditions were primitive all through the mountain valleys. The bed that Coleman shared near Banff was luxurious compared with that along the tote road in the Rogers Pass through the Selkirks (later to become "Glacier" Park). He found "a ragged little clearing of burnt stumps with some big tents and square stacks of baled hay". One of the tents had a sign "Dew Drop Inn", so he did.

> The big tent was undivided, but the rear opened into a little tent where one could observe the whole staff of the hotel — proprietor, clerk, cook, and waiter — embodied in one dirty

man in his shirtsleeves, engaged in frying bacon over a cracked stove. The supper of hot bacon and beans and tea, with stewed dried apples as dessert, was soon on the board, and as soon eaten by the half dozen hungry guests who then gathered round the box stove, for the rainy night was cool four thousand feet above the sea.

A little later every one unrolled his blankets and chose his bed on the earthen floor, picking a spot where no stream dripped from the roof. The hotel sign was not unwarranted, for the dews of heaven "dropped in" at many places, and I shifted my bed more than once before securing a permanently dry corner.[6]

Coleman also thought an "uglier place probably never existed" than Revelstoke in the 1880s. The city was six months old, but fire had already destroyed canvas and log buildings and "many square miles of splendid forest". The remaining log buildings were blackened by soot, and "dismal black trunks" rose into a sky "still grey with smoke". The streets were paved with dust and ashes, and the residents frequently stopped work to "liquor up". In Revelstoke, though, Coleman had the comparative luxury of his own room. Instead of "clambering up to a bunk with all of the rest of the lodgers in the big chamber above" he was given one of a "dozen little chambers" in a lean-to of whip-sawn cedar. He could see his neighbour's candlelight through the cracks between the boards, but was otherwise private.

THE RAILROAD AND TOURISM

As the railroad was built, general manager William Van Horne worked with Prime Minister Macdonald to ensure its profitability. Van Horne thought the mountains could be a world class tourist attraction, and wanted to ensure that the CPR benefited economically. Current conditions in the mountain towns, however, would not meet the expectations of international travellers. Van Horne wanted to control development in the mountain valleys, to protect the scenery from squatting and enable the CPR to monopolize development.

Van Horne decided that a park reserve would provide development control and monopoly. He knew of the national parks movement in the United States, and of the parks at Yosemite and Yellowstone. In 1883, travelling west on his new railway, Van

Horne saw the Bow valley. He passed Lac des Arcs just after a fresh snow fall. The scenery impressed him. He asked William Pearce, a surveyor with the Canadian government's Department of the Interior, to arrange for reservation of a park. He suggested that title of the land for the park could rest with the CPR or with himself, to stop "despoilation by the advances of civilization in the guise of miners or lumbermen".[7] Van Horne would then "build a fine house on the island in the lake".[8]

Surveys were incomplete, so a park could not yet be reserved. Van Horne changed his mind when he saw Lac des Arcs the following spring. The snow was gone and the lake level very low, and Van Horne could hardly see the lake or the island because of a dust storm caused by high winds. Nowhere along the CPR mainline is there as much "swerving high wind" as at Lac des Arcs. For some time people chuckled as they passed "Van Horne's Park". Today a huge cement plant stands at Exshaw, where Van Horne wanted to build his national park.

THE HOT SPRINGS ARE DISCOVERED

Others with little capital and even less influence had found a more promising site for a park. After their meeting with the Healy's, the three prospectors, the McCardell brothers and Frank McCabe, rafted across the Bow River. The water was warm, and the men looked for a hot spring. They found a natural rock basin, filled with warm water from a natural spring. Beyond the pool they found a cave. They climbed down into it to find another pool even hotter than the first, roofed by sparkling stalactites. The three men enjoyed a bath, and dreamed of developing their discovery. William McCardell believed that "the visitation of anyone to this marvellous health resort" would be the only advertising necessary: "In a flare of vision we felt that this place would become one of the most famous resorts for both health amd pleasure for people from every part of the continent as well as people from every part of the world".[9]

The men made some minor improvements. They hauled the calcified logs out of the basin, and built a log platform and railing "in harmony with the natural environment". They inscribed a post with the announcement that W. M. McCardell, Thomas E. McCardell and Frank McCabe had "discovered and located" the cave and basin on the 7th of August, 1883. Visitors began to arrive, first a few prospectors. Then as the railroad approached the mountains, they heard construction echoing down the valley. The men visited the various camps, and invited men to the hot pool. One old friend congratulated them: "You fellows have the world by the tail with a downhill pull! Why this magic basin and pool have no computed value. It is the greatest thing I have ever seen. The Arkansas and the Yellowstone Springs is nothing in comparison with this wonder."

The three men tried to secure their claim to the springs. They tried to homestead the land, but were told there was no home-steading in the mountains. They tried to stake a mineral claim, only to be told it was not a "mineral property". They asked for rights as discoverers, but received only "evasive" replies. While tangling with government red tape, and trying to raise money for development, they made sure that one of them remained at the site to enforce their ownership. They built a cabin, using it for two years. Early in 1884 they found the upper hot springs, again mark-ing their find on a nearby tree.

The potential of the pool did not become more widely known until the three men squabbled. Frank McCabe got into "a disas-trous matrimonial arrangement", and needed money to buy him-self out. He forged his partners' signatures on a sale of his interest in the hot pool for $1,500, to D. B. Woodworth, a member of par-liament from Nova Scotia. The McCardells received legal help from James Lougheed, and Frank McCabe was arrested. He was released into William McCardell's custody, but continued to sell shares in his interest in the hot pool. The Minister of the Interior, Thomas White, was brought into the squabble. He visited the springs, but was less than encouraging. The government clearly wanted to take over the pool, and White suggested that the $1,500 for which McCabe had "sold" the cave and basin would be used to determine any compensation due to the discoverers.

The minister was followed by other important visitors. Two members of parliament, James Trew and S. Hesson predictably extolled the beauty of the scenery, and the glorious natural roof of the cave. They promised to help the men obtain homestead rights or some form of ownership of the hot pools. Van Horne also arrived. He was a heavy man, and McCardell put a safety rope around him when he climbed into and out of the cave. Van Horne commented: "These springs are worth a million dollars!"

Van Horne now knew that the cave and basin should be the

focal point of a park reservation. He again contacted William Pearce, who fully sympathised with Van Horne's objectives for development of the railroad company.[10]

A PARK RESERVE IS CREATED AT BANFF

William Pearce visited the cave and basin, and assessed the work by McCabe and the McCardells. He noted that the makeshift ferry across the Bow River was built from CPR railroad ties and telegraph wire. The "ladder" into the cave consisted of a spruce pole, with the branches cut six inches from the trunk. The stalactites were marvellous, and the pool "delightful to bathe in". Pearce "strongly recommended that a reservation be made". He drew up the order in council that established the park on 25 November 1885.[11] The creation of the reserve meant the discoverers had to be compensated. McCabe's claims, and claims of those to whom he had sold shares, were challenged by the McCardells. Squatters around the cave and basin also claimed a right to compensation. Pearce held a hearing, with himself as the "neutral" judge.

David Keefe, who had operated a boarding house near Banff station, was developing a hotel near the springs. The park would preclude such a development (at least by anyone other than the CPR), so he was awarded $100. McCabe and the McCardells received $675 to recognize their expenditures improving the springs and protecting their interest. Woodworth, the MP who had acquired rights (possibly through a forgery) from McCabe was awarded $1,000 to acknowledge his payments to McCabe and his financial outlay towards establishing a hotel.[12] Later McCardell signed a "quick claim" for $900, most of which he had already paid out in legal fees. In the end McCardell also got that year's rights to the hay along the railway tracks, which he sold to the mounted police. Then he went to work in the coal mine at Anthracite, just outside the new town of Banff.

Potential competitors to the CPR, and all the encroaching "miners and lumbermen" that might sully the scenery, had now been bought out. Although Van Horne did not hold title to the park, he had the next best thing. The government held title to the land, and was essentially sympathetic to the railroad and its friends — for the solvency of the CPR was essential to the electoral success of Macdonald's conservatives. Only the CPR and its friends and dependencies were to be allowed to do business in the park. Any business detrimental to CPR interests, such as McCardell's under-capitalized private development of the cave and basin, were excluded. First choice of location was given to the railroad company, in Banff National Park, and in all the other national parks established in the "Canadian Pacific's Rockies."

A CANADIAN PACIFIC PARK

A year after the creation of this first park reservation at Banff, in 1886, Prime Minister Sir John A. Macdonald returned from his first trip through the Rockies on the new Canadian Pacific Railway. He had ridden part way in the engine's cowcatcher, and had been deeply impressed by the scenery: "There may be monotony of mountains as there is of prairies, but in our mountain scenery there is no monotony. You go up from Calgary and climb to the summit of the first range of the Rocky mountains, and you see one description of grandeur. You plunge into the valleys, and rise up another range, and you have quite a different character, equally sublime. You plunge into another valley and then come the Selkirks, of unsurpassed beauty and grandeur, of magnificent and almost eccentric changes. You plunge into the valley of the Fraser and the magnificent canyons."[13]

He outlined his plans for a profitable mountain showplace: "I do not suppose in any portion of the world there can be found a spot, taken all together, which combines so many attractions and which promises in as great degree not only large pecuniary advantage to the Dominion, but much prestige to the whole country by attracting the population, not only of this continent, but of Europe, to this place. It has all the qualifications necessary to make it a great place of resort." This "great place of resort", though, was to benefit the CPR rather than the Canadian people.

BUSINESS DEVELOPMENT IN BANFF

The Canadian government had an agreement with the CPR giving the railroad the right to a large parcel of land adjacent to each station. In the park the government would not give the railroad outright ownership, but agreed to a 999-year lease. Leases for other homes and businesses in Banff lasted only 42 years. The CPR built the Banff Springs Hotel in 1887, and rebuilt it after the fire of 1926. The railroad company was also given a lease on land in

Banff townsite, which "could only be used for railroad purposes". In the 1930s this was exchanged for land adjacent to the hotel which is now used as a golf course. The land in the townsite was returned to the government, but only for park purposes.

The CPR's company doctor, R. G. Brett, was also given special privileges in the new tourist town. Brett had left school at 16, to apprentice to a doctor. He had made a fortune, and lost it again in Winnipeg's real estate boom of 1881. He joined the CPR as a doctor, to cover his debts.[14]

Brett arrived on the first CPR passenger coach to cross the Bow River in Calgary, in 1883. He set up business in the tent city on the CPR right-of-way at Banff, and by the end of the year he had established his first "Brett Hospital". When the park was established in 1885 he was not bought out by the government, but was offered his choice of locations for a combined hospital and hotel. Doctor Brett chose a prime site where the administration building now stands. The "sanitorium" (as it was then called) was, in the caustic words of one oldtimer "part hotel, part hospital, part pool room and part bar".

Dr. Brett's business grew, and he wanted to expand to the upper hot springs. A man called Whitman served meals from a tent there, and built a log cabin in 1886. His patrons "lolled on stretchers and soaked their aching limbs in a small pool within a cave". According to a grandson of Woodworth, the MLA from Nova Scotia who had purchased McCabe's interest, Dr. Brett "caused Mr. Whitman to leave the area". Dr. Brett established his second hotel, and built a log-lined pool for his patrons. Hot-spring water was piped down to his sanitarium below, and for twenty-five cents his patients could also use the publicly operated pool at the cave and basin first discovered by McCabe and the McCardells.

Brett was also responsible for the health of the miners in Bankhead and Anthracite, who had their pay docked to retain his services. Business developed steadily, and by 1909 Dr. Brett built a new hospital, also bearing his name. He also spent a period as MLA for the Northwest Territories and another as lieutenant governor.

Banff's primary attraction, both to Dr. Brett and to his patrons was the spring waters. The water was similar in content to the reknowned waters of Bath, England. Everyone knew, apparently, that either drinking or bathing in the waters improved the constitution. Brett hoped Banff would be as popular as Bath. His prospectus for investors suggested:

The popularity these Springs have attained among invalids for the cure of rheumatic and neuralgic afflictions, skin diseases and disorders of the blood, leaves no doubt as to the fact that a most profitable return will be made on this outlay. The proposed thermal establishment will be conducted along the lines of the celebrated German Spas, and will be the first of it kind on this side of the Atlantic, combining the treatment of these establishments together with the dietary treatment of the famous Battle Creek, Michigan, Sanitarium.

A government brochure also suggested the radioactive content of springs at both Banff and Bath could "ameliorate" various diseases. On the hillsides around the upper hot springs were discarded canes and crutches, and testimonials describing the miracles were written into rough boards:

"I had to be carried up to the springs", said one of these, "I could not bear even the motion of a carriage. I had not walked for two years and every movement was an agony. In three weeks after coming here I walked down to Banff, and in five I ran a foot race. Praise God."

"I threw away the crutches I had used for four years" said another of these testimonials to the healing of the Springs, "after I had been here ten days. I walked with a stick for two weeks and then threw that away too."

"A month after I began to take the baths", says another, "I climbed to the top of Sulphur Mountain. For five years before then I had not been able to walk without a crutch."[15]

Brett also represented to his investors the benefits of business within one of Canada's national parks: "Large sums of money are spent annually by the Dominion Government in beautifying [the park]. The Government has lately decided to enlarge the boundaries of the surrounding National Park of Canada, and to erect a museum, new Government Offices, Observatory Station, etc., etc. Plans are also being made to extend the system of excellent roads and trails which were laid several years ago, thus opening new fishing grounds and giving the tourist access to some of the most beautiful parts of the mountains."

Others also prospered under protection of the government and the CPR. Bill Brewster senior was first hired in Banff, in 1886, to do tricky "Swiss style" carpentry for the government's new bath houses at the cave and basin. The CPR was also preparing to build, and the community would expand. Brewster wrote his brother John that there were no milk cows between Calgary and Revelstoke. There was a promising opportunity for a dairy. John arrived, and did blacksmith work while he set up the dairy. He faced a problem, since park regulations allowed no more than two milk cows per lot. The town and the new hotel needed the milk, though, so he was allowed to rent pasture from the government at $100 a year. John's two sons, Bill and Jim, helped with the herd and explored the mountains with a Stoney Indian called William Twin. Their school work took a back seat, particularly after they found that money could be made guiding visitors on fishing and hunting expeditions. The CPR referred people to them, though their competitor Tom Wilson was the only one with the right to call himself "Guide to the CPR".

In 1900, financed by their father's dairy profits, they set up as outfitters and guides, complete with horses, equipment and manpower. The CPR sent them to a sportman's show in Madison Square Gardens, to promote travel in the Rockies, and this improved their business. A packing contract with a mining company involving Dr. Brett also produced a small profit. Then the CPR decided to unload its own outfitting services, and sold the Banff concession to the Brewsters. This allowed the brothers to build a large outfitting and livery empire under CPR protection.[16] The Brewsters outlived the railway age, becoming even more powerful in the age of the automobile.

THE CPR AND PARK REGULATIONS

In 1887, the year the reserve at Banff was confirmed as a park, William Van Horne, now vice-president of the CPR, asked a consultant Dr. J. S. Lynch to investigate Banff's "qualities as a resort for invalids and tourists, but especially in its relations with the Company's enterprises there, and more particularly with the hotel now being erected". Lynch was enthusiastic. He found that the medicinal properties of the springs had been tested and "proven beyond doubt to be highly beneficial in a large number of afflictions which cannot be treated at home". They were comparable to the most celebrated European spas. The scenery was "unrivalled", the valley a "perfect amphitheatre", and the great forest of pine trees were good for "pulmonary afflictions". Dr. Lynch, however, was anxious that the company's interests be protected, since after all as he wrote: "The interest of your company in all that affects the region, or for a long time at least, be larger than any other single interest, or rather will form a greater part of the public interest than any other represented there, it is reasonable to suppose that you desire to be in a position to ask of the government the adoption and carrying out of such views with regard to the development and management of the place as in your opinion you may consider most advantageous."[17]

Dr Lynch recommended government ownership and operation of the hot springs, to ensure they would be "salutary, safe and cleanly", and (of course) accessible to CPR customers. Water should only be leased to "hotels of reputable character" and hospitals under license and inspected by the government. He detailed minutely the kind of bathhouse to be built, with a place for cooling off, an attendant, and clean towels. He recommended a layout for the park, with more "short roads" for visitors, through the pine forests and to Lake Minnewanka. To ensure an appropriate tone and atmosphere he recommended the "local government of the Park should be a wholesome terror", with a police force, licenses for all hotels and boarding houses and strict regulations to ensure that livery companies, stablekeepers and hackmen had "sound vehicles and tractable animals". And "as for roughs, gamblers, improper female characters and saloon keepers, they should not be allowed to obtain a foothold at all, and their complete exclusion cannot be commenced too soon".

By 1890 new regulations were ready. Parks officials told Dr. Brett he had "pretty much" what he wanted, but to keep it to himself "until the regulations are out".[18] The regulations of 1890 required a license for all business activities, set standard tarrifs for the commercial use of horses and horse-drawn vehicles, and confirmed the bathing business regulations in the Rocky Mountain Parks Act of 1887. The road to Minnewanka suggested by Lynch was one of the first to be built, and a steamboat placed on the lake.[19] Lynch's suggestions to Van Horne, it seems, had been communicated to government and carried out.

These recommendations made Banff a very different place. Gone were the "Dew Drop Inns" and "Summit Houses" Coleman had visted five years earlier. There were none of the gambling dens or moonshiners of Silver City. Banff would not be a lively working men's town, but a tourist town of beauty and decorum, a place suitable for middle- and upper-class young ladies and their arthritic elderly relations.

Another hot spring in the Rockies, that at Radium in British Columbia, remained outside the national parks until 1922. Experience at these pools shows what might have happened at Banff, if the profit-oriented CPR had not persuaded the government to create a park to control tourist development. By 1900 the bathhouse at Radium consisted of a blanket on a pole. When the blanket was "up" someone was already bathing. People brought their own blankets, and could stay in tents for two dollars a week, and were given enough hay for a bed. Candles stuck in whiskey bottles provided light. The pool was a favourite place for road workers and lumberjacks to sweat it out after a bout of heavy drinking. Most customers were men, and drunken brawling was common. This was hardly a suitable place for the class of tourist sought by the CPR, and was what Lynch intended to avoid.[20]

Promoting the Canadian Pacific Rockies

The CPR began promotion of the "Canadian Pacific Rockies" with an invitation to the Canadian Medical Association to hold their annual meeting in the Park in 1888. A group of leading journalists were invited, and a special coach toured all the CPR's hotels, including those in the parks. Editorials followed in many leading North American newspapers, praising the Canadian Rockies. Church leaders were also invited to travel CPR through the Rockies. The enthusiasm of one of this party, Mr. Leggo, was worth more than any advertising copy:

> The generosity of the authorities of the Canadian Pacific railway in offering to the delegates of the late Provincial Synod a special car, with liberty to "lie over" when and where we desired, was too tempting to be passed by.... the mountain scenery of the Banff district — perhaps the most delightful of the whole route, where the eye travels from the vast distant ranges, faintly visible in the distance, and gradually comes to the foreground with infinite varieties of tone; the exciting passage of the more tumultuous river through the Kicking Horse Pass, the silent grandeur of the Selkirks, the terrific rush on through the 125 miles of the Thompson and Fraser canyons, and then the placid flow of the latter to the oceans, form a diversity of beauties which travellers admit to be unrivalled on the coast.

The churchmen breakfasted at Dr. Brett's sanitarium — "a very pleasant and excellent house". They spent "all day doing the springs and the park", returning to their "moving home" in the evening. They met the park superintendent, and his wife, and watched an artist sketching the scenery — though the mountains were too unbelievable to be captured in a painting!

European tourists were another target of CPR promotion. But a country described as "our lady of the snows", was in reality more like "homeless grandeur" to one English poet.[21] Another traveller wrote to his mother on the Banff Springs Hotel notepaper, complete with a fine engraving of a stag. He complained of crowded and uncomfortable Pullman cars, and pine forests "mostly burned, with sticks on end and new growth about half the height". The weather was cold. But he was still enthusiastic. The sun shone, the Rockies were wonderful, and the snow the finest he had ever seen.[22]

The promotion was effective, and Banff prospered. The town soon had a boat-house on the Bow River; a general store, a newspaper, a plumber, a painter and a tailor; several hotels in addition to the CPR's Banff Springs; the various businesses promoted by Brett and by the Brewsters; and Banff's first souvenir shop, the Goat Curio Shop owned by Norman Luxton. Visitors increased steadily. In 1887 3,000 visited the park, increasing to 7,250 in 1891 and levelling off at around 8,000 in 1901. In 1888 5,000 bathers each paid twenty-five cents to use the cave and basin.

MORE CANADIAN PACIFIC PARKS

National Parks Created Before 1910

National Park	Year	Location
Banff	1885	Western Alberta, on CPR through Rockies
Yoho	1886	Eastern BC, on CPR through Rockies
Glacier	1886	Eastern BC, on CPR through Selkirks
Waterton Lakes	1895	Extends Glacier Park, US, into Canada
Jasper	1907	Western Alberta, on CN through Rockies

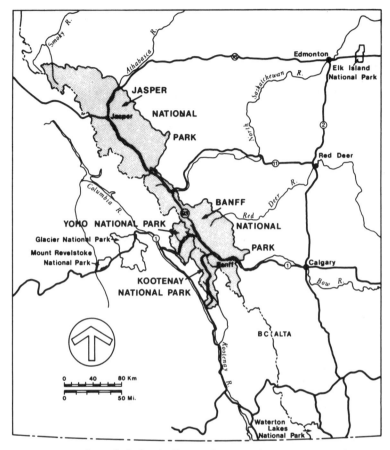

Source: Parks Canada: Planning Scenario for the Four Mountain Parks, 1984
Map 2: The Canadian Pacific Parks

While Banff was the primary showplace in the "Canadian Pacific Rockies", national parks were also created along the railroad throughout the western mountains. In 1883, Sandford Fleming, the CPR's chief engineer before Van Horne, was inspecting the Rogers Pass through the Selkirks and proposed another park. In 1886–87 thirty square miles was reserved in the pass, including Mount Sir Donald and the Great Glacier. The railway company wanted to lighten the dining cars hauled over the Rogers Pass; they built Glacier House two miles west of the pass. By 1888 1,000 people had stayed there. In 1890 the hotel was expanded to thirty-six rooms, and by 1898 12,000 had stayed there. A town of 7,000 developed, housing railroad and construction workers.

But the Rogers Pass was a hostile place. Avalanches killed eight in 1899, and covered the town again in 1910. Then the rescue party was caught in another avalanche. Sixty were killed, and the CPR decided to tunnel under the pass. The workers moved to the west end of the tunnel, in the Illecillewaet valley. The Rogers Pass fell into disuse. Glacier House was now accessible only to enthusiastic mountaineers. Much to the chagrin of the Alpine Club of Canada, which had enjoyed the remote mountain pass, the hotel was closed in 1928. Glacier Park became a wilderness once more, and remained so until after the construction of the Trans-Canada Highway through the Rogers Pass in the 1950s.[23]

Yoho Park, which borders the western edge of Banff National Park, was created in the same year as Glacier. Tom Wilson, a guide who had competed with the Brewsters, had explored Yoho in 1884, with two prospectors, Coldwater George and Hotwater Jimmie Hanson. His companions achieved their notoriety because of their longstanding argument about the best way to drink water — in hot whiskey or in cold! The CPR built Mt. Stephen House in Yoho in 1886, but Banff remained the main focus of their tourist development. Tom Wilson wanted the CPR to bring more pack-train business his way, into Lake Louise and Yoho. So, in 1897 he paid a German professor, Jean Habel, to take photographs and write an article.[24] But Banff remained the tourist centre, and the Brewster's business expanded faster than Wilson's.

In the Yellowhead valley, north of Banff, hot springs were found at Miette. Jasper National Park was created when the Grand Trunk built a second transcontinental railroad through the Yellowhead Pass. Grand Trunk was an old rival of the CPR, but less successful. The company was forced into receivership in 1916, and its assets were combined with those of Canadian Northern in 1920 to form Canadian National. This crown corporation still operates Jasper Park Lodge today, although few passenger trains reach the townsite.

The only early park without a railroad was Waterton Lakes. The United States already had a popular national park, known as "Glacier Park", on the south side of the Canada–United States border. A lake straddles the international boundary, and boaters from the United States visited the Canadian end of the lake with no Canadians ready to sell them anything. Waterton Lakes National Park was created to take advantage of this commercial opportunity. The area was also popular with south Albertans, who fished and hunted around Waterton. After the park was created roads were built, and Canadians could also visit more easily. The park was successful, with 2,000 visitors in 1910, and 20,000 by 1921.

ENJOYING THE CANADIAN PACIFIC ROCKIES

The experience of visiting the Canadian Pacific parks is epitomized in the published travel diaries of Gordon Brinley. He travelled by train to Banff with his wife, a painter who illustrated his books. She was delighted by the observation car: "It is fine on such a blue and golden day to be sitting out of doors while travelling through beautiful country. This observation car is built with an open section at each end and a closed section, mostly glass, in the middle. Indoors or out one can see everything. Dan and I, of course, are sitting in the open section at the end of the car, and of the train, which at this moment is skirting through the wide flat green land that rises on each side to rolling hills. All is blue above us; only a few opalescent clouds are to be seen where hilltops meet the sky."[26]

They enjoyed the tea-houses introduced by the CPR, and now sold to others. They visited some of the lodges in the wilderness that had also belonged to the CPR, such as the one still existing at Lake Ohara. Their experiences were very different from those of Coleman in this same valley before the creation of the park. The Brinleys experienced a luxurious and civilized view of the Canadian mountains. They travelled with the Brewsters, and stayed in the CPR's hotels. At Château Lake Louise, Brinley and his "Duchess" looked into the mountains through polished glass, over flowered terraces and a well kept lawn:

> If you have ever sat at a table for two beside a window in the dining-room of the Chateau, you'll feel again as you read this what the Duchess and I felt at breakfast on our first morning at Lake Louise. You will remember the high, wide windows, so clear one does not realize glass is between the tables and the tall spires of blue delphinium outside; rather, one seems to be out of doors gazing at the peaks of Lefroy and Victoria mountains that tower 11,000 feet above their reflections in this loveliest of lakes.
>
> On the morning I speak of the delphinium and mountains

were not all the picture upon which we gazed while enjoying what might be called a "pontifical" breakfast. There were yellow poppies that swept down terraces to meet emerald lawns, which in turn ran to the edge of the lake's blue waters, stopped by the mirrored likeness of dark forest, shining peaks, and snowy Victoria Glacier.[27]

With the advent of the automobile, the railroad's monopoly on passenger transportation would end. But fifty years of control and favoured treatment by governments had allowed the Canadian Pacific Railroad, and to a lesser extent Canadian National, to build on the best sites, to finance the best facilities, and to control their business and physical environment. When the Brinleys visited the parks in 1937, and even when we visit them today, they are still to a large extent the "Canadian Pacific Parks". They were built not to preserve a natural landscape, but to centralize control of that landscape in the hands of the railroads. That control was used to reduce competition in the parks, and to restrict access to the mountains. Businesses that might be patronized by the working class were not sufficiently aesthetic. Access to the mountains was provided instead to upper- and middle-income tourists willing to pay substantial sums for a sanitized view of the mountains.

CHAPTER TWO

Mining the Parks

*T*OURISM IN THE MOUNTAIN PARKS was financial icing on the CPR cake. In the 1890s less than half of CPR earnings came from passenger traffic. Much of the remainder was from real estate, or from carrying freight.[1] The most crucial source of CPR income was to be from transporting western resources. Tourism could not be allowed to interfere with the exploitation of natural resources. Coal was needed for export, to fuel the CPR's own trains, for domestic use in the mountain towns, and to generate electricity. Coal mining continued in Jasper National Park until after the First World War, and in Banff until after the Second. Access to other mineral resources was permitted in all the national parks — and extraction of oil, silver, copper, talc and potash was attempted. Gravel and limestone from the parks were used for local construction. Timber was culled from berths throughout the parks, for use by the mines, the railroads, and for house construction, firewood and fence posts.[2] The national parks were to be a tourist attraction, certainly, but not exclusively.

COAL MINING

Coal was the most plentiful and profitable of all the minerals in the mountain parks, and was second only to gold in value of production in Canada in 1899. The cascade coal basin straddling the valley around Banff had been discovered in 1883. Commercial mining began when the CPR was fully operational in 1886. The coal was "anthracitic", and very near the railway line — described by the Geological Survey of Canada as "a circumstance of great economic importance". In the Bow valley around Banff coal was mined at Anthracite and Bankhead, both in the park. Coal was also found east of Banff, at Canmore, in the park until 1930. Further north, in the Athabasca valley around Jasper, the CN railway also had access to Rocky Mountain coal. The Pocahontas mine operated in Jasper park from 1910 to 1921.[3]

Politicians and CPR officials accepted coal mining in the parks. At first the park officials also welcomed the mines as "added attractions". After 1910, however, the new parks commissioner, J. B. Harkin, tried to prevent coal mining and other mineral extraction in the parks. He failed, and mining continued until the bottom fell out of the coal market in the early 1920s. By this time the railroad could get coal from outside the park, in the less twisted seams of collieries at Drumheller and Lethbridge. The only large commercial mine continuing in the park, at Canmore, was excluded in 1930 when park boundaries were redrawn.

The mines and company mining towns coexisted in Banff and Jasper national parks with tourist towns intended for wealthy visitors. The two kinds of communities were very different. One had luxurious hotels and recreational facilities, and the other bunkhouses and shacks. The working people were discouraged from visiting the tourist town, particularly when in a rambunctious and celebratory mood. The tourists, on the other hand, were invited to tour the "quaint" mining towns, producing paternalistic comments about how neat and tidy everything seemed.

Anthracite

When the Canadian government reserved the area around Banff's hot springs as a park, the coal companies moved quickly. By the time the park legislation had been confirmed in 1887, the Canadian Anthracite Company had gained title to 1,600 acres of coal land in the park. Their company town, Anthracite, had a peak population of 1,500, with three hotels, several stores, a small church, a number of large houses, a company boarding house to house 200 miners[4] — and inevitably for those wanting female companionship — "Blanche Maloney's House". In 1897 the company expanded mining operations for a half mile in all directions, even though parks legislation should have prevented further development.

Anthracite was very different from the prestigious spa at Banff, and was the model for *Black Rock,* a novel written by Ralph Connor in 1898. The community was consumed by "the devil liquor", but eventually restored to teetotal sobriety by a Scots Presbyterian pastor and a saintly widow with a strong soprano voice. In the words of the fictional cleric: "Poor fellows!" he said as if to himself. "Whiskey is about the only excitement they have, and they find it pretty tough to give it up, and a lot of the men are against the total abstinence idea. It seems a lot to them."

The town was a grim place, particularly to those who had known better: "Any break in the long weary monotony was welcome. What mattered the cost or consequence? To the rudest and least cultured of them the sameness of the life must have been hard to bear; but what it was to men who had seen life in its most cultured and attractive forms I fail to imagine. From the mine, black and foul, to the shack, bare, cheerless, and sometimes hideously repulsive, life swung in heart-grinding monotony till the longing for a 'big drink' or some other 'big break' became too hard to bear."

In fictional *Black Rock* the miners all sign a teetotal pledge. Whiskey barrels and liquor bottles are smashed, and the clergyman marries the widow. But in the real town of Anthracite, and in most lumber and mining towns of the Canadian west, men continued to escape into alcohol. Teetotalism was a descent into the "unmentionable depths of propriety" and a "sad retrograde toward the bondage of the ancient and dying East". Inability to get drunk when you chose was regarded as a "personal grievance".

Anthracite declined after 1897, as the coal seams petered out, and the mine finally flooded. Miners moved to Bankhead or Canmore. Over the next forty years park officials tried to erase the ghost town at Anthracite and restore a more natural landscape. They tried to buy back the land, to remove the buildings and flatten the slag heaps. But even as they sought to blot out the town of Anthracite, someone else was using the remaining coal. In the 1920s an ex-resident, Frank Wheatley, returned to find another excellent coal seam. He worked under the lease of the Canada Cement Company, and produced coal for local domestic use. The mine flooded in 1944–45, but Wheatley found another seam, and produced over 10,000 tons of coal over the next eight years. When natural gas came to Banff, the local demand for domestic coal declined, and the Anthracite mine closed.

Bankhead

In 1902 the CPR's Natural Resources Department employees went prospecting, hiring the Brewsters to pack their provisions into a camp on the Cascade River about ten miles from Banff. The Brewsters had to remain close-lipped, for rumour buzzed through the town. This was no ordinary prospecting trip — the CPR was looking for coal for its own railroad,[5] and wished to beat Drumheller in getting coal to market. They found coal only four miles from Banff townsite, and called the place "Bankhead", using a Scottish term for the head of the coal seam. As cited in CPR papers, "The Bankhead field, as a mountain field, appears to show an unusual regularity and persistency. Its chances for making a large mine of first class coal appear good."[6]

Around five million tons of good coal, both semi-anthracitic and soft coal, would be produced. The CPR, under a subsidiary, built a mine and company town. Neither government or railroad saw any incompatibility between national parks and coal mines. Over the next two years they gave the company coal leases of over 5,000 acres around Bankhead, right in the heart of the park. Some did suggest Canadian parks should be preserved "from spoilation of all timber, mineral deposits, natural curiousities or wonders within said park and their retention in their natural condition",[7] as in national parks in the United States: "You cannot have a public park, with all the wild animals preserved in it, and have mining industries going on at the same time; you cannot have trade and traffic, involving railways going to and from the mines and at the same time keep the place for sport. If you intend to keep it as a park, you must shut out trade, traffic and mining."[8]

But the call for preservation was weak. Most Canadian leaders argued for exploitation of all the resources in the parks, in every profitable way. Minister of the Interior Clifford Sifton wanted "the wealth of the field and of the forest and of the mines exploited in vast quantities". It was unfortunate that coal had been found in the park, but in the words of another politician, "We have to deal with them as we find them" because "it is in the interest of the country that they should be developed and become one of our most important industries".[9]

At its peak Bankhead was bigger and better serviced than Banff itself. The townsite was laid out by park superintendent Howard Douglas as a "model community" with "rows of comfortable cottages", and a "palatial boarding house, provided with all modern conveniences".[10] Bankhead was lively and bustling, with 1,500 people, many of whom were immigrants, and a $45,000 monthly payroll.[11] The mine added a briquette plant in 1907 to supply fuel for locomotives. By 1914 the mine employed 430, with 275 underground and 155 on the surface. With sewer and electricity, with ninety homes and several boarding houses, a school and a church, Bankhead was "very pretty in the summertime",[12] and so "colourful" that Hollywood used it for a silent film, complete with a distressed maiden in a mine tunnel!

Superintendent Douglas thought the mining community could be a tourist asset: "The new village of Bankhead, instead of being a detriment to the beauty of the Park, will, on the contrary add another to the many and varied attractions of the neighbourhood. . . . Nestling under the shadow of Cascade, with its beautiful homes and its teeming industrial life it has already become a popular stopping place for tourists."[13]

But Bankhead was far from idyllic. The town was like Black Rock *before* the miners took the teetotal pledge. Men could get "a pint of grog on the sly" in any one of "numerous blind pigs".[14] Even teetotallers accepted the rights of others to get drunk if they wanted. By 1915 unlawful liquor consumption threatened the tourist trade. Men arrived drunk in Banff, looking for more drink, and "making themselves obnoxious to the citizens and tourists". The Parks Department's solution was not that of a Scots Presbyterian minister. A hotel was licensed in Bankhead itself, so the men could get legally drunk without disturbing tourists.[15]

Bankhead had other imperfections. Some Chinese workers, to save money, established a "Chinatown" at the base of a large waste pile of coal. The park superintendent and a local medical health officer decided the shacks were a "disgrace to civilization", and the kitchen-bathhouse with pigs grubbing around "most unsanitary".[16] Several months later another inspection revealed improvements. Some shacks had been burned, and others were to be demolished. The camp kitchen had been hooked up to the sewer, the paths spread with cinders, and the place generally cleaned up.

Canmore

The Marsh Mine operated briefly in Canmore in 1884,while the town was outside the park reserve, but the coal was poor grade. In 1889 William Pearce noted Canmore's potential, and reserved "ample grounds" for mining and for a railway right-of-way to the coal lands. The government could make $2,000 from selling lots in the townsite, but both the mining company and the CPR were given the right to change the plan.[17] The mine was sold to the CPR in 1890, and in 1902 the park was expanded to include Canmore. When Anthracite closed, more men moved to Canmore. When Bankhead closed in 1922, Canmore grew again. In 1929 a briquette plant was opened. Canmore would add to the tourist value of Banff national park: "From a distance, the white houses of Canmore, set in the woods of this spacious valley, have a beauty one rarely associates with a mining industry. The mining paraphernalia are lost in this gigantic valley. Round about the town are meadows in which cattle graze. The Bow is a broad and peaceful stream — the banks wooded, the water clear except at flood."[18]

Park officials built another model community.[19] The town had a "government" section, laid out by superintendent Douglas, and the "company town", with "monotony of architecture and colour", where the miners had their smaller homes. Dr. Brett operated another "neat little hospital".

LABOUR DISPUTES AND THE COAL GLUT

Labour unrest was the official reason for closing coal mines in the early 1920s. Labour had organized in British Columbia in the first years of the twentieth century. In 1906 the deputy minister of labour, Mackenzie King, was the neutral conciliator.[20] The coal companies organized their own Western Coal Operators Association, and with King's help (he witnessed the documents) signed a two-year sweetheart deal in 1907 with the United Mine Workers of America. The UMW would keep out the unions that had been "irresponsible" in British Columbia (the American Labour Union and the Western Federation of Miners).[21]

In 1911 Parks Commissioner J. B. Harkin tried to tighten national parks legislation. Mining was now officially incompatible with tourism. This could mean closing mines in the parks. But both industry and the CPR needed coal more than the tourist income generated by a landscape free from industry. War made the need for coal even more acute, and in 1914 the government renewed licenses for all mines operating in the parks.[22] Harkin had to wait to end large-scale commercial mining in the parks.

The cost of living rose during the First World War, and the miners asked for a "war bonus". The companies refused, but the government knew of the need for additional coal in wartime. The War Measures Act allowed them to give the workers a bonus, and to compensate the companies with a coal price increase. The government also insisted on an open- rather than closed-shop system, hoping to weaken worker solidarity.[23] Labour unrest continued, and by 1918 radicalism was evident in the Alberta mines. The federal government brought owners and miners together, to achieve "a larger measure of co-operation between capital and labour".[24] The companies wanted to roll back wartime pay increases, but miners were in short supply. Many had not returned from the trenches, and those who had returned expected more money. An Alberta Commission supported the miners, and pointed to poor housing, educational and sanitary facilities, and inadequate pay.[25] Miners began to sign with the One Big Union, which struck at Canmore and four other mines. The government authorized a 14 per cent retroactive increase for all miners returning to the United Mine Workers of America. The miners threw over the One Big Union, and with the assistance of the company, got rid of the "reds".

The men had a pay increase, but the root problems of mining in the West had not been solved. The CPR knew, and governments knew, Alberta was just producing too much coal. The mines all had men working short time for less than half a year. Canada needed less coal than in wartime, and so did everyone else. Mines would have to close. William Pearce was now a statistician with the CPR. In 1921 he advised his employer that 14.5 per cent of the world's supply of coal was in Alberta, and there was no rush to get it on the market. The coal would "not deteriorate with the effluxion of time",[26] and the CPR would make more profit from coal at another time. Bankhead closed first, because the men were already on strike, but Pocahontas soon followed.

The CPR sold off houses in Bankhead. People wanted to move them into Banff, but Parks officials thought miner's shacks unsuitable ("objectionable from a sanitary standpoint") for an international class tourist resort. An architect prepared four standard plans for remodelling the shacks, and recommended they be allowed in Banff if only one of each model were moved into each block. In addition, Bill Brewster was allowed to move the Bankhead railway station into town, and the Bankhead store also took on a new life in Banff. But some were not moved, and in time these reverted to the Crown. The only remains of Bankhead are the concrete walls and foundations, although the area now attracts visitors again — as an historic site.

The mine at Canmore was not closed, and the town's future was settled in 1930, when the Prairie provinces took control of their natural resources. The boundaries of all the mountain national parks were redrawn, to exclude the working mine at Canmore, but leaving the closed mines of Anthracite, Bankhead and Pocahontas within the parks. Mining in Canmore continued until 1979.

Coal mining could still be reintroduced in the four mountain parks. The coal is still there, and in one instance is still retained by the CPR. As part of its land grants for building Canada's first transcontinental railroad, the CPR was given title to ten square miles in Banff's Cascade valley. These lands contain timber and about twenty million tons of coal, and the CPR retains the right to extract coal and cut timber.[27]

THE CEMENT PLANT AT EXSHAW

The cement plant at Exshaw is still obvious to anyone travelling the Bow River corridor. In 1905 Western Canada Cement, with CPR support, leased 200 acres for limestone quarrying. Over the next seven years the company built an industrial plant of reinforced concrete, changing forever the view of Lac des Arcs that had delighted William van Horne twenty years earlier. The park superintendent hoped the new plant would bring more money into the community, and provide better building materials. He enthused: "Beautifully situated on a gentle slope overlooking Lac des Arcs, the town of Exshaw, the centre of a great manufacturing industry, has arisen out of the valley of the Bow River".[28]

With the Forest Reserves and Parks Act of 1911, the department decided there would be no new mining leases. They knew "by experience that the establishment of large camps of men invariably leads to trapping and snaring and in fact to almost every possible breach of the laws for the protection of game".[29] However, while officials wanted to exclude mining, politicians did not. The plant at Exshaw closed briefly in 1916, but was reopened, presumably after pressure from the industry.

Exshaw, like Canmore, was removed from the park in 1930,[30] but the cement company also held title to land near Banff townsite that remained in the park, even after the changes of 1930. The company did not attempt to use the land and the issue was not discussed until 1956. The company wanted to develop a plant similar to that at Exshaw, on land just inside the boundary of Jasper National Park. The company wanted to exchange their land in Banff park for land in Jasper. But, this time the Parks Branch firmly protected the parks. Eventually the government bought out the company's land in Banff, but without relinquishing any property in Jasper.[31]

GRAVEL EXTRACTION

Extensive extraction of gravel still continues in the parks. Most of it is used by Parks Canada itself, by the Public Works Department and in the case of the mountain parks, by the two railroad companies, CN and CPR. A recent report acknowledged this damaged the parks, but did not recommend it be stopped. The more obvious forms of extraction, such as at Exshaw, no longer takes place in the park. But less obvious forms that can be scattered in corners of the parks have been accepted.[32]

SILVER, ZINC AND LEAD

Silver City was described in chapter 1, and became a ghost town before many tourists had detrained at Banff. However, hope persisted of finding silver in the Bow valley. In 1915 a silver mine was started at Eldon, across from Silver City. The First World War stalled the project, and Parks officials prevented the mine from starting up again.

In Yoho Park in British Columbia, however, mining continued. Lead, zinc and some silver was mined sporadically from 1884 to 1952 from the Monarch Mine in Mount Stephen and from the Kicking Horse Mine on the face of Mount Field. The mine entrance was high on the mountain, and the rock was carried down a spectacular series of cableways and conveyors to a smelter on the valley floor. These mining rights were only surrendered when the recoverable minerals were exhausted. Ten years later the Parks Branch wiped out the remaining evidence of the mine's existence. In 1961 the pile of tailings was pushed into the river, and the camp buildings flattened and removed.[33]

Kootenay Park, also in BC, was not established until 1920 and many mining claims already existed. Some staking continued even after the park had been created — in one instance by a Parks employee. He was reprimanded, but his partner appealed to senior officials and politicians. Officials held firm: there would be no new mines in Kootenay Park.

The department treated those whose claims had preceded the park differently. They waited until the claims had been unworked for several years. Then they could be extinguished without compensation or expropriation. Zenith Mines, on Tokum Creek in Kootenay Park was an example. The owners continued assessment work on a small scale for nearly thirty years. Parks officials even seemed to have forgotten about them, until in 1940 the owner asked for permission to bring in explosives. The department checked the value of the assessment, and found the owner's reports padded. The province of British Columbia was persuaded that the claim had been allowed to lapse, and no longer existed.[34]

The Rogers Pass, too, was the site of prospecting, both before and after the creation of Glacier Park. Thirty claims had been recorded by 1916. All but three lapsed over the next forty years. One claim continued to be well worked, even though it was within a park, with $35,000 invested in 1929. Then, with the economic collapse the work was abandoned. The department inspected the claim in 1951, found it had potential, and renewed the license for another two years. The owner then agreed to sell the claim to the government for park purposes, for $12,000, or about a fifth of the value of improvements. Here matters stalled, until it was realized that the unsightly workings were visible from the new Trans-Canada Highway. Officials leaned on their deputy minister, and a firm offer was made and accepted. Another Rogers Pass claim also remained active until the 1950s, when the owner asked permission to drill. Since the claim was in a remote area, he was given permission as long as supplies were brought in by helicopter. The department hoped the claim would prove worthless and lapse at no public cost.

Other claims were also staked, but did not prove profitable. One between Yoho and Kootenay parks, in the first range of the Selkirks, for example, contained iron, titanium and silver, but without economic importance.[35] Talc, used in cosmetics and in insulation, was also present in the mountains. Some was found at Red Earth Creek and at Marble Canyon, and development began in

1921. But the Parks Branch prevented the mines from proceeding. Wartime demands led the government to relax restrictions in the 1940s, when Canada needed talc for electrical insulation. The mines have not been worked since. In Waterton National Park there was a short-lived oil boom in 1901. Other searches for oil continued sporadically, but by the time the park was created in 1910 no more had been found.[36]

GYPSUM IN WOOD BUFFALO NATIONAL PARK

Only one national park now contains mineral resources (apart from coal, which can be found throughout the Rockies) of major economic significance. The boundaries of Wood Buffalo were set long before the mineral was found. Established as a game reserve in 1906, the park contains a very large (500 million tons) gypsum deposit, a mineral used in building materials. The 17,300 square mile area was declared a national park in 1922, which should have locked the door to further exploitation. However, Wood Buffalo has been managed more as a game reserve than a park. The bison herd has been culled, to control their numbers and fill native larders. For twenty years there was a commercial goldeye fishery on Lake Claire. Timber leases were let in the park as late as 1951, so that by the time the gypsum was discovered in the 1960s the park's resources had little sanctity.

The provincial government wanted a full-scale resource inventory in the park, as a prelude to industrial development. The Canadian government wanted to satisfy aboriginal land claims by transferring the gypsum desposit to the Indian band, to whom it had significance as a burial ground. The province, in turn, blocked this move. Land removed from a park would automatically become provincial land. In 1978, with no formal agreement, the Cree Chipewyan squatted in the park, claiming rights to 19,000 acres around the gypsum deposit. The province says they may have surface rights, but no mineral rights. Other native groups have both surface and mineral rights, so the issue awaits general resolution of land claims.

TIMBER LEASES IN THE PARKS

While mining the parks for minerals is not generally accepted today, timber is not as sacrosanct. The pressure to cut trees in the parks came first from the railroads, particularly the CPR, which needed railroad ties. Then, as the coal mines developed, the demand for pit-props seemed unending. The government sold the right to cut timber over defined areas known as "berths" in return for a small annual fee and a royalty or tax paid to the government when the timber was actually cut. Those holding berths were supposed to operate six months of the year, and to have a saw mill. But in the early years this was rarely practicable, and the government did not enforce the requirement. Timber leases were granted in all the mountain parks, and some are still valid. Other national parks, such as Riding Mountain in Manitoba, and Prince Albert in Saskatchewan, began as forest reserves, and contained working timber berths before they became parks.

Before Banff Park was created in 1885 nearly 100 square miles of timber land had been rented out in berths all along the Bow valley, and through the Spray and Kananaskis valleys. However, the timber was poor in comparison with that across the continental divide in British Columbia. Also, much timber had already been wiped out by fire. The mountains were "grand and majestic" but "almost totally devoid of vegetation, except for a few trees growing apparently out of solid rock". The biggest company in the Banff area, Eau Claire, operated from 1887 onwards, and the CPR itself also had active berths.[37] The potential of exchanging these for other more productive berths was discussed as early as 1889, and Eau Claire gave up two. However, the boundary extension of 1902 brought more timber berths into the park.

The conservation movement between 1905 and 1930 increased awareness of the need to conserve forests, whether within or outside the national parks. Exploitation of all the berths along the eastern slopes of the Rocky Mountains was curtailed by the growing awareness of the significance of forest cover in water conservation. The front range of the eastern slopes of the Rockies was protected from cutting, and permits were only given for taking dry or dead timber. Mine props, posts, rails and cordwood could be taken, but only by the user — not for resale.[38]

This decision not to harvest the forest in the national parks presents a particular problem in Banff. After the fires of a century ago the trees have grown back too close to one another for the comfort of the wildlife or the beauty of the scenery. Now the park managers face a dilemma. Do they thin the forest, taking some of the overmature or unsound trees? Or do they allow the present growth to deteriorate with time, producing a shabby forest landscape for another fifty years? If they cut into the forest, they will be attacked by those who want their parks natural, even if the result is less beautiful. If matters are left as they are, the tourist value of the landscape will be affected, and the park increasingly prone to fire.

Today in Banff only the CPR property in the Cascade valley remains open to cutting. Berths also existed in most other national parks. In Riding Mountain Park in Manitoba timber was "harvested" for more than fifty years, both before and after the creation of the park. Until 1937 the park contained several saw mills, and the last two timber berths were not surrendered until 1947. Local residents were still permitted to cut timber for firewood and fence posts, but by the sixties quantity and quality were unacceptable. Applications for permits declined, and in 1964 the government decided to issue no more.[39] Depletion of the resource made it possible to prevent its further exploitation, because exploitation was no longer an economic proposition.

In the 1940s the Parks Branch tried to prevent automatic annual renewal of timber licenses in the parks, but was stopped by political pressure. In 1952 the annual rent was increased from ten to fifty dollars a square mile, a fireguarding charge introduced, and timber royalties increased. A decade later new regulations prevented cutting within 200 feet of a road or right of way. Then finally in 1964 another new park policy explicitly committed the department to acquiring the remaining berths, acknowledging that "the existence of timber limits is not consistent with the purposes of National Parks".[40] Finally, in 1969, with the support of a more conservation-oriented Trudeau government, the department purchased several of the remaining timber rights.

MINING THE PARKS AGAIN?

The press and the conservation groups reacted with consternation when Suzanne Blais-Grenier, as Conservative minister responsible for the environment, including parks, in Mulroney's government, mused about the need to review policies forbidding mining and lumbering in the parks. She would have found that the parks are not fully protected from resource exploitation. Older parks contain a few unextinguished mineral leases, and a scattering of timber berths. Some new parks created since 1969 have included timber leases and mining claims — and not all have been extinguished. In Wood Buffalo and Terra Nova, two of our middle-aged parks, commercial timber rights still exist, and in Wood Buffalo they are used. Such rights even exist in the core of Banff National Park. In the words of one senior CPR official, the area's timber and mineral resources are too rich for the railroad company to reliquish them easily: "The Cascade Mountain property contains significant tonnages of bituminous and anthracitic coal, which our geologist has established at some 20 million tons. In addition, there is valuable timber on the land. If the federal government has coal and timber lands outside the park, we would be happy to consider it on an exchange basis but if, as seems likely, this is not the case, we would prefer to hold onto this property for subsequent technological development in coal mining and recovery."[41]

So, despite Parks Canada's efforts to eliminate resource development from the national parks, the potential remains for another Bankhead. Right in the core of Canada's oldest national park of Banff the CPR retains the right to mine coal, to strip the forest, or do whatever appears profitable. At present, most of Canada's national parks are without active mineral or timber exploitation. Our governments have tried not to lock economic resources into the national parks. Instead, resources have either been exhausted before creating the park; or park boundaries readjusted to exclude the resources; or, in some instances, the resources have been exploited to exhaustion, in spite of being in a park. In Canada our national parks have been mined for profit, both literally and figuratively.

CHAPTER THREE

The
First Conservation
Movement

*T*HE PARKS needed saving from resource exploitation. For a quarter century two fiery autocrats, both absolutely committed to their own convictions, engaged in a medieval tilting contest to determine the future of Canada's national parks. One wanted to preserve the parks, and the other to maximize their profitability. Both had begun their careers as part of the vast army of surveyors mapping the Canadian West. William Pearce had worked as the Canadian government's chief western bureaucrat. In 1904 he joined the CPR, working first in the irrigation department and then as a statistician. While in government service he had been sympathetic to CPR interests. Now CPR interests became his own, and he equated both with the "public interest". Some called him a CPR lackey. He was committed to irrigation to increase the value of prairie farmland (and hence increase profits from CPR land sales). The watersheds of the Rocky Mountain parks would be needed for both irrigation and hydro development.

The second knight, tilting for the cause of preservation, Arthur Wheeler, had also been a surveyor with the Department of the Interior. However, Wheeler did not leave government service to work for the CPR, but to become a virtually unpaid executive director of Canada's first environmental group, the Canadian Alpine Club. This organization of hikers, campers and climbers led the battle to protect the parks from water management and hydro development schemes. Arthur Wheeler was their chief. Some said he *was* the Alpine Club.

WILLIAM PEARCE AND ARTHUR WHEELER

William Pearce had been born in Ontario in 1848, beginning his surveying career there and travelling West in 1874. His capabilities led to his promotion to the position of inspector of land agencies, a member of a two-person board created by Prime Minister Macdonald in 1882. He served briefly as inspector of mines, and also investigated the causes of the Riel Rebellion. He knew the West, and was a trusted government adviser and close to senior CPR officials such as William Van Horne.[1]

William Pearce, whether serving government or the railroads, believed in leaving a good paper trace. He drafted long memoranda, sending copies to his member of parliament, R. B. Bennett, to the minister of the interior, to the Alberta premier and members of his cabinet, and to a variety of trade groups in southern Alberta and British Columbia. William Pearce was the first Canadian to fully appreciate the potential of tilting by mail. His own files were organized as an arsenal in the battle to advance CPR interests. Multiple copies were filed under various headings. To file a letter in one place, he believed, was as bad as throwing it away.

William Pearce was an "organization man" par excellence. Arthur Wheeler was more of a Don Quixote — and even tilted at windmills, Pearce would have said. What could be more quixotic than forsaking a promising bureaucratic career for the executive directorship of an impoverished non-government organization! Wheeler was the eldest son of an aristocratic Protestant family, which immigrated to Canada after living beyond their means for a generation or two in Ireland. Wheeler's father had not expected to have to earn his own living, but had to accept a position of harbour-master in the Great Lakes port of Collingwood, Ontario. Born in 1860, and twelve years younger than Pearce, Arthur Wheeler could remember a childhood before the pressures of employment limited one's freedom.[2] His mid-career shift showed he preferred the free-wheeling life of a person of independent means, pursuing his own interests rather than those of an employer.

Like Pearce, Wheeler was deeply impressed by the wilderness, and came to love the outdoor life. Like Pearce he began surveying in northern Ontario, continuing his apprenticeship in the Northwest Territories. He eventually returned to Ontario in 1884 as "third class clerk" in the Department of the Interior. He learned a skill which took him back to the mountains that would be the focus of all his creative activity. He was taught by his boss, the surveyor general, to use a camera in surveying. Instead of doing all the measurements in the open, photographs were taken and the calculations were done "back at the office".

When the Riel Rebellion hit the headlines in the Eastern Canadian press in 1885, Arthur Wheeler, a handsome and spirited bachelor of 25, turned patriotic. He signed up for the surveyor's corps. His family was told he had been killed at Batoche. But he arrived home to tell his family that reports of his death had been greatly exaggerated! He returned with a sore shoulder and with some bad memories.

Wheeler's major survey for the Department of the Interior was of the mountain range beyond the Rockies, the "incredible" Selkirks. He was taught mountaineering by Swiss guides loaned by the CPR. He used photographic methods, although continually frustrated by smoke from forest fires. Like Pearce, he left a paper trace, not in memoranda but in his two-volume book, *The Selkirk Range* (or more appropriately — "How I surveyed the Selkirks"), published by the government in 1905, with gold leaf cover, a box of maps, and photographs of snow sheds, mountain passes, crevasses, climbers and forests — the latter mostly stripped by fire.[3]

Canada's western mountains were popular with alpinists, most of them American. Wheeler met climbers from the alpine clubs of England, Switzerland, and the United States, and saw the potential for an alpine club in Canada. He drafted an open letter proposing a Canadian branch of the American Alpine Club: "In looking over the list of recorded climbs, the names of Canadians are chiefly conspicuous by their absence. It would seem that we are not yet fully alive to the glorious heritage of snow-clad peaks, shining glaciers, dark blue forests and rushing mountain torrents found in this enchanted wonderland of Crags and Canyons that we possess — a possession that is already proving, and will prove, a veritable and inexhaustible gold mine".[4]

Elizabeth Parker of Winnipeg, was incensed. To join an American organization would be unpatriotic. She asked Sir Wilfred Laurier for support. The prime minister was decidedly uninterested in the project — the mountains had less appeal to Laurier's

Liberals than to Macdonald's Conservatives. "You write to me" he said, "on a subject as to which I have to confess I am very little familiar. In so far as I understand it, I have no hesitation in sending you my sympathy with your intentions and action."[5]

Elizabeth Parker's lobby for a purely Canadian club was successful. As a journalist she could promote her views in the *Winnipeg Free Press*. The Canadian Alpine Club first met in 1906, selecting Arthur Wheeler as president, and Elizabeth Parker as honorary secretary. The group organized annual camps for climbers of all levels of skill. Many women were active, in addition to Mrs. Parker. A chapter of Wheeler's *The Selkirk Range* was on women climbers, and they participated in many of the club's climbs in the "Canadian alps". Members came from across Canada and from abroad. A $1,000 annual grant showed government support, and the CPR provided guides, train passes, and other help. The club became a group favoured today by Parks Canada — a "co-operating association"[6] of private individuals supporting and supplementing the work of Parks staff.

Initially Wheeler was allowed to help the Alpine Club as part of his regular government duties. In 1909 the government threatened to withdraw this permission. But, after an outcry from the club,[7] he was given "time off" to supervise their annual camp. Then in 1910, with the creation of a separate Parks Branch, Wheeler was told surveyors could no longer "do Alpine Club work". Wheeler gave up his civil service position to become the club's executive director.

The club was committed to providing Wheeler with a salary, for although he had the attitudes of the independently wealthy, he lacked the wealth. They asked Prime Minister Laurier to triple their annual grant to $3,000, to support their new director. CPR facilities were too costly, they argued, for most Canadians. Alpine Club camps were cheaper.

> We do not wish to criticize in any way the charges made by the railway company in this connection. They may be fair and just and a legitimate profit on the investment. We merely wish to emphasize the fact that those among the less wealthy but most intelligent and appreciative classes of Canada's citizens are barred out from this cause.
>
> In support of the above case we may cite the fact that four

annual camps have been held by the Alpine Club with an atten-
dance limit of 200 persons. At the first, 112 were placed under
canvas; at the second, 157; at the third, 177 and at the fourth,
190. In all six hundred and thirty odd.

What did we find?

That the camps were promptly taken advantage of by profes-
sors and teachers in schools and colleges, by clergymen, by
students, by artists and photographers and, generally speaking,
by those whose means prevented their visiting the mountain regions under the existing tourists conditions which are only for
the wealthy.[8]

Emphasizing the club's non-profit nature, they described its con-
tributions to the parks, building a club house, and attracting visitors from other countries. Elizabeth Parker sent the letter to
"twenty-one principal newspapers in Canada". Since government
had no change of heart, Wheeler was appointed at the "highest
salary the club could afford".[9] That was not very much, so
Wheeler hustled survey contracts from provincial and federal governments, and from the CPR. He also developed a small pack-train
business alongside the Alpine Club camp, carrying provisions and
providing rides to tired hikers.[10] Others in the pack-train business,
particularly the Brewsters, thought his competition unfair, and
protested to the Parks Department. Wheeler was told to give the
Brewsters some Alpine Club business, if he wanted any more co-
operation from the Parks Department.

Wheeler did not mellow with middle age. Rather the reverse.
His aristocratic manner became imperious, and his temper short.
He blustered through life, impatient with those who could not
match his pace.[11] Pat Brewster said of his competitor: "He was a
meticulous autocrat, and one of my greatest difficulties was trying
to find men who would be willing to go out with him on various
trips. Sometimes it was necessary for me to go out myself; I understood the man and appreciated his strong points."[12]

Another to see the rough side of Wheeler's tongue was a clergyman's son from Ontario, a summer student hired by the Alpine
Club and later retained as Wheeler's assistant. Paul Wallace wrote
to assure his parents that he still had the three bibles they had sent,
and needed no more. Then he described his new boss:

Last Sunday Wheeler spent testing his cameras on the golf links. I attended. His language was theological all day — the only time he has been that way.

On the first place the wind was too strong; in the second place the air was too thick with golf balls; in the third place the sun wasn't quite right; in the fourth place the tripod screw would not fit in one camera, and after we had worked on it half an hour, it got worse and wouldn't fit either; in the fifth place, after piling up the tripod with stones to make it absolutely firm, Wheeler slipped, dropped the camera, and fell heavily on the tripod, knocking everything golly-west.

His language reminded me of an old fashioned Methodist sermon.

In the sixth place, he handed Mr. McGaw a plate and Mr. McGaw sat down very suddenly at the critical moment that the plate was passing from one hand to another.

Wheeler picked the plate up. It wasn't broken, but you would not have known that from what was said.[13]

Wallace quite liked "the old man" to start with. But the relationship deteriorated when Wallace became Wheeler's year-round assistant. Wheeler expected him to work far into the evenings. Eventually Wallace refused to work longer than 8:45 a.m. to 6:30 p.m. Wheeler "roared" around demanding that this "narrow-minded pig-headed idiot" resign. "You needn't think you're secretary of the Alpine Club. I am the Alpine Club. What would it ever be without me? Name a man who could take my place?"

Wheeler would make no distinction between work for the Alpine Club and his other affairs, such as work for the Conservative party. Wallace, paid by the Alpine Club, felt he should only work for the club. Dr. Coleman, an executive member, reminded Wallace that Wheeler was not *the* Alpine Club. Wallace refused to go to a Conservative constituency meeting.

It begins to look as though I had been properly fooled by the old man, doesn't it? He apparently was more anxious to have somebody to do his work than the work of the Alpine Club. He says I must not consider myself at all independent of him, and of course I won't submit to that for two minutes. He has told me more than once in confidence during the summer that he always gets his own way, and I suppose he figures on getting it in this case.

. . . . He indulged chiefly in the language that might be applied either to an African slave or a dog, but I have translated it into what was probably at the bottom of his mind.

Wheeler got his way, and Wallace left, commenting in a final letter home that "Mr. Wheeler ought to be kept in the mountains; it's his only element". Wheeler's strongest supporter was Emmeline Savatard, whom he married after his first wife died in 1924. Wallace thought Ms. Savatard, or the "chatelaine", typified "all that is vulgar and offensive in the English character". She was a "devil incarnate", who never spoke, only shrieked, and lectured him for not smoking or drinking. Wheeler met his match in his "Emm".

The Wheelers, with people like Elizabeth Parker and Dr. Coleman, led the battle to save the Rocky Mountain parks from power and irrigation dams. William Pearce, promoting development, was to match Wheeler's outspokeness, bluntness and tyrannical disposition.[14]

The battle between these two men and their ideas was fought against the backdrop of Canada's first conservation movement. The idea of "conservation" had become current in the United States, and as is often the case with new ideas, overflowed into Canada. The major Canadian forum for conservation issues was the Commission of Conservation meeting from 1910 to 1918 under chairman Clifford Sifton. The Commission brought together provincial and federal representatives, academics and various other interests.[15]

The commission's concept of "conservation" did not mean preservation through non-use, but maximizing future profits through good management today. Conservation implied managing forests for perpetual profits; mining coal to minimize waste; capping gas wells so less gas would be lost; retaining forests on watersheds to guarantee a more steady water supply for agriculture; and farming such resources as fur, oysters and buffalo. The concern was primarily with the "scientific" use of resources for long term economic gain.[16]

Both Pearce and Wheeler claimed to support conservation. For Pearce conservation was the economic principle advocated by the

Commission of Conservation. Agricultural irrigation, his long term enthusiasm, now gained legitimacy. Hydroelectric developments were also entirely consistent with his idea of conservation. Pearce joined other more powerful interests, with influence in Ottawa and the provincial capitals, which wanted to maximize the economic exploitation of all Canadian resources, including those which might by some mischance be found within national parks.

But for Wheeler, and others enjoying the mountains and other wilderness areas, conservation justified the preservation of natural wilderness. Wildlife protection became a general and popular concern. The idea of preservation took on an aesthetic and moral character. Wheeler, and other Alpine Club supporters, opposed hydro development in the parks. They wanted more and larger parks, managed with more attention to preservation.

The conservation movement changed Canadian forest management, particularly on federal crown land in Alberta, Saskatchewan and Manitoba. In the Prairie provinces the federal government controlled land and natural resources, and "scientific" forestry led Ottawa to create forest reserves on land unsuitable for agriculture. The largest, Rocky Mountains Forest Reserve, created in 1910, surrounded Banff Park, and extended north to Jasper Park, and south to the United States border. The Prince Albert and Cypress Hills reserves in Saskatchewan were created, and those at Duck Mountain, Porcupine Hills and Riding Mountain in Manitoba.

Multiple use of the forest reserves was regulated to maximize long-term economic benefits.[17] Mining, lumbering, quarrying, pasturage and haylands, reservoirs and hyrodelectric sites were all permitted, but agricultural homesteading and tourism were not. People who wanted to enjoy the scenery would have to visit the parks.[18]

The forest reserves were crucial for the future expansion of the national parks. Because homesteading had been forbidden, new national parks could be created without expropriation costs.

THE FIRST PRESERVATION PARKS: WILDLIFE CONSERVATION

The conservation movement's concern for wildlife preservation also affected Canada's national parks. For the first time parks were created purely for preservation, with little concern for profit. A number of species were threatened. In 1914 naturalist W. T. Hornaaay (sometime guest of the Alpine Club) predicted extinction of the pronghorn antelope. Three antelope reserves were established, one in Saskatchewan and two in Alberta. With hunting forbidden the species recovered. Their objectives met, the reserves were then eliminated, and the land handed over to the provinces for more profitable exploitation.

Alberta's Elk Island National Park also originated as a game reserve. W. H. Cooper, territorial game warden, knew of a small herd of elk in the "Knob and Kettle" country east of Edmonton, and in 1903 asked his minister for permission to fence a reserve to protect the herd from extinction. Nothing was done, and hunting continued in 1903 and 1904. Then seventy local residents petitioned their Member of Parliament, Frank Oliver, and the Minister of the Interior, Clifford Sifton, for a sixteen-square-mile fenced enclosure around Astotin lake.[19] Nothing was done, and hunts continued.

In 1906 five Fort Saskatchewan residents put up a $6,000 bond to enclose at least twenty elk in a four-mile fenced area. The elk enclosure was included in the Cooking Lake Forest Reserve in 1906. But, although the land was unsuitable for agriculture, it was also unsuitable as a forest reserve. Fire had destroyed the original tree stands. The reserve was to be crucial in preservation of another species, the buffalo. In 1908 a herd was bought from a Montana rancher for $250 a head. Some were sent to the Elk reserve until fencing was ready at Wainwright. A few eluded recapture, and were still prospering in the 1920s, when Elk Island was declared a national park.

The herd at Wainwright increased in the 1920s, and thousands were sent north to a new wildlife park, Wood Buffalo. The Wainwright park was closed, after overcrowding caused disease and parasites. and is now used for military exercises.[20] The herds at Elk Island and Wood Buffalo have been "scientifically" managed, and limited by periodic culling. Northern natives have eaten their meat, and used skins for buffalo robes and other clothing. The herds, though, have not been profitable. At one point the supply of skins so far outran demand that thousands rotted.

The Canadian Commission of Conservation was also a forum for those advocating bird sanctuaries. In 1915 a recommendation was heard to create sanctuaries at Point Pelee in Ontario, and Percé Rock and Bonaventure Island in the Gaspé area of Quebec. Nesting birds were being shot and needed protection.[21] Point Pelee, as the southernmost part of Canada, attracted particular attention. The proposal was endorsed by the Advisory Board on Wildlife Protection in 1916. Conservation groups, such as the Essex County Wild Life Protection Association, the Essex County Game Protective Association and the Canadian Association for the Protection of Birds all supported the creation of a park.[22] Point Pelee was a naval reserve, and already federal crown land. The Canadian government created the park in 1918. However, Point Pelee became more of a recreation area than a bird sanctuary.

IRRIGATION

Since 1883 Pearce had believed the semi-arid region of southern Alberta would not be fully profitable until it was irrigated. He had seen successes with similar lands in Utah, and recommended a comparable program for Canada. However, he had been told to keep quiet. The government feared that no one would want to settle out West if they suspected it was too dry for agriculture.

Pearce was vindicated in the prolonged drought from 1884 to 1896, and in 1892 he was asked to head up Ottawa's new irrigation branch. His ideas were embodied in the Northwest Irrigation Act of 1894, then the most advanced legislation of its kind in the world.[23] Its controversial element was supression of riparian rights, or the rights of those adjoining streams. The government would decide who should have water and how much, not those fortunate enough to live next to streams. Irrigation works were built, but forgotten when the rains came in 1897. By 1904 none of the original projects were in operation. Pearce had been ahead of his time.

The end of the Macdonald era and the advent of the Liberals reduced Pearce's influence in government. His deputy minister and friend, J. S. Dennis, left government to work for the CPR, so Pearce joined him 1904. His ideas about irrigation gained widespread support with the advent of the conservation movement. Pearce advocated water management for irrigation, flood control and hydro development, and to increase the value of land held by his new employer. As a CPR employee, Pearce had more freedom to speak his mind — and did so.

In 1907, a year after Wheeler and Parker had created the Alpine Club, the first convention on irrigation in western Canada took place in Calgary. The minister, elected representatives from the federal government, from British Columbia and the two new provinces of Saskatchewan and Alberta all attended. Municipal governments and agricultural and trade organizations were represented; the media was there, and (of course) the railways.[24] The Western Canada Irrigation Association was created, with Pearce as an executive member. Water management was also on the agenda of the Conservation Commission. In 1914, for example, the Commission looked at both watershed management and hydroelectric development. Pearce's ideas were gaining legitimacy.

But Pearce's schemes had become more grandiose over time. As usual they were widely distributed in lengthy memoranda in multiple copies. He described his mission: "I have been trying to hammer into the public for more than thirty years, viz, that there is not a drop of water that can be made available for irrigation purposes in any of the three prairie provinces that should be allowed to go to the Hudson Bay, Arctic Ocean, or even into the Mississippi drainage, via the Milk river".[25]

Pearce's continuous pressure produced government surveys, but not on the scale he sought. The publicity also produced some misunderstandings, as press coverage of his comments upset senior CPR officials. One defended Pearce:

> Article Edmonton Journal very misleading. . . .
>
> What the government is doing is carrying out a promise made by Mr. Meighen to Mr. Pearce in the spring of 1919, that he would see that surveys were made to ascertain whether or not Mr. Pearce's proposition regarding irrigating the immense tract of land lying in Alberta and Saskatchewan [is feasible]. . . .
>
> Nothing was done in 1920 owing to alleged insufficiency of force qualified to make surveys and appropriation by Parliament. Pearce has been urging as strongly as possible on the present Minister to have the necessary surveys made. The result is that several parties have been put in the field but no intimation has been given Pearce as to the scope of their investigations. Pearce fears that possibly the men are not the best possible and may not carry on the investigation on the lines that he thinks they should be. He states that as soon as he can obtain time he proposes obtaining from the Department full details of what they are striving to do this year. Of course as soon as he does he will report.[26]

Pearce continued to urge water storage in the Rocky Mountains and elsewhere. He was frustrated as Banff and Jasper parks expanded, and new parks were created at Waterton and in British Columbia. These, he believed, would ultimately have to be flooded for irrigation, flood control, and hydroelectric development.

THE SPRAY RIVER PROPOSAL

The issue finally came into focus, for both Wheeler and Pearce, with the proposal of 1923 to dam the Spray Lakes for hydro development. Calgary Power Company, organized in 1889, already had power dams on the Bow River's Horseshoe Falls, at Lake Minnewanka and at Kananaskis Falls, all within Banff Park. The Minnewanka dam, in the heart of the park, was permitted in 1912 because of periodic low water at the Horseshoe Falls. Cottages had been moved back to the new shoreline. The agreement protected the park from negative side effects:

> This work shall be carried out in such a manner that the purpose for which the Rocky Mountain Park was set aside shall be adequately safeguarded, and it will be necessary to incorporate in the agreement conditions calculated to effectively provide for the preservation of the beauty of the scenery.[25]

Lot owners were also protected, and the landscape restored. The dam was maintained and any timber that might end up under water was removed. Lake Minnewanka retained its beauty and popularity, and supporters of the Spray Lake proposals claimed this showed hydroelectric development could be consistent with park values. Another hydroelectric development was permitted in the Kananaskis Falls Agreement of 1912.

But by 1923 Calgary Power again needed more power, and looked to Lake Minnewanka for further electricity. The government turned down their application, but opposition leader Arthur Meighen ridiculed the opponents of hydroelectric development in the parks: "I have seen articles in American and Canadian magazines about the profanity, the blasphemy of harnessing Niagara falls and thereby diminishing the flow of water down this great cataclysm of nature. Well, I consider that rubbish. Imagine the people of Ontario today with their own backs and hands doing the work that the falls of Niagara are doing, in order that wedding couples could see more water falling over the top. That seems to me ridiculous, and the same is true of Banff national park."[28] Calgary Power Company proposed instead to dam the Spray River, also in the park, and east of the town of Banff. The minister hesitated, admitting he was in a double bind: "I am speaking neither for nor against them. I am in a difficult position, having to make a decision, because I have within my department the Water Powers Branch, who look at this matter from the standpoint of power, . . . the advantage of having cheap power for the development of industry, and on the other hand . . . the Parks Branch, whose business it is to preserve the scenic beauty of our parks for tourist purposes, and as a playground for the people of Canada, and the views of the two branches are widely at variance on this question."[29]

The minister's ambivalence gave both supporters of the scheme and opponents time to organize. Supporters included, predictably, the power company itself, the Province of Alberta, the Canadian government's Water Powers Branch and Calgary City Council. William Pearce and various public power enthusiasts also supported development. The opponents of the Spray Lakes scheme were not as powerful, but they were numerous. The Alpine Club, and Wheeler in particular, goaded people into action. The group had covert help from Parks Commissioner Harkin, whose own opposition was public.

THE CANADIAN NATIONAL PARKS ASSOCIATION

At the end of their annual meeting in 1923 the Alpine Club organized a second organization, the Canadian National Parks Association, to protect the national parks. The new group immediately told the minister of the interior of their resolve: "That a National Parks Association for Canada be formed with objects consisting of the conservation of the Canadian National Parks for scientific, recreational and scenic purposes, and their protection from exploitation for commercial purposes".[30]

The new group, with Arthur Wheeler on the executive, claimed to represent many organizations. But William Pearce felt it was only Wheeler's mouthpiece. He wrote to his MP, R. B. Bennett: "Mr. Wheeler is, of course, entitled to very great credit for the organization and effectiveness of the Alpine Club of Canada, which I think is a most excellent institution. Through his influence with that club he is continually having resolutions passed — many of them going outside the influence of said club — and this opposition (to the Spray lakes proposal) is one of them. The said Club is not directly a tourist organization, and should follow the lines which its name implies."[31]

Writing to Wheeler, Pearce asked: "How many members who participated in the passing of the resolution have seen the Spray Lakes?"[32]

But Wheeler was fighting for a principle. He replied: "It is not a question of opposing the Spray Lakes power scheme, but rather a desire on my part to carefully preserve the National Parks of Canada from spoilation, and I am now fighting for the recognition of a great principle which principle at the present is threatened".[33]

Pearce found this illogical and absurd. People were obsessed with the idea that parks should be maintained as nature left them. No one would be able to use them, except a few backpackers. There could be no fires and no tents. Nor any improvements, and in the Spray valley the dam would be an improvement. A "marshy, mosquito breeding area" would be "converted and maintained in perpetuity, summer and winter, as an attractive sheet of water with a firm margin all round".[34]

The National Parks Association felt they were neither illogical, nor adsurd. They wrote to Parks Commissioner Harkin, who had attended their first meeting. They asked for publications "which would be of interest and assistance"; to be informed of development applications; and for the commissioner's opinion on how the new association could assist the Parks Branch.[35] The National Parks Association was behaving like a typical Canadian pressure group — seeking an alliance with one branch of government in order to oppose the plans of another.[36]

This new group might also help Commissioner Harkin, as he manoeuvered through the internal government politics, as long as it was kept at some distance. It might become a liability, particularly with a volatile personality like Wheeler. The Parks Branch took memberships in some associations. One staff member asked if they should join the National Parks Association, to "keep track" of the group. Harkin said no. The branch "might conceivably have some difference of opinion in the future regarding some government action concerning National Parks". Grants to the Canadian Alpine Club would continue, but would not be extended to the

new group.[37] Again, this typifies the Canadian custom of manipulation of interest groups by public administrators.

The National Parks Association campaign began with a mass of
letters to the minister of the interior. Most were form letters
acknowledging support for the organization, but a few were
individualized.

> I can assure you that Mr. Wheeler has the interests of our
> parks at heart, and when it comes to a stand-up fight, he is there
> with the goods. Personally I am opposed in any degree to the
> destruction or disfiguration in any possible way of the Domin-
> ion or Provincial parks, which we perhaps do not expect to
> enjoy to the fullest, but our future generation may.[38]

Wheeler, as executive secretary, prepared the association's first
"Bulletin". This contained by-laws, a membership form, and
details of the Spray Lakes controversy. The association, said
Wheeler, had no quarrel with the power companies, but flooding
the Spray valley would damage the "scenic attractions" of Banff,
and be a precedent "most injurious to the future of the National
Parks". The Alberta government, he said, wanted to control the
Spray Lakes basin. But Alberta had enough coal to produce electricity, without "disfiguring" the national parks.

A telegram to Minister of the Interior Charles Stewart early in
1924, referred to the more preservationist policy in the US national
parks:

> In United States, where utility and value national parks more
> fully appreciated and where similar situations have arisen, the
> Government is absolutely pledged to integrity of its National
> Parks system. Should your Department feel disposed toward
> granting request of promoters of Spray Lakes project we urge in
> strongest possible terms deferring action until Parliament con-
> venes, when through their representatives the voice of the peo-
> ple may be heard, National Parks being the heritage of the
> Nation and not question of mere local concern.[38]

But even Wheeler was reluctant to defend the parks in purely non-
economic terms. He cited the classic comments of Parks Commissioner Harkin that parks are for profit — though profit was from
tourism rather than hydroeletric power: "From a straight commer-

cial standpoint, our parks are one of our most important resources. The public has no conception of their value".

He calculated the revenue from tourists visiting the parks: "Capitalize that revenue (from tourists) at 5%, and on that basis the Canadian National Parks are worth in actual dollars $360,000,000. . . . I emphasize the commercial side because I find that the general public persists in the idea that National Parks are simply frills and luxuries. Nevertheless, on the basis of cold blooded commercialism, I don't think there is an institution in Canada that pays as big a dividend as the Canadian National Parks."

Many organizations joined the Canadian National Parks Association: Banff Citizens' Council, the American Association for the Advancement of Science, anglers clubs, automobile clubs, boards of trade, service clubs, naturalist clubs, the local council of women, and Alberta's provincial Liberal association. The net was wide.[39] Wheeler also hoped the coal producers would agree that electricity should be produced from coal rather than hydro power. He wrote to the Western Canada Coal Operators Association, representing the mines facing a slump in Alberta: "Unless the Canadian National Parks Association in Alberta have the support of the coal operators in the province one of our strongest arguments against the desecration of the parks by handing concessions to Calgary Power will be lost".[40]

Producing electricity from coal could be more expensive initially, but Wheeler claimed it would provide more jobs and Alberta had plenty of coal. Two years later the mines asked the province to postpone approval of the Spray Lakes proposal until "the advisability of the development of power by the utilization of small coals" had been studied.

Pearce was busy also. He wrote letters everywhere. The CPR headquarters asked Pearce's supervisor to tell him that his public pronouncements were embarassing the company in Ottawa. Pearce justified his support of irrigation and flood control as in the public interest and in the interest of the CPR:"In view of the active part I have taken in that connection for now nearly forty years I would not feel warranted in stating I refuse to give my assistance. Further — it would not add to the popularity of your Company if it were known that said Company requested me not to."[41]

His letter writing continued. Reservoirs and dams would not damage the scenery: "If the creation of reservoirs meant the destruction or injury materially of our parks as playgrounds or tourist resorts, I could understand the objection from the Parks authorities, but I believe that I am as competent as any of the Parks authorities and very much better qualified than most of them to vizualize what will be the results of the establishment of these reservoirs".[42]

Pearce was impossible to silence.

The province of Alberta, together with the other Prairie provinces, complained of having no ownership or control of land and natural resources. These had been retained by Ottawa when the province was established in 1907. The Prairie provinces wanted these resources handed over, but Alberta felt it would be severely penalized if Ottawa kept the national parks. The parks contained the resource base for provincial economic development; timber, coal and hydro potential. Without control of the Rocky Mountain watersheds, the province would also be without water for irrigation and unable to control flooding. Alberta wanted the parks so they could be managed for provincial purposes.[43]

Those who believed that power should be developed by the state also intervened. Socialist J. S. Woodsworth was ideologically committed to public power: "I would urge upon the department that there should be no further alienation of any water power but rather that in view of the great need there will be for water powers for electrical development in the days to come, we grant use of any of these powers only under the strictest supervision".[44]

A public power movement had developed in Ontario, advocating government intervention to protect the interests of industrial consumers of electricity. Government involvement in power projects in the national parks was doubly necessary: "[Private] interests would be primarily concerned with getting their money out of the project and getting it as rapidly as possible; whereas. . . . the government would also be interested in maintaining the park value of the area in which the power privileges exist".[45]

Pearce wrote a lengthy technical analysis of water storage and flooding problems in southern Alberta. He traced the history of flooding and drought, and predicted that Calgary could be flooded out. The Spray valley lacked scenic value, was marshy and damaged by lumbering and by fire. He distributed the report widely, in multiple copies. Some went to Charles Stewart, minister of the interior. R. B. Bennett and Fred Davis were each given twenty-five copies to distribute among fellow MP's, and members of the Senate.

Other ministers, and provincial and municipal politicians all received copies.

The technical strength of Pearce's analysis helped convince policy makers, particularly the minister responsible, Charles Stewart. He discredited claims about the beauty of the Spray valley. The Alpine Club and the National Parks Association were going to "extremes" and were "most unfair".[46]

FEDERAL–PROVINCIAL NEGOTIATIONS

The issue was debated for the rest of the decade, but was eventually resolved in a typically Canadian fashion — in a federal–provincial conference. Under Sir John A. Macdonald the country had been run by the government and the CPR. In 1930 a different alliance was necessary. The crucial transfer of resources agreement was negotiated by the provincial premiers and the prime minister. They traded across the table for the natural resources in Alberta, Saskatchewan and Manitoba, allocating of those provinces' forests, water powers, mineral resources and national parks. These negotiations set a pattern for future federal-provincial diplomacy in Canada which has not changed much since.

Alberta, Manitoba and Saskatchewan were given ownership of and responsibility for the land within their boundaries, complete with timber, minerals and water rights. The coal of Alberta, all the forests, including the vast reserve on the eastern slopes of the Rockies, and the smaller reserves in Saskatchewan and Manitoba. Royalties would now belong to the Prairie provinces, just as in the other provinces.

The Spray Lakes controversy was also ended. To satisfy the supporters of the National Parks Association and Commissioner Harkin, there was a new National Parks Act. This would ensure the parks remained "unimpaired for the enjoyment of future generations". No mining would be allowed, no hydroelectric dams, and no commercial forestry. Even the provinces promised to do nothing outside park boundaries to lessen waterflow through the parks.[47]

The national parks in the Rockies, and in eastern British Columbia would remain under federal protection. The game reserves of Wood Buffalo in northern Alberta, and Elk Island near Edmonton would become national parks. Prince Albert National Park was developed in a forest reserve in Saskatchewan, for the benefit of

Prime Minister Mackenzie King's constituents. For Manitobans a national park in the Riding Mountain reserve provided a summer resort around Clear Lake.

Even today parks enthusiasts see the legislation of 1930 as a landmark achievement in protecting Canada's parks. And the elimination of mining, lumbering and hydro development was taken more seriously after 1930. However, for Wheeler and Harkin the decision was a major defeat. The agreement reduced the size of the parks so that no minerals remained of economic value, and the Spray Lakes project could go ahead, but just outside Banff Park.

The legislation was explicit, if ponderous.

> The Government of Canada will introduce into the Parliament of Canada such legislation as may be necessary to exclude from the parks aforesaid certain areas forming part of certain of said parks which have been delimited as including the lands now forming part thereof which are of substantial commercial value, the boundaries of the areas to be so excluded having been heretofore agreed upon by representatives of Canada and of the province.[48]

Areas of "commercial value" included Canmore and its coal mines, and the coal mines east of Jasper. Exshaw, with its cement plant, was taken out of Banff Park. More than 1,300 square miles of timbered land was taken out of the parks, and contributed to Alberta's resource base. So also was the Spray valley, with its hydro potential. Boundaries were redrawn to exclude them all. William Pearce had been influential, for the Spray valley *would* be flooded. But not as influential as he had hoped. The Bow valley and Waterton Lakes remained in the parks and were now more securely protected. Pearce could see Harkin's "Italian hand" behind suggestions that water storage was inconsistent with the "amenity or utility of the parks".

Politicians claimed that little of any value was left in the parks, except the scenery: "This land is very desirable from a scenic point of view [but] as far as we know the area has no mineral value".[49]

With commercially valuable land removed, the scenery in the parks could be preserved. At least, preserved from mining, lumbering and hydroelectric dams. But, Harkin and Wheeler had not argued purely for the intrinsic value of the scenery, for the preservation of natural landscape. They had used one economic argument to counter another, insisting that beautiful scenery was in itself a source of profit — a source of tourist dollars. This argument dominated decisions about Canada's national parks through the thirties and forties, and prevails even today. Wheeler and Harkin saved the national parks from one kind of exploitation, but by ensuring their exploitation from another. In 1930 the new National Parks Act entrenched a system and philosophy of parks for profit.

CHAPTER FOUR

Autoparks

THE RAILROADS' dominance of passenger transportation was soon threatened by a new and more flexible means of travel. The automobile was destined to displace the railroads from priority in Canada's older parks. People in cars can decide when to leave, and how fast to travel. They can select their route (within the limits of the roadway system), and where and when to stop. They can find the cheapest gas, a preferred hotel or a new experience on a lake boat or hiking trail. An automobile could stop just outside the park, amd use cheaper facilities than those in the park. The automobile introduced competition into the business environment of the parks. New small entrepreneurs served autotourists, and advocated new parks and new roads to those parks.

DEFENCES AGAINST THE AUTOMOBILE

Established businesses in the older national parks tried to limit competition from the automobile. First they tried to protect their existing monopolies by forbidding cars in the park altogether. A couple of tourists from Boston brought a private car into Banff in 1904, and both the CPR and the livery stables protested. Cars were noisy, dangerous, and would frighten the horses and wildlife. There were not enough roads, and existing ones were unsuitable for automobiles. The government agreed to ban automobiles from the parks, protecting the railroad monopoly for seven more years.[1] But the automobile age was inevitable. Cars began as toys for enthusiasts, but by 1910 they were legitimate and convenient transportation. People were investing in cars, and developing businesses to serve motorists. A coach road was being built from Calgary to Banff, and in 1909 the Calgary Auto Club deliberately defied the regulations and brought their cars into the park, driving all around the town.[2] The car could not be stopped. Entrepreneurs in the parks had to find another way to protect their business interests. The railroads and other businesses in Banff tried to protect their monopolies by enlarging the parks. With boundaries further from the townsite the government controlled development across a larger area, and limited new commercial development which might compete with Banff's established businesses.

A major expansion in 1902 increased Banff Park from 260 to 4,400 square miles. The Rocky Mountain Parks Act of 1911 reduced this again, to bring the park within the administrative capacity of the Parks Branch. However, after debate and discussion the park was expanded again in 1917. The upper Red Deer River, the Panther watershed and the Kananaskis valley were added. The 2,751 square-mile park now contained Canmore, the Spray Lakes, the cement plant at Exshaw and the hydroelectricity site at Horseshoe Falls — uses today considered unsuitable in a national park.

Jasper Park was drastically reduced in size in 1911, with boundaries parrallel to and ten miles from the Grand Trunk Pacific railway line. But "scenic marvels" such as Medicine and Maligne lakes, Mount Edith Cavell and the alpine heights of the upper Athabasca and Sunwapta rivers were all left out. Railroad officials objected, as did the Alpine Club. Commissioner Harkin said the park was so narrow it was a joke! In 1914 the park was increased to 4,400 square miles. The railroad companies and their friends could for a while keep competition at a distance, beyond the park boundary.

These strategies eventually failed. The railroads, the Brewsters, and the Parks Branch all recognised the automobile's inevitability. All three became advocates of services for automobiles in the parks. The railroad companies wanted more roads, and lobbied for routes through their own property and beside their own railway line. The Brewsters, and the other outfitters, traded in horse-drawn carriages for gas-driven buses. The Parks Branch built roads through existing parks, and created new parks accessible by road rather than rail.

J. B. Harkin and Autotourism

The inevitability of the automobile age was obvious to Commissioner James B. Harkin. "Bunnie" (to his intimates) had been a journalist, rising to be the city editor of the *Ottawa Journal,* with membership in the parliamentary press gallery. In 1901 the minister of the interior, Clifford Sifton, had asked Harkin's editor to help hime recruit a political secretary. Harkin was recommended, and he joined as a first-class clerk. In 1904 he became the minister's private secretary, also serving Frank Oliver when he became minister in 1905.[3] Harkin recalled:

> It was in June, 1911, that Hon. Frank Oliver, then Minister of the Interior, called me into his office and told me that he was considering the creation of a new Branch of his department. The number of visitors, he said, who are coming to see our Canadian Rockies is increasing every year and the government feels that we should be doing more to protect this magnificent region. As you know we have one legally constituted area at Banff set aside by Act of Parliament as a "National Park", and four others set aside by Order-in-Council as scenic reserves. The Government has decided to bring down a Bill creating them all "Dominion Parks" and establishing a separate Branch headed by an executive who will have full power to administer and protect them.
>
> "How," he said, "Would you like to take on the job?"
>
> Overcome by surprise I could only say that I doubted my ability since I knew nothing about the parks or what would be expected of me.
>
> "All the better", said he in a laconic way, "You won't be hampered by preconceived ideas, and you can find out."[4]

The possibilities caught Harkin's imagination, and he accepted. Oliver's new parks commissioner lacked ties to the railroad and to other businesses benefiting from CPR protection. Harkin had no vested interest in the park monopolies. He was to turn railroad parks into automobile parks.

Harkin was different from the CPR's Pearce and the Alpine Club's Wheeler. Pearce and Wheeler were both volatile and outspoken. Although Harkin had strong convictions, he was even-tempered and careful. Wheeler and Pearce had been surveyors, with a love of wilderness. Harkin's preferences were more civilized: he played golf.[5] He was also creative, storing "good ideas" on cards for future development. In 1928 he suggested the tar sands of northern Alberta be used to surface roads![6]

Harkin took charge in the horse-and-buggy era, when coaches swept from Banff to Lake Louise over the park's only good gravelled road. But motorists already wanted the old "tote-road" from Calgary to Banff to be improved for cars. Motor roads were also needed in the parks.[7] In 1911 Harkin cancelled the prohibition on automobiles and introduced motor vehicle regulations. Car owners would pay twenty-five cents registration. Speeds were limited to 8 m.p.h. in the townsite, and 15 m.p.h. elsewhere. The railroad, though, still had influence. Cars were only allowed to travel from Calgary on the Calgary–Banff coach road, and were then to follow Banff Avenue and Spray Avenue straight to the CPR's Banff Springs Hotel.[8] Harkin further extended the freedom of the automobile in 1913, allowing their use to visit the golf course and private homes. A five dollar annual license was paid by those using a car within the park, and one dollar paid for a single trip. Two years later even more roads were opened to automobile traffic. In 1915 these regulations were extended to include all the national parks. In 1919 the speed limit was raised to 25 m.p.h..

Commissioner Harkin's enthusiasm for automobiles was expressed in 1914 in a thirty-four page document which guided his decisions for the next twenty years. The parks had two purposes, commercial and humanitarian. While the commercial concern for profit should be subordinate to the humanitarian, Harkin recognized that political support would be related to profit rather than humanitiarianism. Parks had to be a "solid business proposition", providing plentiful opportunities for profitable enterprise. The enterprise would be, of course, "autotourism". Harkin cited US experts, including railway executives, civil servants and politicians. He described the "See America First" movement, which encouraged Americans to spend their tourist dollars at home rather than in the "Canadian Pacific Rockies". Harkin quoted one US railroad president: "Thousands of Americans go to Canada every year for things they might just as well get here in the United

States. They go there for holidays and they go there to see the scenery in the Canadian Rockies — 95 per cent of the people going to Canada are Americans. The reason for it is the advertising which is being done by the Canadians. In the future we all want to go ahead and do a great deal more in the way of advertising. This will change the current of travel from Europe and Canada to this country."[9]

Harkin wanted to maintain and extend the flow of American tourists into Canada. A new Canadian association published a magazine promoting tourism in Canada. Three million American tourists visited Canada each year, bringing over two million dollars to Montreal alone. In Harkin's estimation, roads would increase the profitability of tourism in general, and of the national parks.

> In connection with the commercial side of National Parks automobile traffic appears to provide a means of immensely increasing the revenue to be derived for the people of Canada from the tourist. The Parks Branch is shaping its development work on lines calculated to make the unrivalled scenery of the Rockies accessible to automobile traffic. Consideration of the expansion of recent years with respect to motors and motoring cannot fail to convince one that adequate trunk roads through the mountains will inevitably mean a huge automobile traffic and consequently a large expenditure of money by autoists. Statistics indicate that in the United States alone there are about a million motor cars — a car for every hundred of the population.

> It is a well established fact that most motorists spend their holidays in their cars. Many facilities already exist which bring the motorists to the foot of the Rockies. What motorists will be able to resist the call of the Canadian Rockies when it is known that he can go through them on first class motor roads. And what a revenue this country will obtain when thousands of automobiles are traversing the parks.[10]

Throughout his career Harkin spoke of the profitability of national parks. He compared selling scenery with selling other Canadian natural resources, even calculating the dollar value of an acre of parkland. Scenery was worth $13.88 an acre, whereas wheatland was only worth $4.91.[11] And, scenery could be sold again and again, without diminishing its value. But, the key requirement would be accessibility. Harkin knew that to sell scenery Canada would have to build good roads into and through the parks.[12]

Harkin also justified roads into the parks on humanitarian grounds. Criticism in the House of Commons suggested the parks were for the rich, inaccessible to ordinary Canadians: "If these sites or parks happen to be the playground of the people of Canada, who are the people who are able to use them as a playground? At the present time these parks are practically situated in one place in Canada, with the result that there are thousands and thousands of people in Canada who are not able to visit them. As far as Saskatchewan is concerned at the present time I have no national park or no national playground that we can visit. Yet we have to help bear the burden. . . . a large amount of money is being spent almost entirely on one spot, to induce tourists from the United States."[13]

Government subsidized parks for wealthy foreigners. Harkin agreed parks had been the preserve of the wealthy, but the car would change all that. "In the past it has been a matter of regret that situated as they were, the parks could not serve all the people of Canada. With the coming of good roads and the low priced automobile, they are within easy reach of practically half the country."[14]

His minister also explained that the automobile, particularly the Ford, would open the parks to all income levels. "Some of the visitors to Banff come there in Ford cars. They are provided with camping facilities. I was simply amazed to find how many people camp in that way, and visit in Banff park at very little expense."[15]

"Bunnie" Harkin spent twenty-five years as parks commissioner building and maintaining roads to and through national parks. Building and maintaining the Calgary–Banff coach road, for example, was a major concern, absorbing a substantial portion of his parks budget for many years. The road was first completed in 1911, when a Calgary newspaper reported the "Good News": "Autos can run the Banff Park. The road from here to Banff Village is now very good. Change made in the Rules of the Park. Only One Bad Spot between here and Banff. It will be fixed."[16]

Maintenance was difficult. In 1913 the Calgary Automobile Club asked for the road to be finished "properly", but a Navy bill held up funds for park roads. The park superintendent promised to "repair the auto road from Kananaskis to Banff" so club members could "run autos into Banff from Calgary",[17] but ran out of funds and stopped work. In 1914 the road between Exshaw and the park boundary was again "in bad shape".[18] An appeal to their MP, R. B. Bennett, finally succeeded, though he "had a terrible time getting the Government to agree to go on with the work at the park".[19] Improvements were completed in 1914, but in 1916 the road was washed out. Repairs were slow, because of the wartime labour shortage. The superintendent telegraphed Harkin:

> Have gangs presently working on Banff–Calgary and Banff–Minnewanka roads. Have combed Exshaw, Canmore and Bankhead for men without success but have every available man working on the roads. Cannot get a gang for Banff–Castle [i.e. Banff–Lake Louise] road and Howard has only four men on surfacing work at Castle Laggan. We are doing best we can in face of labour shortage.[20]

Harkin wanted the impossible. He replied:

> Because of tourist traffic give priority to Banff–Kananaskis:

and:

> Essential put roads in good condition but our appropriations are limited:

and:

> With the park being heavily advertised among automobile owners on the Prairie this year, a large influx of these is expected, and I think we should make this job the very first. It is reported that two or three cars had to turn back at the boundary (of the park) last weekend.

and finally:

> If any bad spots on the automobile road do your best to put them in good condition for automobile week.[21]

His superintendent eventually did the impossible, and a Calgary newspaper headline read:

Road to Banff in Good Shape Motorists Say; Alberta Motor
League Tourists Make Run to Mountain City in Quick Time.

Motorists could now make better time on roads in the parks than
on those outside. In 1918, after a couple of timely showers, the
superintendent reported the Banff–Kananaskis road was in "better
shape than at any time since the introduction of motor cars". He
lacked workers, but got the job done anyway.

The CPR and the Automobile

William Pearce also promoted roads on the CPR's behalf. In 1913 he
returned from a convention on national parks to report that United
Kingdom and United States representatives were emphatic on the
inadvisability of letting automobiles "roam at will" through the
parks. However, as "arteries of communication connecting one
centre with another it would be idle to try and prevent the automobile roads being established and utilized". Cars could not be
prohibited, so roads should be put where they would be most useful to the CPR. Roads would increase land values. Selling land to a
man "stuck in a mud hole" would be a "dangerous proposition".
But if he had "bowled along comfortably at a high rate of speed for
some hours he could safely be tackled by a land agent".[22] Pearce
was told to advocate roads through CPR-owned land, so the
railroad could benefit. "To insure that the main automobile road
through the mountains be located on Canadian Pacific Railway
territory certainly appears to me to be to be a thing of importance
to the company, and I would welcome any suggestion from you as
to actions which we might take to bring about this desirable
result."[23]

In 1926 the Canadian government decided to build a road
through the mountains. Pearce proposed it be build adjacent to the
CPR right of way. This would have a number of advantages. A road
built on the flat, said Pearce, would be easier to build. The flattest
route was alongside the CPR tracks. Most of his recommendations
were uncontroversial, because they were the most feasible. However, the choice between the Rogers Pass (which was high, but
contained the CPR right of way) and the Big Bend (which was
longer and flatter) attracted debate. Pearce, of course, proposed a
road through Glacier Park in the Rogers Pass.

Typically he wrote letters everywhere: to the premier of Alberta and the federal minister of roads; to the commissioner of irrigation and the Calgary Board of Trade. He spoke for the Calgary Automobile Club at the Canadian Good Roads Convention, on the need for roads through the Rockies. He wrote to MP R. B. Bennett. He was so persistent that Bennett felt harassed, replying: "I only marvel at the amount of work you are able to get through, but I think if you had to live down here for two or three weeks you would understand what a destroyer of time the House of Commons really is."[24]

Pearce also ran a public campaign. Headlines read:

> William Pearce Favours Rogers Pass Route:
>
> Veteran Engineer Sets out Reasons for Choice of his plan;
>
> Big Bend Road not favoured by Expert;
>
> Sees Great Attraction to Tourists in Summit Highway.[25]

But Pearce was not impartial. The route was of great interest to the CPR. Avalanche hazards had led the company to dig the Connaught Tunnels in 1916, taking the trains under the Rogers Pass. No trains stopped in Glacier, and only the hardiest alpinists reached the railroad company's hotel. Business dwindled. A road through the Rogers Pass would restore the popularity of the CPR's hotel. The CPR offered their disused railbed for the road. Pearce mobilized support in Regina, Kamloops, Revelstoke and Calgary, and even the British Columbia Automobile Club supported the route through Glacier as both more scenic and more direct.

The only community support for the longer Big Bend route came from the Alberta Motor Association, based in Edmonton. They wanted a road through Edmonton to the west, and the Big Bend route would be part of it. Within the federal government, Harkin also supported the Big Bend road. The Rogers Pass route would cost more, even though several miles of disused railway grade could be used. Also, snow slides would close a road in the Rogers Pass.[26] Road enthusiast though he was, Harkin still felt automobiles should be kept out of one national park. "I might say that this Branch is not favourable to the adoption of the Glacier Park route. It is felt that one National Park should be kept free of motor traffic and Glacier Park affords the last opportunity of doing this."[27]

Finally, and most important, the British Columbia government preferred the Big Bend route because it opened promising mining country. The Big Bend route around the Selkirks was chosen, rather than the Rogers Pass. The railroad company cut their losses. Glacier Hotel was closed and fell into disrepair. The Alpine Club members were upset, for it had been a favourite. Arthur Wheeler mourned: "The chief charm of this hotel was its homelike atmosphere and the informal hospitality that led to a fine feeling of camaradery and good fellowship. It is too deeply to be regretted that for the time being the hotel is not in operation and that climatic conditions have caused the present building to be condemned."[28]

But a hotel without access by train or by car was unprofitable. The Rogers Pass, and Glacier Park, remained deserted until the new Trans-Canada Highway was built through the Rogers Pass in 1962.

The selection of a route opposed by the CPR was significant. By the mid-twenties the CPR had less influence than at the turn of the century. Then the railroad companies had been able to negotiate many advantages — whether land grants, townsite locations or national parks. Now the automobile competed with the train, and the railways had lost their transportation monopoly. Loss of monopoly brought loss of influence. New interests, concerned with the new form of transportation, competed for the ear of government.

THE BREWSTER EMPIRE

The automobile was a new and exciting opportunity for the smaller enterprises that had developed under protection of the railroad monopolies. While the CPR was trying to influence the location of roads, the Brewsters were using those roads to expand their own empire. The Brewsters and other livery companies had capital invested in horses and equipment. The Brewsters had "three 'hotel buses', twelve tally-hos, nineteen three-seaters, twenty surreys, eighteen single rigs and numerous miscellaneous rigs, baggage wagons and cartage wagons — as well as 146 head of driving horses".[29] Automobiles should be gradually introduced. In 1910 the Brewsters wanted to use a "horseless carriage" between the station and the hotel at Lake Louise. The trail was steep, and "representatives of societies" were "complaining of the cruelty to animals driven on the road".[30] They got permission, but the CPR put in a tram line instead.

In 1915 Jim Brewster bought a Canadian-made Baby Overland. He liked its "climbing abilities". In 1916 he bought five more, but wanted to continue using horses on narrower trails. Brewster's competitors wanted to use automobiles throughout the park, and said all roads should be widened and all restrictions lifted. The Brewsters had too much invested in horses. The CPR supported Brewster's request for reservation of some roads for horses only. But Harkin had no allegiance to the railroad or its dependencies. The roads were widened, and cars and buses were allowed everywhere. Brewster still did not give up his old tally-ho's. He bought several trucks, and stripped them down, mounting the upper framework of the tally-ho on the truck chassis. The drivers got new top hats and coats, and Banff's first "auto tally-ho" was born.

Tourism slumped in the First World War, and the Brewsters had financial trouble. But still, with the end of the war they risked further additions to their fleet. They joined the "Grey Line" in 1928, and had half a million dollars in assets by 1929. The company came close to collapse in the depression, but prospered after the Second World War. Greyhound purchased it in the 1960s for a million dollars. The Brewsters had made their million on the roads of Canada's western national parks.

BUSINESS DEVELOPMENT IN BANFF

Others also profited from the protection offered by the park. The Banff Board of Trade (later Banff Advisory Council) spoke for these business people. The board had a "Good Roads Committee"; promoted events such as Indian Days; and advocated development of the golf course and the recreation grounds.[31] They insisted that groceries not be sold at camp grounds, so people had to come into Banff. They opposed increases in the cost of leases, and tried (unsuccessfully) to stop anyone advertising cut-rate expeditions. They wanted to keep outside bus companies out of the parks. They wanted to limit competition in the taxi business, by introducing tests that included knowledge of the "sights", and restricting taxis to taxi stands. They opposed construction by the CPR of another line through the valley, so that Banff remained the only commercial centre. This was not "free" enterprise, but a system of protection for the benefit of existing entrepreneurs. The only competition sought by the Banff council was a second railroad serving Banff, to compete with the CPR. They wanted the cheaper prices resulting from competition, without subjecting themselves to a competitive environment.[32]

New businesses had to break into this environment without help from the government or the CPR. For some the automobile had brought a decline in profits. Wheeler operated a commercial walking tour, supported by pack trains, for several years. In 1925 he asked the Parks Department to subsidize his operation, because of a drop in business. He blamed the motor car, because "people who have them feel bound to use them". The Parks Branch refused to help, not wanting to be unfair to other pack-train operators.[33] Free enterprise for Wheeler, but protection for his established competitors.

Patronage was also important for anyone doing business in Banff National Park. R. B. Bennett as MP responded to local constituents like Brewster, and CPR employees like Pearce. Bennett also provided lists of suitably Conservative candidates for employment, and suppliers of such things as gasoline engines and sewer pipe. He intervened on behalf of those wanting to quarry, to provide a massage service, or to sell advertising space in the park. Commissioner Harkin had Bennett's support for expanding the park and forbidding billboards on park roads. Bennett was horrified by that possibility: "Any person who would request the privilege of erecting a bill board in a National Park must have a very poor idea of the eternal fitness of things".[34]

But working through their local Conservative association, the Brewsters tried to discredit Commissioner Harkin. Brewster, and another businessman, Norman Luxton, boasted of their "influence" with Harkin. The commissioner explained to Bennett that the complaint was probably related to his purchase of supplies in Calgary rather than Banff. Harkin said he favoured no one: "It seems absurd to hold me responsible for what Brewster and Luxton may say. Last year I personally told Brewster that if we ever caught him killing game in the Park I would personally see that he was expelled from the Park and kept out. This talk about influence at Ottawa may be simply clever work on his part (and Luxton's too) to put one over on me. You are well aware of his methods. He is strong on giving things a certain steer and sitting in the background while his catspaws do the rest."[35]

R. B. Bennett remained interested in the national parks. In the depression of the 1930s, as prime minister, his Public Works Construction Acts produced many of the park facilities (including roads) that we enjoy today.

PARK POLITICS

New roads opened up the parks to new visitors. Only the wealthy had been able to visit the Canadian Pacific Rockies, and use the luxurious railroad hotels. Now the middle class could use their cars to go camping. One such visitor, Jennie McAllister wrote to the park superintendent:

> I have had the most wonderful trip home from the East coming by motor from Banff and I do want to tell you how very wonderful it is that such men as you have seen so far ahead and to have made it possible for motorists to enjoy the very grand and gorgeous scenery bestowed by Our Maker in the very great Province of BC to have such a highway already traversed by tourists from Ontario, Quebec, New York and hundreds from the South bringing money and people into Canada through this great Province. We met thousands during our trip, and when that link from Golden to Revelstoke is finished we will have thousands we now lose who turn south into United States and not coming by rail as it is too expensive. $27 is a big item and when that is added to by train tickets and meals for 4 or 5 passengers, not many will pay it so of course we (Canada) lose all that extra.[36]

Visitors like Mrs. McAllister were good for business. Not necessarily for big companies like the railroad or even for the Brewsters, but for small tourist shops, service stations, grocery stores and motels along the highways of western Canada. As the small business sector grew national parks became good politics, as well as good economics. The middle-class Canadian tourists who used their cars to explore the parks were all voters (once women obtained the vote). A politician responsible for creating a park they had enjoyed, or building a road they had travelled, would be favoured. Politicians creating a park within an afternoon's drive earned constituent support. Their leadership would be remembered with gratitude during an afternoon's drive on a good road, on a warm summer day by the beach, or during a hike on a fine fall weekend. Those memories might translate into votes, come election time.

Local politicians asked for national parks, in Revelstoke for example. Provincial politicians in Saskatchewan, Manitoba and the Maritimes, wanted national parks — as long as costs were born by Ottawa. Members of Parliament asked for national parks for their constituents. In 1909 a Saskatchewan MP asked for a game reserve and some buffalo, "as we have no land at present reserved for park purposes as in other provinces of the Dominion". By the 1920s the requests became a flood. In 1924 a Nova Scotia MP wanted a park in the Maritimes, as did other MPs from Eastern Canada. Members from all over the country asked for national parks,[37] or for roads to make existing parks more accessible.

Not all requests succeeded. The government would not create parks in an opposition constituency, where the political credit could be taken by another party. Also, although Ottawa could unilaterally create parks on the prairies (until 1930), elsewhere land for a national park required provincial agreement. In central and eastern Canada, and in British Columbia the province had to hand over the land, unencumbered by private ownership, timber leases or mining claims. Most provinces refused. If land was acquired it was for a provincial park. Then provincial politicians would get the political credit, not the federal government. Also, in a provincial park the province could continue to exploit all the natural resources. The only way to persuade a provincial government to accept a national park was the promise of road construction — roads that could be used both for tourists, and as part of the infrastructure for provincial economic development. Roadways became more important than railroads in park politics.

A Road to Jasper

Jasper National Park had two railways, Grand Trunk Pacific and Canadian Northern, until the two were merged under state ownership in 1923. Survey work for park roads began in 1911, and by 1924 gave access to Maligne Canyon, Mount Edith Cavell and several nearby lakes. But there was no road linking Jasper and Edmonton, no northern equivalent of the Banff coach road from Calgary. Edmonton business people set up the "Edmonton Auto and Good Roads Association", to promote a businesslike approach to city government (a typical objective for civic groups at that time), and road development. The construction of a road to Jasper was a favourite project: "Aggressive action on the Jasper highway was the greatest feature of the 1922 program, and it is satisfactory to be able to note that this action on the part of the Association has had united co-operation of all Good Road advocates; steady aid and assistance from the Council of the City of Edmonton; sympathetic hearing on the part of various Cabinet Ministers, both in Alberta, British Columbia, and at Ottawa; and the undivided cooperation of the local and district press".[38]

In 1924 the Canadian government began its section of road within Jasper Park. In 1925 the minister of the interior, Charles Stewart, was among the Liberals defeated in the general election. The government hung on, and he was successful in an Edmonton by-election. Stewart tried to bolster his electoral hopes through road construction. The federal government finished its section of the Jasper–Edmonton Highway in 1928. But the province did not complete its own section from the park gates to Edmonton. In 1929, just before another general election, Stewart instructed his department to build the provincial section of the road. The Liberals were defeated, so Stewart could not complete the road.

Without road access, Jasper National Park remained the poor sister of the mountain parks. The completion of the Banff–Jasper Highway in 1941 brought the first wave of visitors from Banff into Jasper, but the Yellowhead Highway from Edmonton into British Columbia was not opened until 1968.

MOUNT REVELSTOKE NATIONAL PARK

In 1912 J. H. Hamilton of Revelstoke's Progress Club persuaded his Member of Parliament, and the Member in an adjacent constituency, to get the mountain top set aside as a park. The people of Revelstoke wanted a road to the park, but war limited regular park expenditures. They were not going to give up that easily. In 1915 they petitioned Harkin for a road, repeating their request in 1916. They suggested the work be done by prisoners of war:

> I beg to enclose herewith a copy of a resolution endorsed by the Executive of the Revelstoke Conservative Association, the Revelstoke Liberal Assocation and Revelstoke Board of Trade and the Revelstoke Retail Merchants Association which represents practically all the voters in Revelstoke and vicinity.

Anything you can do towards having an internment camp established here for the purposes of completing the autoroad to the summit of the mountain will be highly appreciated by this community.[39]

The Hague Convention allowed for internees to work, and Revelstoke's new national park seemed appropriate. The place was remote. The people of Revelstoke wanted the road and would presumably welcome the internees. Still, Harkin reminded them, the men were just people who had been at the wrong place at the wrong time: "War prisoners are not criminals, but are in many cases merely citizens of countries with which the empire is at war who happened to be in Canada at the time hostilities were declared. Under international law they may not be treated as prisoners but are entitled to certain considerations."[40]

Harkin was naive, though. He expected that the men would work for twenty-five cents a day. Free men were getting eight times that for work in isolated camps. The men worked through the first summer and fall, but with cold weather they spent more time winterizing their camp than working on the road. They cut and hauled firewood, cut props to reinforce their cabins to carry snow, and eventually shovelled the snow itself. The men got restless. Blacksmiths refused to dress tools. The men became obstinate. Morale sank as the men struggled with frozen tents and heavy snow falls. They were moved into Field until spring. Little work had been accomplished.

The following year Revelstoke asked for the camp to be reopened, to finish the road. But park officials were disenchanted with interned workers. Many had been released and those remaining were unlikely to be productive. The road remained incomplete until the 1920s.

KOOTENAY NATIONAL PARK

Kootenay was created because the provincial governments wanted federal help with road construction. This was Canada's first park with a roadway straight through the middle, but no railroad. Even the government's own publications called it a "highway park".[41] The federal government had agreed to pay for the highways within BC's national parks, and the province and the CPR would pay for the rest. The federal government built its own portion, but BC's section proved difficult and costs exceeded the budget. Work stopped in 1913.

Business groups in communities along the highway, such as Banff, supported the project. The federal government agreed to complete the road, but only if a ten-mile-wide strip of land either side of the highway were set aside as a national park. In addition, British Columbia would have to agree to all the boundaries to other national parks in the province.[43] For British Columbia this road would provide access to resources. CPR land holdings would increase in value. For the federal government the road would be part of a transportation system holding the country together. The agreement was signed in 1919, and "Kootenay" Park established. Nearly 5,000 cars travelled the Banff–Windermere Highway after it opened in 1923.

ELK ISLAND PARK

Elk Island Park originated as a game reserve,[44] but could have become as commercially successsful as the mountain parks. The Koney Island Sporting Company did good business on the edge of the park until 1909. Then the Grand Trunk Pacific railroad carried its first passengers from Edmonton to the north shore of Cooking Lake, south of Elk Island Park. A tourist town boomed, not in the park, but at the railway terminus. Cottages, a hotel and a pier were built. In 1911 Cooking Lake became so popular that special trains took hundreds, even thousands of holiday makers to the steamers and motor boats waiting at the pier. Cooking Lake's glory was short-lived.

In 1922 Elk Island Park was enlarged to accommodate expanding herds of buffalo and elk. The new boundaries abutted the highway from Edmonton. Elk Island Park now became an automobile park, within convenient distance from Edmonton. In 1923 a road was built to Sandy Beach on Astotin Lake. Elk Island's popularity grew as Cooking Lake water levels fell, and the lake atrophied. With purer water and road access, Elk Island's Lake Astotin became decidedly more attractive for swimming and boating.

Elk Island Park became a resort, like others within an afternoon's drive of Canadian cities. Park officials encouraged commercialism, with two bungalow cabin camps, a restaurant, a service station and a dance hall. But Astotin Lake has now atrophied also, and swimmer's itch discourages all but the most determined bathers. Pressure for commercial development has declined with the water quality, allowing park managers to operate the park with less concern for profit. Commercial facilities have been replaced by government operated interpretive programs. Elk Island Park is no longer profitable, and can be the kind of park preferred by environmentalists.

PRINCE ALBERT NATIONAL PARK

Prince Albert National Park, the second prairie park, was created in Saskatchewan in 1927, as a thank you present from Prime Minister Mackenzie King to his new constituents. The prime minister had been defeated in the general election of 1925, and sought a new seat in Prince Albert. Neither the Progressives nor the Conservatives opposed him in the 1926 by-election, and with the support of the provincial premier he won easily over an independent.[45] In the following September he again won easily in a general election, defeating young John Diefenbaker.

The next year, firmly in the prime minister's chair once more, Mackenzie King expressed his gratitude to his constituents. He gave Saskatchewan its first national park, in a forest reserve near his own constituency of Prince Albert. Although development of the new access road was still underway, and the town site was not yet developed, the prime minister officially opened the park himself in August 1928. He was presented with a summer cottage on Waskesiu Lake, and another lake was named "Kingsmere". He wrote in his diary of his hope that the park would help his constituents remember him.[46]

By the next federal election in 1930, boy scouts had a bi-annual camp in the park, and newspaper boys were treated to holidays. King arrived during the campaign, and spent a "quiet" weekend in his cottage on Waskesiu, having listened to a waltz named after the lake. King retained his seat easily, again defeating Diefenbaker, who then gave up trying to get elected in his home constituency. The "chief" did not contest Prince Albert again until 1953. A park, particularly when accessible by road, was a suitable gift to one's constituents, and could produce long term loyalty. National parks could help to stimulate support for government and enhance the private accumulation of capital.

RIDING MOUNTAIN NATIONAL PARK

Manitobans also wanted a national park, and the area first favoured by politicians was the Whiteshell lakeland near the Ontario border. The federal government agreed, but the provincial government would have to build the road to, and through, the park. The arrangement with British Columbia over Kootenay Park would not be duplicated. The proposal was endorsed by all Manitoba's MPs and the Manitoba premier.

But support was not universal. The minister of the interior, Charles Stewart, received resolutions from municipal councils all over Manitoba recommending that Riding Mountain, a forest reserve north-west of Winnipeg and within easy reach by car, be set aside instead. The Whiteshell was too inaccessible, and the wildlife not as interesting. A lawyer from Dauphin, a town just south of Riding Mountain reserve, organized a Riding Mountain Park Committee. Their writing campaign convinced the Parks Branch of support for Riding Mountain as a park, and in 1928 the minister came to look for himself. He addressed a crowd at a picnic: "I am not going to say that we will call this a National Park, but I do say this — you will have all the facilities of a National Park. We will develop a small golf course for you; we will provide facilities for cottages here and give you sufficient ground for a playground and camping ground, and then your committee will have to get to work again to get a road which will provide facilities for people coming in here every day."[47]

Politicians like to respond to popular pressure. In 1929 the Manitoba MPs all signed a memorandum asking for a national park.[48] Riding Mountain was created in 1930, as part of the Transfer of Resources Agreement between Ottawa and the Prairie provinces. The following year the park was visited by 6,000 cars and 12,000 people.[49] But this was the last park to be created on the prairies for many years. The Transfer of Resources Agreement meant the Canadian government could no longer create national parks unilaterally on the prairies. The Prairie provinces, just like the other provincial governments, would have to hand over the land free of encumbrances. Provincial enthusiasm for national parks was rarely sufficient for such a transfer.

NATIONAL PARKS IN ONTARIO

Ontario was unenthusiastic about national parks, and only three tiny ones were created. The province preferred instead to create provincial parks such as Algonquin and Quetico, where multiple-resource exploitation could continue. The three exceptions were possible because the parks were created on land that already belonged to the federal government. St. Lawrence Islands National Park (created in 1914) and Georgian Bay (created in 1929) were both purchased from land held in trust for Canadian Indian bands. Point Pelee was created using land that had belonged to the admiralty.

Point Pelee National Park was created following pressure by conservationists enthusiastic about preservation of birds.[50] But, like other national parks created at the end of the railway age, Point Pelee ended up being more about roads than about birds. The parks commissioner recommended a new road be built near the park, to improve its accessibility.[51] Then he battled with his voluntary park superintendent about the cost of gravelling roads in the park. Then a development company wanted to divert the access road, spoiling the scenery. Lots were subdivided on the point, so residents wanted a road along the east shore, to relieve "acute traffic problems". The "honorary" superintendent and the Toronto Field Naturalists opposed this plan. Then the Essex County Automobile Club wanted the existing road paved. National park status had increased the pressure for access, rather than reduced it.

Once roads were built, Point Pelee was so popular that by 1924 the superintendent was concerned that "the great crowds cannot be kept under control" and feared that the open spaces would "suffer to a large extent by motor traffic".[52] Point Pelee was a playground for people living in the cities and towns of southern Ontario and the northern United States. Parks Commissioner Harkin admitted that bird protection was incidental — Point Pelee was "primarily a National recreation area".[53] In spite of determined efforts by park planners to limit human impact Point Pelee remains primarily a recreation area. Heavy use is still a problem.

FROM RAILROAD TO AUTOMOBILE

In the railroad age the parks had been promoted by the railroad companies, close to the ear of the federal government. Parks had expanded to meet the railroads' needs. By 1930 the CPR and the CNR were losing passengers to the automobile,[54] and losing interest in national parks. Without the enthusiasm of the railroads, national parks slid from the list of national priorities. Support became more diffuse, scattered through local constituencies and expressed by individual politicians. Their enthusiasm on the hustings and in the House produced a few more national parks — but only when a road would be built at federal expense to and through the park. National parks were not created in Quebec, and those in Ontario remained pitifully small. Apart from Wood Buffalo National Park on the border of Alberta and the Northwest Territories, no national parks were created in the North. No parks were created on the BC coast, and creating parks in the Maritimes was a painful process.

Without the support of the railroads, national park budgets were eroded. Parks Commissioner Harkin, and his successors, had difficulty finding funds for roads and other facilities. In 1914 the federal government had spent one-half of one per cent of its total budget on the national parks. Between 1915 and 1947 the average annual expenditure on national parks by the federal government slid to .28 per cent of the national budget. Two wars and a major depression left little for such "frivolous" purposes as national parks. In the post-war period spending rose again, particularly during the construction boom of the 1950s, and after new parks were added by the Liberal government of Pierre Trudeau. By 1981 Canada was spending .37 per cent of the national budget on national parks, still a smaller proportion than was spent in the period before the First World War.

Harkin tried to obtain sufficient resources. While the politicians used parks and roads to solidify their electoral support, Parks Commissioner Harkin used politicians to promote parks. He encouraged them to believe parks would enhance their popularity. His image of playgrounds across the country, accessible to all who could drive a car, was being fulfilled. He had envisaged parks to benefit both entrepreneurs in search of a profit, and city dwellers needing recreation. He promoted the national parks as profitable, as stimulants to Canada's tourist industry, but also with humanitarian purposes. In many parts of Canada people could now visit "a national playground", comparatively close to their hometown.

Politicians did believe they could benefit from the good will of constituents who gave them credit for calling for, or even better, creating a national park. Boards of trade and other small business groups scattered across the country were also enthusiastic about the profits from tourism stimulated by national parks. They sought commercial opportunities in the parks, and pressed for road construction. They told politicians of their enthusiasm. Politicians rose in the House of Commons, in provincial legislatures and in municipal council chambers to call for national parks for their constituents. But, while national parks were politically attractive to those seeking election, they no longer had a central place in national policy. The railroads were no longer interested. The national government, no longer as tied to those railroads, also gave parks less attention. The smaller entrepreneurs who now made up the tourism business were too scattered for their influence to be effective. Harkin's promotion was insufficient to restore parks expenditures, or to create national parks wherever they were lacking.

Harkin and his successors attempted to solve the first problem, that of insufficient funds, by using a variety of special work-creation programs. The second problem, the uneven distribution of national parks, had to wait until the birth of Canada's second conservation movement in the 1960s. Although Harkin failed to ensure that national parks remained a political priority, his initiatives still influence the way Canadian national parks are conceived. The automobile is still the primary means of parks access, and a road is the first development in any new national park.

The concern for autotourism even dominated the organization which had originally been concerned with preservation. None of the parks enthusiasts, not even the Alpine Club or the National Parks Association that had struggled to save the parks from hydro development, resisted the penetration of the automobile into the parks. With the National Parks Act of 1930, and the change in park boundaries that removed the Spray River valley from the park, the leaders of the movement to "save the parks" went to sleep. Some, like Wheeler, were too old, or too familiar to be effective. Preservation looked less important during the economic crisis of the 1930s and the world war which followed. The Canadian National Parks Association did not die but was transformed. In the 1930s the group's members became "patriotic Canadians from coast to coast in support of National Parks and tributary highways".[55] By the 1940s the group supported "National Parks, tributary highways, recreational travel, modern forestry".[56]

Parks were profitable tourist attractions, rather than sanctuaries of preservation. Harkin and his allies (politicians seeking parks and roads for their constituents, and the small business people seeking tourist profits) were noisy, but their influence was diffuse. None had the political access and control that had been available to the railroads. They were not powerful enough to substantially increase the number of national parks, or to ensure the Parks Branch budget kept pace with its responsibilities. Harkin had entrenched autotourism as the major purpose of Canada's national parks.

CHAPTER FIVE

Building the Parks

A LOW PRIORITY at budget time did not necessarily mean a halt to all parks development. The parks were actually a hive of activity. Golf courses were designed, landscaped and groomed — patches of civilized wilderness. Craftsmen used logs to build wardens' cabins, administrative headquarters and gatehouses. Retaining walls were hand-built of rock from the parks' own quarries, and hiking trails were carved out of mountain slopes and prairie forests. Roads were built everywhere, bridging ravines, rivers and railroads. All this was done by a Parks Department with a reduced budget.

MAKING WORK IN THE PARKS

Park development was possible because most men working in the parks had no choice, and received less than the market wage. From 1914 to 1945 thousands were forced into labour camps, in the national parks and elsewhere. They included prisoners in the two world wars, men working for relief and in make-work programs in the Great Depression, and conscientious objectors and Japanese internees in the Second World War. For thirty years these programs provided the Parks Branch with an average of 700 extra workers. That was five times the permanent park staff in 1950, and twice the total park work force in that year.

Table 5.1   *Cheap Labour in Canada's National Parks**

World War One	Workyears
Civilian Internees	813
The Great Depression	
Work for relief	11,429
Public Works Construction Acts	5,208
National Forestry Program	417
World War Two	
Conscientious Objectors	2,025
Prisoners of War	200
Japanese Internees	1,208
Total	21,300

*Table constructed from Annual Reports of the Commissioner of Dominion Parks, and other departmental documents.

These men were stripped of their civil liberties. Some worked hard. Even under work camp conditions they demonstrated craftsmanship, leaving a marvellous inheritance of park buildings and facilities. Others were restless and resentful, and protested by striking. They malingered, or worked slowly. Some tunnelled out, trying to escape. In total, though, whether they worked willingly or under protest, these men left a mark on the national parks. Without their contribution the Parks Branch could hardly have maintained the parks, let alone built the roads, buildings, tennis courts, golf courses and trails enjoyed today.

WORLD WAR ONE

The first unwilling workers were civilians interned in the First World War. In 1914 the War Measures Act provided for internment of anyone suspected of being an "enemy alien". Those who "quietly pursued their ordinary avocations" were "accorded the respect and consideration due to peaceful and law-abiding citizens".[1] About 8,000 were actually interned, but only 2,117 remained in camps by the end of the war.[2]

The Hague Convention provided for internees to work "according to their rank and capacity" on projects having nothing to do with the war. The men were placed in the federal government's forest reserves and national parks. Some worked briefly on the road to the mountain top in Revelstoke Park, and we met them in

Chapter 4. Internees also worked in Field, in Jasper and in Banff national parks. Parks Commissioner Harkin was delighted with his new work force, costing only twenty-nine cents a day for support, and twenty-five cents a day for pay. The typical daily wage in an isolated camp was two dollars, so internees were very cheap.[3] The men could be made to work: "We have supervising officials to see that the prisoners do the work. The work is not voluntary on the part of the prisoners; they are taken and put to work."[4]

But Harkin soon found the men would not work for twenty-five cents a day. The camp at Revelstoke, described above, was closed as winter deepened and the men became more restless. The men were moved to Field in Yoho Park, and the Revelstoke camp was not reopened. The park superintendent in Yoho, Russell, believed the Field camp could be profitable: men would remove sound timber from an old fire burn, for sale as pit props, fence posts and railroad ties. A camp was built, and the railway line extended to take out the timber. Buildings were ready for Christmas 1915, when "the only men not in comfortable quarters" were the park employees.[5] The men were in good spirits, for Russell had agreed to a holiday on Greek Christmas. He wanted to keep them happy: "We can get far better results out of these men if they are contented, but if sulky it is pretty hard to do much with them".[6]

Weather prevented work on all but three days in January. Then a prisoner escaped, and work stopped until guards found him. In the spring work began again, until June floods washed away bridges and the camp had to be moved. Then 129 of 200 men refused to work. They resented internment, because other aliens were "still allowed not only to go free, but also to earn their living". Free market wages had shot up to six, eight or even twelve dollars a day. The twenty-five cents a day paid in the camp looked miserable. The men were sick from typhoid shots. On top of that, they dreaded another winter in camp. The men would obviously not work again without "strenuous measures". Letters smuggled in from other camps showed no internees were working. Russell gave up: "There is no reason to supose that we can expect the Aliens to go to work again, and my opinion is that there is very little chance of their doing so."[7]

Feeding the men wasted Parks Branch money, and Harkin asked the Department of Defence to take over. Then, in a scene straight out of television's "Hogan's Heroes", the men dug their way out with shovels and table knives. They only had eight more feet to go when discovered. The newspapers reported them "unruly and surly for some time."[8] The camp was closed, and the men were dispersed. The labour shortage worsened as war continued, and many internees were released to jobs in industry. Russell had been overly optimistic. The men had produced no pit-props or fence posts. Four miles of right-of-way was cleared, and several bridges built "in a most creditable manner", but not where they could be of use. The new tool house and wagon shed had been built, but would not be needed.

In 1916 two hundred aliens also worked in Jasper National Park. But the men were Austrian rather than German, and of "proven good behaviour". They were released to work for the railways and the coal mines, under RCMP supervision.[9]

The largest internment camp in the parks was in Banff, with almost as many men as had worked there under free market conditions before the war. The road near Lake Louise was repaired and widened. The men cut wood, and cleared brush around the town and buffalo paddocks. In 1917 the Parks Branch took over the CPR's nine-hole golf course, intending to use "alien labour" to add another nine holes. Not much work was done. The most capable men had been released to private industry, and the rest were "dangerous". Later in 1917 the camp at Banff was closed, and the remaining men sent to Petawawa Forestry Reserve in northern Ontario.

Even after this failure, Harkin continued to seek cheap labour. He investigated work programs in US prisons. Prisoners built roads in Virginia for $3,400 a mile, compared with $4,900 for road built by free labour — saving nearly 30 per cent. "Hard manual labour" was beneficial, bringing men "in close touch with nature and its fresh air and sunshine".[10] Some men were rewarded with a "small wage", and others with a reduced sentence. In the South, where "prisoners are of a lower type", the guard system had been cost-efficient in producing a fair day's work! Fortunately, Harkin was unable to obtain prisoners to work in Canada's national parks.

In 1918 the parks budget was restored to the pre-war level of about $1 million. But prices had inflated, and government expenditures rose. Parks expenditures as a percentage of total government costs remained between .28 per cent and .39 per cent, well below the pre-war levels of .50 per cent. Budget limitations and labour shortage lasted into the 1920s. Some park roads were built, but only those with major political backing. The Banff–Windermere

Highway through Kootenay Park had to be built because of the deal with British Columbia. The road to the top of Mount Revelstoke, begun by internees, was finished. And Prime Minister Mackenzie King made sure the new park in his constituency in Saskatchewan was developed. By 1930 around 400 miles of park roads had been built, 145 in the Rocky Mountain parks.

WORK FOR RELIEF

Until the 1930s the Parks Branch provided relief in the parks. The branch was stingy and punitive. In 1924 the mine at Brule in Jasper National Park closed, and Alberta asked Ottawa to help park residents thrown out of work. Commissioner Harkin told the park superintendent to give groceries "if conditions were desperate", but no cash. He should "exercise special care not to encourage further demands".[11] Three families were found in sufficiently desperate circumstances, but the superintendent reported smugly to Harkin: "The total expenditure through Corporal Birks has been very light and he is giving assistance to only the Montray family at present and that (sic) very small. You can rely on us all protecting the Government's interests in this matter."[12]

Unemployment rose again when the railways laid off men. In 1925 the superintendent asked Commissioner Harkin for $1,000 for work-for-relief projects, but was turned down. In 1929 the situation worsened, and the superintendent asked for a $20,000 winter-works program. The Jasper Advisory Council supported him, but Harkin again said, "No". The parks commissioner did not understand welfare matters, and approached his responsibilities with the conservatism and insensitivity of a small-town clerk.

Declining conditions in Jasper presaged the stock market crash of 1929. Crops failed. The price of wheat fell. Canadians, from east coast to west, turned to relief. By 1933 about a fifth of the work force was unemployed, and 15 per cent of Canadians were on relief.[13] Regular parks expenditures were drastically reduced, as governments rescued the unemployed and destitute. The Parks Branch was fortunate that some programs for the unemployed put men to work in the parks.

In 1930 the Unemployment Relief Act introduced a federal work-for-relief program costing $4.5 million in the first year. Most of the funds were allocated to provincial governments. In Saskatchewan and Manitoba the federal relief funds were used to set up work camps in the national parks. Unemployed men from the urban centres were sent to Prince Albert and Riding Mountain. Alberta set up projects in the cities, where unemployment was higher than in rural areas. Only $38,000 was spent on the regular residents of the national parks, who were given relief in return for building and repairing roads, and for constructing bridges, wharves, trails and cabins. Eight hundred men were employed under work-for-relief in the national parks in 1930–31, working a total of nearly 16,000 man days.[14]

In 1931 unemployment worsened. The "short term" program of 1930 was extended. Conditions for Banff and Jasper residents remained desperate, and the prime minister himself added another $33,000 to work-for-relief funds for the mountain parks. Over the year 266,000 days of relief work were provided, compared with 16,000 in 1930. Relief work in the parks now supported some of the unemployed who began to criss-cross the nation in search of work, as well as park residents. The kind of work changed too. Now Harkin could build the major highway of which he had dreamed for two decades — from Jasper to Banff. Also, new park boundaries agreed upon in the Transfer of Resources agreement of 1930 were surveyed and marked. Work was "necessarily restricted", but relief funds paid for "numerous important works" which "would otherwise have had to be held over for better times".[15]

Work-for-relief helped Harkin more than those who depended on it for a livelihood. The park superintendent in Jasper saw the grim reality, as the railways laid off men with twelve to sixteen years seniority, and park residents returned after fruitless searches for work. Transients roamed in search of work. The relief camps paid even less than the market wage. Relief work on the roads earned thirty cents an hour, and marking boundaries twenty-five cents; eight-five cents a day was deducted for keep.[16] Relief workers netted about six dollars a week, about half the contemporary minimum wage in Ontario. To start with the men showed "strong evidence of willingness and thankfulness to work", and with "steady cheerfulness" produced more than expected.[17] But the next winter, with more men in the camps, winter clothing ran out. A visitor wired the Minister of the Interior of the hardships:

> Men in Jasper camps suffering severely through totally inadequate clothing and boots. Some only thin summer cotton un-

derwear, cotton shirts and cotton overalls without coats or trousers. Temperature twenty-two below. Numbers sent back to camp two days on that account within one hour from starting work and draw no pay while not working. Commissariat inadequate since obtaining supplies only as men order and many have old board bills to discharge and cannot buy necessary clothing out of dollar ten a day. No grumbling or unrest but real hardship. Could not advances be made to fit out present men with winter clothing, footwear, etc. at once either through commissariat or direct from Edmonton? Fear sickness from exposure.[18]

Parks Branch officials scurried in defence. Some men lacked winter clothes, but had bought none because they hoped for free ones. The whole thing, they said, had been blown out of proportion by a do-gooding clergyman. Reverend Edwards had "practically all his information from some camp roust-abouts at Camp No. 1 and who were of the grouser type". But Reverend Edwards was not alone in criticizing camp conditions. A Department of Labour inspector cabled his supervisor:

Five canvas camps totally unfit winter quarters present condition. Several tents poor shape and badly pitched.[19]

The Parks Branch officials were very upset. The inspector should have talked to them, before reporting to anyone outside. Cabins were being built, but a road was needed to bring in lumber. Meanwhile canvas camps and some discomfort were inevitable. The Parks Branch tried to improve conditions. Log walls and floors were added to the tents. Complaints continued. The *Edmonton Journal* published a letter from a camp resident complaining that two weeks work was needed to pay for either a "mackinaw or a windbreaker". The "overzealous" Reverend Edwards organized clothing donations, so succesfully that he both clothed the men and supplied a used clothing business![20]

The Parks Branch camps were now ready for official inspection. This report glowed!

I looked around all of the different camps en route and found everything satisfactory and the men all happy and contented. All of the different camps were looking much better than could be expected and the progress being made is excellent. We reached camp No. 7, the most southerly camp, just after the men had had their midday meal and we were served by the camp cook Stewart exactly the same as the men had, and we were all delighted at the excellent menu, service and cooking.

It is assumed that the information given will dispense with, once and for all, the various unreasonable complaints that have been received about our Jasper camps. These were largely instigated by a few malcontents and encouraged by the Reverend Edwards who was according to my information absolutely unfamiliar with winter camp conditions. As far as camp accommodation, commissary matters etc. were concerned I found very few things requiring my attention during my inspection at Jasper, and am very well satisfied with the splendid organization work done by Mr. Mitchell.[21]

But the men were not so forgiving. In February 1932 some went on strike. One man was dismissed after a warning. Twenty-two others stopped work in protest. They were also fired, and appealed to the Edmonton Ex-Servicemen's Association, which interceded with the minister. An internal review supported the firing: "In letting these men go Mr. Mitchell followed the only possible course open to him in the circumstances. . . . he was well advised to take the opportunity of making a firm stand and of showing them that they could not get the upper hand in the control of the camps and the work."[22]

To increase control in the camps Harkin introduced a recreation program. Idleness fostered communism, he believed, and the men should be occupied: "Roughly one third of their time, after allowing for the eight-hour work day and about eight hours for sleeping would be on their hands and probably few of them would know how to employ it. Such idleness might be fertile ground for red propaganda if there should be a few men with Bolshevistic inclinations among the men in the camps. In any case it does not seem to me a desirable condition to have the men sitting around during long winter evenings and Sundays with no amusements or recreation."[23]

The men needed books, magazines and radio sets. Record players, table games and books were donated. Eatons provided a radio and a movie projector, and guest speakers gave lectures with lantern slides. In Riding Mountain Park the men were given shovels and brooms to clear the lake for skating. And Harkin reinstituted the six-day work week, for the men were "better off and more contented when they are occupied".

Reading, games and more work was "healthy", but drinking was not! The superintendent in Jasper sent a list of men on relief to the liquor store manager, asking him not to serve them. But as a federal official he could not instruct a provincial employee. He then wrote directly to the provincial government. But that failed too. The men continued to buy drink if they wished.

Other civil liberties were limited. Those on strike were fired, and collective organization was forbidden. Complaints had to bear only one signature, and could not be presented by a committee: "Organizations of associations the objects of which are to present concerted demands to the authorities in regard to camp maintenance and operation are forbidden."[24]

The men grumbled, but no more major problems arose in the Parks Branch camps. Harkin's paternalistic concern with the men's leisure, and his hard line on strikes both possibly helped. Harkin attributed minor problems to "turbulent characters" who were treated "fairly but firmly", and removed "before the disaffection spread".

ORGANIZATION IN THE RELIEF CAMPS

Provincial relief camps were different. In 1933 the radical Alberta Relief Camp Workers' Union organized the Alberta Relief Commission camps. The men struck, and were threatened with loss of relief for all time if they did not work. The issue, as in the park camps, was free clothing. Work stopped at all six Alberta Relief Commission camps east of Banff. The new union called for the Parks Branch camps to join them, and distributed "the red letter":

Dear Comrades:

We have not yet received communication from your camp so are writing to acquaint you with present conditions.

You can receive union cards from comrade at camp 4A. Comrades returning from camp 6 report that, after working two weeks and quitting they are met at headquarters camp by Police and their free clothes are taken from them.

The Canmore camp struck work on July 3rd, but the Police

came in with the buses and the men came to town, about 25 to 50 remained and went to work.

We are arranging a United Front demonstration for the near future.

A comrade was fired from Camp 15 and 44 men struck and abandoned the camp in solidarity. Camp 14 with 40 men was to be moved down there to fill in but only 8 or 10 men went.

The *correct policy* is to go to the camps and organize and stay in the camps and fight.

The BC union reports that they are building a broad united front movement against militarization in the camps.

We suggest that you work on small grievances such as recreation, tent, sport equipment, free soap, the right to go to town and return. Try and organize 11 camps and have a subdistrict committee to meet regularly.

> Comradely Greetings,
> O. "Red" Osslington,
> Sec. ARCWU[25]

This letter, and others like it, circulated through all the camps. Labour unrest was evident everywhere. Miners had struck in Estevan, Saskatchewan. Chicken pluckers were on strike in Stratford, Ontario.[26] In urban centres those working for relief were unruly and restless. In Winnipeg, for example, men sat to pick dandelions on the boulevards. A passing taxpayer objected, and was sworn at and almost beaten up.[27] In Winnipeg the unemployed rioted, and in Edmonton they struck for an increased food allowance.[28] In British Columbia, where relief camps were run by racketeers, both the men on relief and observers protested.[29] The militaristic character of camps run by the Department of National Defence caused unrest, despite regulations forbidding collective organization. Tensions culminated in 1935 in the "On to Ottawa Trek", with a riot in Regina, a commission of inquiry, and a meeting between leading protesters and the prime minister.[30]

The primary demand was for a living wage. Although organizers began with minor issues such as free soap or the right to go to town, their ultimate demands were broader. They wanted the right to wage work, not to relief. The unrest led the government to scale down work for relief, and introduce public works programs employing free labour and paying market wages. By 1933–34 over $1 million had been spent on work-for-relief in the parks. New facilities included roads, telephone systems, wardens' cabins and administration buildings [31] (see Appendix 2). Visitors could enjoy new campgrounds, golf courses, tennis courts, and bandstands.

PUBLIC WORKS CONSTRUCTION ACTS

The Public Works Construction Acts were a tremendous opportunity for the Parks Branch. They could select workers, including craftsmen, to finish pet projects. Skilled carpenters could finish bandstands; stonemasons could build retaining walls; plumbers could work in the new bathhouses; roofers, concrete finishers, gardeners and cabinet makers could all be hired. The Parks Branch no longer had to find the skills it needed among the destitute seeking relief work. The new program was better for the workers, too. Those with skills could use them. The work had the dignity of *real* work, rather than the indignity of relief. The concept of work-for-relief was being replaced by the recognition that, in the absence of work, cash relief was more humane and more practical (see Appendix 2).[33]

As the depression began to loosen its grip, unemployment declined. Work-for-relief continued on a small scale to assist local residents, in national park towns and other municipalities. But the only work-for-relief camp remaining open was hardest hit. The make-work programs also declined in scale. The Parks Branch lost its largest work force. Better times for the country brought retrenchment for the national parks.

THE NATIONAL FORESTRY PROGRAM

The Parks Branch had another idea for cheap labour. In 1936 the commissioner proposed young men be hired for forestry work in the federal forestry reserves and national parks. His superintendents sent lists of possible projects, showing surplus equipment from the obsolete work-for-relief camps. The Youth Employment Commission turned down the Parks Branch proposal, for they wanted programs to involve more training and rehabilitation. Canadian young men had been without work for a long time. "Unfit" and with "low morale", they lacked job skills and discipline, and needed more than a job to make them employable. After tedious negotiations, the "National Forestry Program" was introduced in 1939, for men between eighteen and twenty-two.

Five thousand were hired, one thousand for the federal forests and parks, for the five summer months. But they did not do forest conservation or get much training. The Parks Branch used them as if they were working for relief. Recreation facilities were built, rather than trees planted. They built comfort stations, bridges, picnic facilities and barns. They cleared a ski slope at Jasper, and seeded an athletic grounds at Cape Breton Highlands.[34] An evaluation showed little forestry work, even though young stands acutely needed thinnng: "Very little forestry work was accomplished, and evidently very little was intended in so far as the Parks were concerned".[35]

Some men felt conned. They expected training, not just manual labour. Asked to dig ditches for mosquito control, they went on strike. The superintendent explained "the purpose of the camps and what was expected of them". Four men left for town, but the rest "remained to work". The four men had a point. Mental and physical training were supposed to be part of the program. A half day of lectures a week never materialised. The only lecture given was a radio address by the minister, who specifically asked it be broadcast to the camps. Some even missed this dubious benefit, because "atmospheric conditions" interfered.[36] In four camps the men were trained in fire lookout and firefighting duties, but only one camp tried to instill any understanding of forestry. Those running the program thought the men lacked the education for theoretical instruction.

The parks branch also neglected the physical training component. The evaluator "very strongly" suggested more "recreation" another year. Team sports would "encourage team work, tend to strengthen morale and improve outlook". However, his recommendations could not be implemented. The Second World War began, and the forestry program for 1940 was cancelled. The young men, inured to hard work and discipline, were called up into Canada's armed forces. Their camps and equipment would be available for three other groups forced to work in Canada's national parks.

ALTERNATIVE SERVICE WORK

The National War Service Regulations of 1941, provided for "Alternative Service Work" by conscientious objectors. In the United States objectors could take non-combatant roles in the armed forces. In Canada they were all channelled into work camps for four months in the summer of 1941, and "for the duration" in 1942. In 1941 they worked almost entirely within the national parks, but the following year they also fought forest fires in British Columbia and worked in industry and agriculture.

Most objectors belonged to religious groups committed to non-violence. The largest group was Mennonite, although Seventh Day Adventists, Hutterites and various other smaller groups were also involved.[37] The Mennonites were excluded from service because of an agreement in 1873 on their "entire exemption from any military service".[38] This agreement could have exempted the Mennonites from Alternative Service Work also. One official commented on an *Edmonton Journal* criticism of government generosity to the Mennonites: "Should they insist on 'justice' on their part, then they should not be asked to do any military service, nor any service in lieu of such. We recognize that as citizens of Canada, in common with all Canadians, they now come forward of their own free will and accord to do service and to that extent annul the proviso quoted above."[39]

The Mennonites co-operated that first summer. The Doukhobors did not. The draft board at Regina was greeted with their peace song "Arms Down, Soldiers Go Home". The government offered to exclude them from medical examinations, which the Doukhobors said were militaristic. A promise not to give them military supervision was still insufficient. They refused to participate in Alternative Service Work, and none worked in the parks.

About 700 men did work in the parks. Over 500 were Mennonite, and most were single and of Dutch extraction.[40] They were to do "forest conservation and improvements in the parks". But, as with the National Forestry Program, the men developed the parks rather than improved the forest. They were paid fifty cents a day, much cheaper than "prevailing rate" employees. Pay and maintenance of a regular employee cost $2.80 a day, compared with $1.33 for an Alternative Service Worker.

In addition, this new work force was productive. They did between 10 per cent and 25 per cent more work than regular employees. The firm religious leadership of the Mennonite community followed the men into camp, maintaining their discipline. The men's pastor was encouraged to visit the camp, to keep the men "more contented in their leisure hours". The church wanted to install a resident pastor. The Parks Branch agreed, if church services were outside working hours, and if the pastor helped in the office. Even the pastor should not be idle in a work camp.

The men had religious services every morning, and a longer one each evening. They were asked to conduct services in English rather than German. This request was made in Manitoba, and caused panic among the bureaucrats. German was in the province's schools, and could hardly be forbidden to conscientious objectors![41] However, the men agreed to use English, and avoided a major language crisis. Services included community singing, and seemed recreational. The men's good behaviour amazed parks officials: "With 742 young men between the ages of 21 and 25 years it might be expected that some difficulty might be encountered. It is therefore pleasing to report that everyone connected with the operation of these camps was agreeably surprised by the exceptionally good behaviour."[42]

Camp conditions also added to morale. Summer sunshine, good food, recreational equipment left from the National Forestry Program, more relaxed supervision than in home communities all helped; these pacifists even tried out the boxing gloves. The men also completed a first-aid course. The first summer went well for both Parks Branch and men. But a factor in this success was probably the men's knowledge they would soon be home.

But Canadians would not let "conchies" get off lightly. As Canada geared up for war, public opinion demanded conscientious objectors work for "the duration". In the spring of 1942 the conscientious objectors were again called into service, to remain for the rest of the war. The men were less willing. A summer away from their families had looked like a holiday — several years did not. Also, the men were needed at home to help with spring seeding. Many turned up late, and others disappeared on week-end passes and turned up a few weeks later.

Parks officials planned to keep this new labour force working in the parks. But with the men called up for the duration, they were sought by government agencies and private corporations across the country. Gibson, the director of the National Parks Bureau (Harkin's successor) reiterated Harkin's position. National parks were a tourist asset, and their development was a good investment. The work was healthy. And, parks and recreation were essential to relieve stress in wartime. Parks were good for everybody, including those working in them.

Competing demands for cheap labour were strong, and some men were put to other work. British Columbia feared sabotage would cause forest fires and that Japan would invade. A third of the objectors were sent to British Columbia. Some went back into agriculture, or industry. But, the Parks Banch also retained some men, who built fire trails, telephone lines, bridges, and fencing in the parks. In Kootenay and Banff parks they removed timber destroyed by bark beetle, salvaging the wood for saw-logs and pit-props. By 1945 a hundred objectors remained working in the parks.

Most men had been raised on farms, and toughened by outdoor work. Accustomed to discipline and supervised by their pastor, the men worked hard. These men were the strongest, most co-operative and most productive the Parks Branch had ever employed. Over a five year period from 100 to 700 extra men worked in the parks, at 60 per cent of the cost of regular employees. They completed many projects still incomplete after the major programs of the depression, including roads and trails, buildings, dams and breakwaters (see Appendix 2).[43]

JAPANESE INTERNED IN JASPER

The Mennonites were relatively willing workers. The Japanese were not. The forced relocation of the Japanese living on Canada's West Coast can only be fully understood in the context of the anti-oriental movement in British Columbia. Anti-Japanese feeling had been strong since before the turn of the century. Those feelings were inflamed by racist politicians and community leaders in British Columbia. Japanese immigration to British Columbia began around 1884, reaching significant levels after 1896. In 1891 the province passed a law to slow down their immigration. The federal government feared damage to relations with Japan, and disallowed the law. The provincial government then took away the Japanese and Chinese immigrant's right to vote, arguing: "It is unquestionably in the interests of the Empire that the Pacific province of the Dominion should be occupied by a large and thoroughly British population, rather than by one in which the number of aliens largely predominated and many of the distinctive features of a settled British Community were lacking".[44]

In 1907 the United States government stopped Hawaian Japanese from going to the mainland. Many came to Canada instead. Our first boat people were greeted in Vancouver with riots and parades led by the Asiatic Exclusion League. The legislature again tried to exclude the Japanese, using a language test. The Lieutenant Governor disallowed the bill. However, the riots infected even the federal government, and agreement was negotiated with Japan to limit immigration.

Immigration slowed, but anti-oriental feelings were heightened by the geographic concentration of the Japanese. By 1941 over 8,000 lived in Vancouver, and 75 per cent of the 22,000 in British Columbia lived in the Lower Mainland. Organized labour resented competition from immigrants who would accept lower wages. But this tension declined as the Japanese and other working-class Canadians learned they could work together.[45] The Japanese prospered, developing small businesses, mixed or soft-fruit farms, or buying stores or fishing boats. As the Japanese joined the middle class, they met white-Canadian middle-class hostility. Organizations like the White Canada Association, the Native Sons of BC, and the Asiatic Exclusion League poisoned British Columbia from 1908 until the Second World War. These extremist organizations had political support. In the 1930s the Liberal party in British Columbia joined the anti-oriental cause. Their election material portrayed the CCF as a front for oriental iniquity:

A vote for any CCF candidate is a vote to give the Chinamen and the Japanese the same voting right as you have.

A vote for the Liberal candidate in your riding is a vote against oriental enfranchisement. The Liberal party is opposed to giving the Orientals the vote.

Look behind the solicitor for a CCF candidate, and you will see an Oriental leering over his shoulder with an eye on you and your daughter.[46]

Two strongly anti-Japanese Liberals, Ian Mackenzie and Thomas Reid, were successful in the federal election of 1935. With two other politicians, an independent (A. W. Neill) and a Conservative (Howard Green), they aroused public opinion, and pressured for

Japanese internmeht. Vancouver Alderman Halford Wilson also tried to withold business licenses from Japanese factories, or "sweat shops". He tried to close Japanese schools, saying they were "dangerous to young health". His attacks continued throughout the war and beyond.

Political endorsement increased the legitimacy of anti-oriental protest. As Japan's military readiness became evident, hostility to Japanese Canadians increased. In 1939, on Halloween, white Canadians raided Vancouver's Chinese and Japanese communities, destroying businesses and homes and beating people. The bombing of Pearl Harbour in December 1941 unleashed further anti-oriental feeling. Backbenchers from BC[47] pressured the prime minister to intern the Japanese. Tension mounted until the safety of the Japanese was threatened. After weeks of typical dithering, Mackenzie King announced the evacuation of the coastal Japanese. He may have believed he was protecting them, and their property, from racist neighbours. But he chose racists to implement the evacuation, and they offered no protection or consolation.

Japanese families were herded into the exhibition grounds at Hastings Park.[48] The men were dispersed to road camps in the interior, including several within Jasper National Park. The women and children were sent to ghost towns. Japanese nationals and Canadian citizens of Japanese descent were treated alike, as were single men and those with families. The splitting of family units increased anxiety, and stimulated civil disobedience.

The Parks Branch was asked to find work for Japanese Canadians. But they already had many conscientious objectors, and thought them better workers. However, one project was suitable. The Yellowhead Highway through Jasper National Park, could be completed. About five miles was incomplete within the park, and about twenty miles outside the park. The roadway west of Jasper Townsite was chosen for up to 2,000 Japanese.

The men gathered in Vancouver were sent to Jasper by train. By April over 1,500 had arrived. Life was uncomfortable. Men worked eight-hour days, building camp facilities at first, and then blasting and excavating rock. Building a major highway by manual labour was like levelling a driveway with a teaspoon — but that was what the men had to do. A single man was paid $20.00 to $30.00 a month, after deductions for board. Married men received very little, for another $20.00 was deducted to support their families.

The work was strenuous, and objectionable to many. The Japanese came from all walks of life, and were of all ages. A druggist (who acted as first-aid man), a restaurateur (who became the chef, but was only allowed to cook western style), a science graduate who had won the Governor General's Medal at the University of British Columbia, and the owner of a large strawberry farm: "Some are rich, some are poor. Some had cars and servants; others earned small wages at menial tasks. There are farmers and fishermen, grocerymen and lawyers, university students and miners, barbers and taxidrivers, lumberjacks and druggists, photographers and newspapermen."[50]

Few were used to manual labour, and "back aches and sore muscles" followed their first use of picks and shovels. They seemed "entirely unsuited for work of this nature", being "incapable, physically, of producing a fair days work".[51] Camp rules were also tough. Family members could not visit; private cars were forbidden, as was private use of government vehicles; alcohol was prohibited, and "dissenting meetings of any organization" were not permitted. A curfew was enforced from one hour after sunset to "lights out" at 7:30. No one could leave camp and go into Jasper without written permission. Park trails and the railway line were out of bounds. Fishing was forbidden, and bunkhouse doors could not face the railway (for security reaons). Mail was censored, and had to be in simple Japanese without "obscure" characters. Cameras and radios were forbidden.

Having rules was different from enforcement. The men could not be dismissed, except to jail, so could not be compelled to work. Radios appeared everywhere, though confiscated as fast as they were found. Married men were restless at separation from their families. In spite of the rules forbidding collective organizations, the camps developed committees. They threatened to strike, and demanded changes such as a new foreman, a pay increase, and resolution of many "minor" difficulties.

Rumours of unrest first reached officials in March 1942. News of a strike in one camp was broadcast, but was only rumour. But by April the strike was real, and seven "troublemakers" were removed. The men complained of being treated "like dogs" by a foreman, who had been told to be "tough". The foreman left. There were rumours of hunger strikes. In June the men in one camp struck again. The police removed the "malcontents", but Parks officials complained: "If these people are allowed to continue refusing to give a fair days work proposing trivial and unjustified reasons for striking, it would be more economical for the Government to confine one and all to an internment camp and supply the project with power machinery".[52]

They despaired of getting the men to work. They limited strikers to two meals a day, giving three to those working. But still the men would not work. The strikers broke through their guards, and marched down the railway line into Jasper. The chief engineer met them, to hear their grievances. Money was slow to reach their families, and they wanted to visit other camps and to go to town. They returned to camp, but still refused to work. A few days later the police again removed the "trouble makers". When permits to visit town were given more freely the men went back to work.

The atmosphere remained tense. One Japanese beat up a white teamster. The veterans in Jasper armed themselves, and park officials prepared smoke bombs. Jasper residents demanded military protection, and women feared the Japanese who roamed freely through the town. The problem got worse with each Japanese military success: "The Japanese in these camps are becoming more arrogant and more difficult to handle each day. Radios are plentiful in the camps, and on any success by the Japanese armed forces or the armed forces of Germany, a demonstration immediately takes place."[53]

Singapore fell to the Japanese in February 1942, and a Japanese submarine bombed Canada's West Coast on the twentieth of June. Canadians feared Japanese invasion from the Pacific, and pro-Japanese demonstrations in the camps increased public agitation.[54] Anti-oriental politicians fanned the flames. Member of Parliament T. J. O'Neill called the camp foremen Japanese "flunkies". The internees, he said, had unlimited sugar and canned fruit, even though other Canadians were rationed.

The camp strikes continued through June and July. Even those who worked did not accomplish much. Men deliberately tantalized and frustrated their foreman by slow work:

> They do not deliberately refuse to work, but make it a habit to work for possibly half an hour and then sit down for ten or fifteen minutes to "discuss the affairs of the work in general".

> A certain number of Japanese in almost every camp make it a point to protest against most trivial inconveniences or what they

consider as inconveniences in camp, whereas white labourers working under the same conditions would find nothing to complain about. This, I judge, is due to resentment on the part of many Japanese for being placed in camps at all, and thus taken away from their regular occupations; or in certain cases it no doubt is due to desire to embarass our officials to the greatest possible extent without going so far as to call for arrest and jail sentences.[55]

Intercepted and censored mail described the atmosphere:

Maybe the older men do a bit (of work) but the young guys never do anything. You know about the Mass Evacuation. I thought it was going along fine until they started saying that single men have to remain in the road camps. That sure burned everybody up. Lot of the men are saying to kick the members of the Mass Evacuation Committee out and soon.

or:

The boys up here don't take any shit from anybody.

When anybody gets hell we do less work, or if they slap on any new regulations.

Today everybody was loading gravel on a truck and while waiting for the truck to come back we played poker of five-hundred and the straw boss told us that it looked like hell so that we had to cut it out. We didn't load any more and waited for quitting time. Up here they don't call a Mountie like they do over where you are.

Don't take any shit Jackie. They won't do anything to you. Maybe they'll transfer you to Slocan like the other boys from Solsqua. At least ask for another job under another boss.[56]

Parks officials detected an undercurrent of sabotage in Japanese obstructionism. The road had military purposes, the Japanese believed, and would "carry men and supplies to decimate their brothers in Japan". The unrest led the government to scale down camps nearest to Jasper, and move married men to join their families. By 1943 14,000 Japanese were interned in the ghost towns of the BC interior. Nearly 4,000 had been moved into southern

Alberta and Manitoba, to work in the sugar-beet fields. Around 1,000 single men remained in the road camps of British Columbia, including those on the Yellowhead. Another 1,000 were in prison camps, for refusing relocation.[57] The Yellowhead camps were now smaller, but internees continued to avoid work. The camps became a clearing house, and attempts to make the men work were an admitted charade.

In 1943 the Japanese government inspected the camps. The committee took "a very fair view of the conditions, and was disinclined to encourage the Japanese in any unreasonable complaints".[58] In 1945, after the armistice was signed, the camps were canvassed for those who wished to return to Japan. Frustration, anger and despair led about 10,000 to select "voluntary repatriation". About 4,000 returned to Japan, either of their own will or by deportation. The rest waited another four years for freedom to travel within Canada.

The evacuation and internment of Japanese Canadians in World War Two is one of the worst examples of racism in Canada, a country that today prides itself on multiculturalism. The treatment of the Japanese, though, was not an isolated example of iniquity by a thoughtless federal government. The movement of the Japanese must be seen in the context of a half-century of bigotry in British Columbia, legitimized by certain politicians who fanned the flames of racial intolerance.

The Japanese did leave a legacy, though, along the Yellowhead Highway. The men were on strike much of the time. Unlike the conscientious objectors, they did not acknowledge the legitimacy of their internment. Their pay was lower than that paid to those working on the Public Works Construction Programs, or even doing relief work. They refused work in passive resistance to unjust internment. But, along the Yellowhead Highway west of Jasper the road-bed was begun by Japanese internees. The road was not completed until large machinery was brought in after the war.

German POW's in Riding Mountain

The last group of workers were German soldiers. Most POW camps were in the federal forestry reserves, but in 1943 a firewood shortage developed in Manitoba. The deputy minister responsible for parks did not want to use prisoners of war to cut firewood. He remembered the experience of the first war, when the men did not cut enough wood to keep themselves warm.[59] But Minister of Munitions and Supply C. D. Howe had other ideas. He suggested a dead poplar stand near Whitewater Lake in Riding Mountain National Park be cut for firewood by prisoners of war. In 1943 Alternative Service Workers and some wage workers built a camp on a site used by the National Forestry Program. Thirteen buildings included five large bunkhouses. Parks officials were horrified, by the substantial construction that hardly seemed justified on a project to collect firewood.[60]

But good conditions did not produce high productivity. The men began cutting around three-quarters of a cord per man per day, but soon this declined to half a cord. The men worked to the quota, gaining nothing from cutting beyond it. Their civilian guards just sat around doing nothing, adding to the "general atmosphere of indolence". And to make matters worse, C. D. Howe had overestimated the available firewood. The men worked at a snail's pace for about a year.

Other activities were more interesting: carving model battleships; bee-keeping; building dug-out canoes, which still lie on the lakeshore today. They helped in emergencies, such as forest fires and electric storms that damaged telephone cables. Some tried to escape, but were engulfed by a snow storm and returned voluntarily.

The fuel shortage was over by 1944, but a huge pile of firewood sat in the middle of Riding Mountain National Park, far from civilization or any means of transportation. Even at a snail's pace, the prisoners added to the pile daily. They would have 40,000 cords by the end of the season. The men might do more "useful" work in the park, but Parks officials realized this would require money from the Parks Branch budget. Riding Mountain camp closed in April 1945, having produced expensive firewood in an inaccessible part of Manitoba. The buildings were dismantled or destroyed, leaving only a few concrete floors.[61]

Cheap Labour in the National Parks

Between 1914 and 1946 six programs provided cheap labour for the Parks Branch. Civilian interness in the first war built roads and camp grounds. Relief workers and those employed under the Public Works Construction acts in the 1930s added bathhouses and administration buildings. Young men in the National Forestry

Program groomed golf courses, and dug ditches to control mosquitoes. Conscientious objectors worked all through the parks, building roads and trying to control the bark-beetle infestation. The Japanese laid the foundation for the Yellowhead Highway, and German prisoners of war took firewood out of Riding Mountain Park.

Taken collectively, these programs had a major impact on capital construction in the parks. In the First World War about half the regular parks budget was spent on cheap labour. The relief and make-work programs of the thirties in the parks cost twice the regular Parks Branch budget. In the Second World War the Japanese and the German prisoners were provided at no cost to the branch. The Alternative Service Workers absorbed about 12 per cent of the Parks budget, but provided labour worth twice that.

Around five million man-days were provided over the entire thirty-year period, or 21,000 man-years of work, for a department with 337 salaried employees in 1950, of whom only 137 were permanent. Over the thirty years between 1914 and 1945 the Parks Branch had an average of 700 extra employees a year, more than double their total staff and about five times their permanent park staff in 1950. Though many were not fully productive, for reasons described here, the men's collective contribution was substantial.

Major national crises appeared to justify the work programs. Interning people who had committeed no crime seemed justified; all men had to be called to national service, regardless of their commitment to non-violence; the only solution to unemployment appeared to be relief work. National parks were low on the political agenda, so we did not pay a living wage to those building park facilities. National crises forced men to work in the parks for less than a living wage, and without the rights and freedoms of fellow working men and women.

CHAPTER SIX

The
Second Conservation
Movement

*I*N 1945 federal and provincial governments reviewed the federal proposals for "reconstruction". The "Green Books" made proposals for all economic sectors, and for government programs such as welfare and family allowance. The book on "Public Investment" described the national parks as "natural outdoor museums of wildlife" which would attract tourists, and be important in Canada's postwar development:

> Canada is in an exceptionally favourable position from which to develop a large international tourist travel. She is located alongside a great and wealthy nation, well disposed towards Canada, and much given to tourist travel. Particularly as a result of the war she now has also a status with other nations which she did not enjoy before. There can be no doubt that great numbers of citizens of many lands will welcome opportunities to visit Canada after the war provided suitable facilities are made available and that the attractions are made available and that the attractions which this country has to offer are adequately publicized.
>
> Among these attractions none occupies a more important place than the national parks. These areas of outstanding beauty

and abounding in other qualities which appeal to tourists are already well known among the travel-minded, and much more can be done in the future than in the past to publicize their attractions on a world-wide scale.[1]

Public investments would be needed to prepare the national parks for tourists. More roads in the parks; improved highways, particularly from the United States; more tourist accommodation, within and outside the parks. C. D. Howe spoke of the potential value of tourism, and promised to build the Trans-Canada Highway, highways to the United States, and to and through the national parks.[2] The conference later disagreed over federal attempts to intrude into provincial jurisdiction, but several provinces welcomed federal public works such as roads and parks.

Enthusiasm for tourism, and for the role of national parks was reiterated at a national tourism conference in 1947. Tourism was "big business", and "one of the means which we have of getting foreign capital into this country". About $220 million came into Canada each year from tourists, paid to railways, gas stations, hotels and restaurants. The national parks attracted these tourists, having over a million visitors in 1947. Gibson, the director of national parks, thanked delegates for: "Advertising done by the various governments and the transportation companies; the stories written, the motion pictures shown and the radio broadcasts, all start people travelling through Canada and the National Parks. The National Parks, said Gibson, were one of the greatest tourist lures in Canada."[3]

Articles like that in the *Saturday Evening Post* headlined:

> Luxurious Wilderness: Grizzlies Roam Freely in Sight of Pampered Guests; and Golfers sometimes have to Kick Black Bears off the Green. Here is Canada's Paradoxical Zoo without Bars.[4]

Parks Canada cringes if such stories appear today, but thirty years ago they revitalized tourism in the national parks.

Eroding the Parks

Government policies did not reflect this enthusiastic public posture. The Trans-Canada Highway was built, but the national parks were not protected from resource exploitation. In 1947 the federal government eliminated two national parks, reduced Waterton Lakes National Park by sixteen square miles, and Prince Albert National Park by 380 square miles. C. D. Howe, so ethusiastic about parks and tourism in 1945, explained: "The maintenance of national parks by the federal government is a considerable obligation. There are certain standards to be maintained. We have standards of protection and of development, and we have certain standards of improvements. As I understand the situation from the officers of the department, the purpose of the bill is to reduce the parks to an area which can be kept up to the standard set by the government for these national parks."[5]

In Waterton the sixteen square miles lay in another watershed, and was difficult to patrol. Alberta welcomed the additional resources. The muskeg to be removed from Prince Albert National Park in Saskatchewan was unsuitable for park purposes. Timber was ready to be cut, and part was to become an Indian reserve managed for "fur conservation". Also, thirty square miles on the south side of the park was promising farmland. The two parks eliminated had been wild-life sanctuaries, and were expendable because the herds had recovered.[6] After pressure from the Alberta government similar legislation two years later withdrew a further twenty square miles from Banff National Park, so Calgary Power could develop the Spray valley. The federal minister was: "Satisfied that the area excluded from Banff National Park in 1930 is insufficient for the proper development of the project, and that it is necessary in the public interest that the further area of 21.2 square miles proposed to be withdrawn from Banff National Park by section 2 of the present bill be excluded from the park in order that the proposed project may proceed. The said further area is all on the edge of Banff National Park, and contains no features making essential its retention for park use."[7]

In 1956, again at provincial request, a Nova Scotia park was made smaller. The province had scanned the mineral potential of Cape Breton Highlands, and asked that 13.3 square miles be returned.[8] In 1958 Nova Scotia asked for the return of more parkland, this time for hydroelectric development. The local Member of Parliament (on the government side of the house) wanted park expansion, but the province's request was granted.[9]

So scenic resources were not sacred. The legislation of 1930 had prohibited resource development in the parks, but exploitation continued. Timber berths continued in Glacier, Yoho, and Revelstoke,[10] and were leased out in Wood Buffalo National Park as late as 1959.[11] The Parks Branch tried to end nonconforming uses. Some timber berths were purchased, and mining leases were purchased or allowed to expire.[12] But resource inventories were promoted in the parks, to reveal their hidden costs. One MP referred to the natural resources "underlying" Canada's national parks; "It is a fact, of course, that there is no development of any national park in that sense. Naturally it is not expected that we should immediately open gold mines or oil wells in national parks, but I think we are going to have to recognize that certain areas of our parks represent vast natural wealth under the surface. . . . Unquestionably the government is today losing money by way of royalties which they could well use."[13]

One Member had been approached by Shell Oil, grumbling about not being allowed to take rock samples. A small rock would never be missed! Parks were to be "maintained and made use of so as to leave them unimpaired for furture generations". This policy, he claimed, was inflexible and outdated! "The parks were set aside for the benefit, education and enjoyment of the people of Canada. I read that from the act, but so far I cannot see that we are getting a great deal of enjoyment out of them. After all, when we buy a new suit I do not think we are inclined to take the new suit, hang it in a cellophane bag, put it away in a closet and save it for our grandchildren. Nor do we build ourselves a new home and say that we are going to save it for the generation that is going to follow some time after the year 2060, which would be 100 years from now."[14]

Trucks had to detour around the parks, interfering with lumbering and mining. Only about 100 yards of parkland was needed each side of the highway. The rest, he judged to be poor value.

This period was difficult for the national parks. Canadian public policy was concerned with economic development through exploitation of natural resources. C. D. Howe presided over construction of the Trans-Canada Highway, built the country's first oil pipeline and the St Lawrence Seaway. Timber, wheat, minerals, energy resources such as electricity, coal, oil and natural gas were priorities. The large resource corporations, many multinational, were favoured by government. National parks eroded whenever resource development appeared more profitable.

The only defence of national parks was an economic one based on increased tourism. But the small business people involved in tourism lacked political clout, and were no match for C. D. Howe or the resource sector multinationals. Many pressured their MPs to ask for a national park, but ineffectively. The Conservative party, the party of small business, had been in opposition too long. Small business received little attention in public policy. There was no public defence of the parks nor any internal opposition from parks officials. The National Parks Association, originally an active opponent of the Spray Lakes development, was unconcerned. Amalgamated with the Canadian Good Roads Association, the group was concerned with road construction and tourism not preservation. The national parks were eroding, piece by piece.

THE TRANS-CANADA HIGHWAY

Canada's first major coast-to-coast highway was as important to Canada's national parks as the Canadian Pacific Railway built eighty years earlier. The highway stimulated a tourist boom, producing demands for new development, first from businesses in the parks, and then from larger outside corporations.

Tourism was only one reason for putting the Trans-Canada Highway through the national parks. Another had to do with federal provincial relations. In the 1920s, when British Columbia sought federal help to build a road into the interior, Kootenay National Park had been part of the bargain. The federal government built the road through the park. That was the precedent for the Trans-Canada Highway. The provinces wanted the highway to go through the parks, because there Ottawa would pay all construction costs, rather than the half they paid outside the parks.

The debate was just like earlier ones on the CPR and the Big Bend Road: a new highway through Banff and Yoho parks or a northern route through Jasper park. Edmonton, of course, favoured the Jasper route, while Calgary prefered a southern route taking the highway through their city. The mayor of Edmonton protested being left "in the cold". A protest meeting sent a telegram to the minister. A caravan travelled the Yellowhead route to meet the Royal Commission on Transportation.[15] They argued the northern route was easier, and they were not acting just from "sectional pride and personal cupidity". Alberta Liberal Harper Prowse recommended a fact-finding commission to select the route.[16] But the Canadian government had its own priorities. The Trans-Canada, like the CPR seventy years earlier, and like the first rough "autoroad" through the mountains, was built through Banff and Yoho.

Construction of the Trans-Canada Highway took ten years. In 1960 the sections through Banff and Yoho Parks (in the Rocky Mountains), Revelstoke Park (in British Columbia) and Terra Nova Park (in Newfoundland) were completed. The more difficult portion through Rogers Pass in Glacier Park took a little longer.[17] With the completion of the Highway, tourists arrived, and business picked up.

THE TOURIST BOOM AND ALVIN HAMILTON

The Trans-Canada Highway was begun by the Liberals, but completed under Diefenbaker's Conservatives. The minister coping with the demand for more park facilities was Alvin Hamilton. Unlike his Liberal predecessors, who had chipped away at the parks whenever it was economically or politically advantageous, Alvin Hamilton was committed to the principle of national parks. Preservation of their beauty, and access for ordinary Canadians, were his priorities. He heard the demand for expanded facilities: "The federal government can no longer indulge only in provision of recreation for the leisured classes but rather it must provide recreation for the leisured masses as well".[18]

Hamilton saw opportunities for development. Glacier, deserted since the tunnels rerouted the CPR under the pass, would now need new visitor facilities. So would Revelstoke, also fully accessible for the first time. Construction was under way in Cape Breton National Park. Banff had a new civic centre and a curling rink, and wanted to offer the Winter Olympic Games. Ski areas were proposed or under construction. Motel owners wanted to open all year round. Enthusiasm was limitless. Hamilton was complimented "for the tremendous boost he has given the tourist industry" for "money spent by the government for national parks to provide better facilities and make tourists welcome is an investment that will pay us well in the years ahead".[19] Even his Liberal opponent, Pickersgill, was encouraging. Of Terra Nova Park he said: "The minister need have no doubt that anything he does in the park to make it more attractive will be repaid as it is in the other parks, by an increase in the tourist traffic, something which I know he has very much at heart and which he is trying hard to promote".[20]

Hamilton listened to this enthusiasm for tourism. He also heard complaints the parks were "hampering industry". Alvin Hamilton knew that both tourism and resource development could threaten the national parks. A conflict was inherent in national parks policy. He pleaded with his fellow MPs, and with Canadians who used and loved the parks:

> As I listen to this discussion this afternoon I could not help but feel the necessity of a national parks association doing education work among the members of the house. Hon. members should be aware of the fundamental purpose of the parks, which is to preserve, as they were in the beginning those beautiful scenic areas of our country in order that our children and our children's children for generations to come may go there and find certain areas where the country is the same as its original discoverers found it. That is the primary purpose of the national parks.
>
> At the same time there is a second function of those responsible for the administration of these parks, and that is how to make these beautiful places as accessible to the Canadian people as possible. There is a clash between these two purposes. The parks department has had to stand up in favour of these basic purposes against those forces which would like to exploit the parks and use up all their resources quickly in their lifetime and leave nothing for the generations that will follow. I as a minister, want to make it abundantly clear that I stand for the primary purpose of these parks. At the same time I will do everything possible to make these beautiful parks available to the people of Canada.[21]

Hamilton recalled tenting at minimal cost in the national parks. All Canadians could enjoy their natural beauty by camping and hiking. Parks were not for "honky-tonk recreation", for mining or forestry, or for people who want to "shoot off bullets at a rifle range". These opportunities exist outside the parks. However without support a minister could not resist the pressure to develop the parks, "unless the people who love these parks are prepared to band together and support the minister by getting the facts out across the country".[22] In 1960 Alvin Hamilton called for a pressure group to help withstand the pressure for resource exploitation in the parks. He asked for help in preventing mining and lumbering and inappropriate commercialized tourism.

MIDWIVES TO THE NATIONAL PARKS LOBBY

Parks officials also hoped a national parks association would be created. In 1947 the director had commented on the various groups concerned about parks — of the Canadian Parks and Recreation Association and the Canadian Camping Association, for example. He wrote: "I think we should continue to display polite interest in these organizations. Some of these days they will get together and form a worthwhile national parks association."[23]

But "polite interest" could not create an association. In 1958, however, Canada's new Conservative prime minister, John Diefenbaker, announced a national conference on conservation. In 1961 governments and experts from across the country met to discuss management of Canada's renewable resources. Eighty background papers were prepared by various experts, in forestry, agriculture, water management, fisheries and recreation. These "Resources for Tomorrow" participants were flattered by a keynote address describing them as "the fathers of conservation", and listened to provincial resource ministers outline the need for multiple use of the scarce land resource. "More intensive use of and greater return from resources devoted to recreational purposes" was needed.[24] Conservation was the intention, not preservation.

Spooner, the Ontario minister, said mining, wilderness, hunting, fishing, camping, agriculture, parks and timber could all co-exist. The province's Algonquin Park was an example.[25] National park supporters were alarmed by this commitment to multiple use. A recreation workshop, like Alvin Hamilton's speech of a year earlier, called for a pressure group to support the national parks: "There is a need for an informed, organized, nongovernment association to promote the interests of park development and perform as a 'watchdog' over those areas now reserved for parks purposes".[26]

Those present became a nucleus for the National and Provincial Parks Association of Canada (NPPAC). The Resources for Tomorrow Conference in Canada was followed by major conservation initiatives in the United States. In February 1962 President John F. Kennedy's message to Congress focussed on "natural resources", and outdoor recreation.[27] The United States sponsored the First World Conference on National Parks, with the president giving the introductory address.[28] In North America, both in Canada and the United States, the nations' leaders had introduced from the top the new conservation movement.

The creation of a national parks association was slow, though. In 1962, a year after the Resources for Tommorrow Conference, the provinces again pushed for prospecting and resource development in the national parks.[29] Conservation groups were becoming active. The Canadian Society of Wildlife and Fishery Biologists published a "Wilderness Policy for Canada". The Federation of Ontario Naturalists' statements on wilderness were read into the parliamentary record.

In 1963 a nucleus finally formalized the National and Provincial Parks Association of Canada. Incorrectly described by a Member of Parliament as "a spontaneous response of the people of Canada to the Conference", NPPAC would do the job outlined by Alvin Hamilton in 1960,[30] and by the parks director in 1947. NPPAC was a "voluntary group of citizens that will assist in encouraging public opinion in the fundamental purpose of our national parks system".[31] Government gave the group start-up funds and a small annual grant.

In 1965 the Association hired a small staff, and began publishing *Park News.* The NPPAC also "successfully" opposed the use of Banff for the 1972 Winter Olympics. The Association matured with sponsorship (jointly with the University of Calgary) of the "Canadian National Parks: Today and Tomorrow Conference", in 1968.[32] Conference papers remain major sources on the history, development and purposes of Canada's national parks.[33] Jean Chrétien, responsible for the national parks following the election of Trudeau's Liberals, congratulated those present: "Conferences such as this one are indicative of the country's concern for the state of our environment, and they can do much to add to the level of public discussion and debate".[34]

Chrétien was to benefit from the initiatives of Diefenbaker and Hamilton. Active pressure groups supported preservation of the national parks, and Chrétien was a good enough politician to use that support well.

Saving the Townsites from Tourism

The first struggle to save the national parks from tourism was in the townsites of the old western parks — Banff, Jasper and Waterton Lakes. This struggle involved primarily the existing business people of Banff and the other park townsites, National Parks Branch bureaucrats, and the various ministers responsible for parks. Environmental groups participated to some extent, and the Alberta government also took sides.

The national parks towns were unique. Parks policies, established to preserve the monopoly position of the CPR, gave the government tools to be a "wholesome terror" in the towns. Land was owned by the federal government, and leased for twenty-one or forty-two years to those developing houses or businesses. For many years these leases involved minimal payments by the tenants, and many included a clause allowing for "perpetual" renewal. Prime Minister Sir John A. Macdonald had suggested people would not build houses of a suitable standard without stability of tenure. The leases were almost indistinguishable from freehold ownership.

There was no municipal organization in the townsites. The Parks Branch ran the towns with the help of advisory councils. This both minimized the local tax burden, and caused local complaint. Whenever residents disliked a Parks policy they complained of being deprived of democratic rights. Taxes equivalent to municipal taxes were raised in Banff only after 1950, to "offset the costs of services such as water, sewerage, garbage collection and the like".[35] Community leaders opposed taxation without representation. They demanded local self-government. Political scientist Grant Crawford, author of a local government text, was hired to study the problem. He told the advisory councils in the three towns that tax increases would result from self-government. The councils decided against "local autonomy with the taxes that entails". They had a "fortunate financial position . . . in the matter of their costs for community services under present arrangements".[36] Financial advantage was more important than esoteric concerns with self-government! The status quo was maintained. Banff and Jasper were also studied by star planner Peter Oberlander.[37] Recommendations for a town manager, for pedestrian routes and improved traffic circulation were implemented. The Oblerlander studies, though, were soon overtaken by new political and economic events.

In 1962 the Parks Branch planners began an exercise with far-reaching implications. They drafted an alternative to "piecemeal" national park policies. They wanted to "correct" rather than "create" policies with "stability and continuity". But here for the first time, the Parks Branch made explicit the tension between townsite development and park values. Only essential roads, townsites and "artificial recreational developments" would be permitted. Townsites would provide minimum visitor services, and accommodation only for those serving tourists. Townsites would not expand "to a point where visitors who would not otherwise come to the park are attracted".[38]

The Liberals, returning to power under Lester Pearson in 1963, met a bureaucracy which wanted to curtail townsite expansion. The new government was sympathetic.[39] By 1964 the House had accepted a parks policy based on the draft of 1962. They intended, according to Arthur Laing's parliamentary secretary John Turner, to preserve the "sanctity" of the national parks from commercialism and "the pressures of profit". The automobile, the dangers of easy access, were to be avoided. Private development would not prevent "the ordinary man, woman and child" from using the parks. Also: "It [was] not the purpose of the national parks to provide summer residential subdivisions, cottage lots, or shack tent areas for the exclusive use and possession of private individuals".[40]

The lease system introduced by Sir John A. Macdonald was to be the key mechanism for controlling townsite growth. Many had acquired leases, according to Laing, for private purposes, not intending to serve visitors. There would be no more perpetual leases or automatic lease renewals. Holders of most existing residential leases would be compensated, and their property managed by the crown as a rental unit. Holders of commercial leases would have to pay a rent related to market value.[41]

The new policy deprived residents of rights that had been effectively indistinguishable from freehold rights. Opposition was vigorous. The Conservatives blamed the department for the poor relationship between the town and the government. The Parks Branch, said Conservative MP for Bow River, Eldon Wooliams, was "tight knit". He knew from talking to townspeople that the minister was not to blame, for many had failed to "prevail over" the park superintendent. Parking tickets were distributed too liberally, to tourists and to Wooliams himself. Leases were in confusion. People were threatened with taxes. Profits and free enterprise were endangered.[42]

The Banff Chamber of Commerce complained that Ottawa had no sense of responsibility. Banff had no right to elect a council or to appeal departmental rulings. The government was unsympathetic to tourists, businessman and Albertans.[43] The chamber wanted security of tenure with forty-two year leases, with guaranteed renewals and unlimited transferability, zoning for more intensive development, compensation for changes in policy, a town manager so decisions need not be referred to Ottawa, and equal treatment of all businesses.[44]

The tension heightened when the Parks Branch approved a motel proposed by William Hawreluk, the Liberal mayor of Edmonton. The site had not been zoned for a motel, and Banff Advisory Council demanded the minister's resignation. Laing responded that Oberlander had recommended the site for a motel.[45] The difficulty in the parks, for Laing, was "resistance to competition". As minister he had to decide how much competition was enough.[46] Laing, though, postponed approval of another proposal for Jasper until he had studied reports by Oberlander, and the chamber of commerce.[47]

Opposition MP Dinsdale accused bureaucrats of "continually quarrelling with democratically elected groups in the townsites".[48] Horner, MP for Jasper–Edson, said six thousand second class citizens had been created of people who only wanted "a few acres of freehold so that they could run their own show".[49] Laing retained the parks portfolio after the 1966 election, and the opposition groaned. They charged him with being completely insulated from people's concerns. His policies did not "make sense, rhyme or reason".[50]

Banff, Jasper and Waterton Lakes chambers of commerce, Banff Advisory Council, Banff Parks Citizens' Association and Waterton Lakes National Park Advisory Council presented their case in a series of leaflets. One read: "Confiscation without compensation: its unethical and un-Canadian".

This was the new national parks policy in a nutshell! Alberta's Premier Manning suggested the federal park policies infringed on provincial property rights. The province submitted a widely published brief suggesting: "National Park Policy is unfair to the citizens of Alberta and of serious detriment to the third largest industry in the province — tourism".[52]

Alberta had ten times more parks than other provinces; tourism and recreation were increasing; visitors to the mountains had little to do after dark; accommodation was insufficient; the policy preventing accommodation near the ski slopes discouraged business; and to call the Banff School of Fine Arts undesirable was ridiculous![53]

Laing published his reply widely. Alberta's parks were a national resource, not just provincial. The Canadian taxpayer had spent

$100 million over a decade in these parks. Use had increased and would continue to increase. Banff, Jasper and Waterton towns would remain their present size, with new centres added if necessary. Expansion plans were flexible, and expansion of the School of Fine Arts had already been approved. The government was not anti-development.[54]

In 1967 Laing made matters worse by proposing a "Leaseholds Corporation" to manage the leased properties at arm's length. The town's access to redress would be further reduced, so the town decided to challenge in court the government's reinterpretation of the leases. A parliamentary committee went to listen to the leaseholders. Banff Chamber challenged the concept of "impairment" used by the Parks Branch, and complained of the government monopoly on land.[55] But the committee, of course, supported the government. The opposition called this "kangaroo court" a "sham", for advocating expropriation without notice or compensation.[56] The Alberta MPS said new businesses would not move into Jasper or Banff without security of tenure. In Banff the superintendent called protesters "rabble rousers" and threatened to close their stores.[57]

Early in 1968 the Banff Park Citizens' Association published a proposal to transfer Banff town to Alberta. The association wanted "their democratic rights". All nonconforming uses in the park would be consolidated in a single municipality, containing the townsite, golf course, air strip, sight-seeing lifts, the remains of Bankhead, and the power dams on Lake Minnewanka and Two Jack Lake.[58] All profitable ventures would be consolidated within control of a single municipality — and out of control of the Parks Branch.

In 1968 the new prime minister Trudeau selected Jean Chrétien as minister of Indian Affairs and Northern Development, a portfolio including national parks. This appointment brought no joy to the townspeople. Chrétien reintroduced the Leaseholds Corporation Bill and increased rents. One business received a 4000 per cent increase. The initial rent had been nominal so the increase was not substantial in dollar terms. Chrétien wanted to put the interests of Canadians in general before the profits of particular business people. In 1969 he published a revised National Parks Policy confirming restrictions on townsite growth. The National Parks Act had been interpreted as encouraging "artificial recreations", and development of parks "along resort lines". He believed that this was inappropriate. Urban facilities should be introduced only where necessary, and always with minimal impairment. No townsites would be introduced unless needed by visitors, and should not provide: "The extra entertainments and services common to urban living throughout Canada. . . . [Parks would not] attract people by virtue of the townsite who would not otherwise have come."[59]

The opposition spoke of colonialism, and of callous policies that turned off developers. Western business people were not avaricious and predatory. "The impression has evidently been widely held that these communities are largely populated by vultures preying on the innocent tourist, whose park residence has constituted if not a license to steal then at least a license to print money".[60]

In 1970 the courts upheld the "perpetual" park leases. The government lost its key control for managing the park townsites. The opposition crowed.[61] The Leaseholds Corporation Bill died on the order paper, and Chrétien admitted that although he still wanted to gradually eliminate perpetual leases, he was now approving every renewal and transfer.[62] The government would use a carrot rather than a stick. People signing agreements to transfer their leases only to people working in the national parks were given lower rents. Others would pay full market rents.

In 1972 two school boards in Banff and Jasper, as the only elected governments, petitioned for municipal status. The Alberta legislature unanimously supported them. Studies of Banff and the other park townsites followed. In 1976 a board reported that limited local self-government would be a "possible and acceptable way of minimizing operational problems". The town could control its own planning and urban development, and such services as traffic, garbage collection and street lighting. Also, land rents would be 10 per cent of appraised fair market value. A plebiscite, twinning of the Trans-Canada, perpetually renewable leases for Canadian citizens and "bona fide" residents were also recommended.[63]

The Parks Branch authorized a new urban development plan for Banff, explicitly based on the concept that the townsite was "an intrusion" in the park. Growth would be limited to infill and redevelopment within the existing "land use structure". New hotels and motels would only be permitted in areas already designated for the purpose. All such developments would have to provide staff housing, to reduce the pressure for more housing in Banff.

Canmore, just outside park boundaries, would be a service centre. Only those who actually worked in the park would be encouraged to live there. Once again, though, the government would have to use financial incentives, rather than disposition of expired leases, to attain their objectives.[64]

Policy on Banff and the other townsites was reaffirmed in the draft Parks Canada Policy released in 1978. Leaseholders would pay economic rent. Land needed for public purposes would be taken over "through negotiation". Banff and Jasper townsites would be limited within existing boundaries, and no new townsites would be developed. Limited local government would be encouraged for service administration. The 1978 document also contained a commitment to citizen participation, to consultations and to public hearings.[65] The government had been burned by the political fallout from the leaseholds issue, by public outcry over proposals for Village Lake Louise (see below), and by messy disputes over new national parks. Public participation would anticipate and accommodate opposition, and ensure that environmental groups, as well as economic interests, participated. The new Parks Canada Policy was itself subjected to the new participation processes. Copies were distributed to interested groups, to other federal departments, and to the provincial and territorial governments. Briefs were submitted and public hearings held. A final document, little changed from that of 1978 was published a year later.[66]

The most recent exercise to affect the townsites of Banff and Jasper has been the "Four Mountains Park Planning Program". The process involved extensive public hearings and consultation. Fifty-six briefs were received, primarily from groups wanting to use the parks. Hang-gliders, bicyclists, snowmobilers, hostellers, hikers, riders, campers and cavers — all wanted policy changes to increase their opportunities. The input and information was condensed in 1984 to three planning options. Option A, emphasizing natural qualities of the parks, prevented expansion of existing facilities or development of new ones. Existing facilities which created "undesirable impacts" would be changed or eliminated. Option B provided for expansion on the bases of existing facilities, both public and private. A finite limit would be set on visitor accommodation. No new facilities would be permitted. Option C would increase the number of visitors, and the tourist value of the parks. Increased private development would be dispersed, with inevitable impact on the natural environment.[67] Option B, of course, was the only option consistent with the National Parks Policy of 1979.

Over 3,000 people responded. Nearly half selected the minimum development option A, and 1,000 preferred option B. Only 15 per cent selected the tourist option C. A draft planning scenario placed before the minister mixed the three options, so that preservation in the backcountry combined with development near existing roads and towns. A new Conservative government has been elected, and a new minister responsible for national parks appointed, since the Four Mountain Parks planning program began. In December 1986 the minister, Tom McMillan, introduced new parks legislation in the House of Commons. He has chosen to permit more development within the boundaries of the existing park towns, while preventing expansion beyond those boundaries. This compromise appears to reflect both McMillan's earlier experience as Minister of State for Tourism, and concern for preservation of the natural parks environment. Also, he has reinforced policies to protect wildlife and the ecological integrity of the backcountry.

In 1962 parks planners wanted to limit development of the towns. However, restrictions were vigorously opposed by people with livelihoods and capital investments to lose. A great deal of energy was invested in opposing government plans. Opposition MPs, particularly those from Alberta, supported them. The Alberta provincial government also supported the business people of the park towns. Parks planners and politicians, and the environmental groups met this challenge. Citizen participation was extended to ensure environmental groups could present the case for the public interest in preservation rather than profit. Presentations of various groups concerned about wildlife, about wilderness preservation or about "natural" forms of recreation, were weighed against those of the more sectional interests of business people and residents in Banff and Jasper.

The scales balanced to the advantage of the business people of Banff and Jasper. Development in the towns is still limited, and Ottawa is still the ultimate landlord, but security of tenure is established. Skillful manipulation of vague policies for "development within the existing framework of land use" will allow improvements of and extensions to existing facilities, and limited new development. Although the towns still lack full municipal autonomy, they control some local services. They complain of limited business opportunities, but conditions for existing businesses are close to optimal. Parks Canada policies have limited competition, providing a considerable advantage to entrepreneurs already in the towns. Grumble they may, but existing businesses have retained and reinforced exclusive rights to profit from park visitors.

But the environment groups are not pleased. A profitable commercial sector is again politically legitimate. The towns will not be removed. Policies to reduce the impact of towns have been rejected. The environment groups protest that most respondents to the planning process prefer preservation. The economic interests of a small number of business people, they say, have been given primacy over the wider public need for natural environments uncontaminated by urban development or the profit motive. Environmental groups, parks planners and several federal ministers tried for twenty years to save the parks *from* profit. They failed, managing instead to save the parks *for* the profit of a limited group of entrepreneurs. A protected business environment begun under the CPR monopoly has been inherited by today's business people in the park townsites. The business people of Banff and Jasper still benefit from the limits to competition ensured by Parks Canada policy.

DOWNHILL SKIING: THE NEW MONOPOLY

Skiing involved other bigger players — large corporations developing Canada's most lucrative natural resources. The Spray Lakes had been the issue of the twenties, with Calgary Power Company challenging the groups concerned about national parks. Now Village Lake Louise was to be the issue of the seventies. Several resource corporations proposed huge downhill-ski resorts at Lake Louise and Sunshine, and were opposed by a array of environmental groups.

A ski development is a monopoly rather like a railroad. The location of ski lifts, their starting and ending points, and the pattern of grooming on the slopes, all determine the paths to be chosen by all but the hardiest downhill skiers. The company owning the ski tows has a captive market. Skiers also have to use the company's food facilities and bars, equipment rentals and sales, ski instructors, buses and even overnight accommodation. In a national park, where the number of competing ski resorts is restricted by government policy, the company operating a ski development is in an even better competitive position.

Four downhill ski resorts now exist in the mountain national parks, Marmott in Jasper National Park, and Sunshine, Lake Louise and Norquay in Banff. Skiing began in the 1930s as a small proposition. The first tow on Mount Norquay was run by a group of Calgary businessmen called Canadian Rockies Winter Sports Limited. The second was at Sunshine, operated by Jim Brewster.[68] Sunshine had a lodge in 1930, a rope tow in 1940, and a modern lift in 1957. In 1966 Calgary Power became involved in Sunshine. Opposition MP Eldon Woolliams commented on government favouritism to large corporations:

> Canada (sic) power can go in and develop a great skiing enterprise. But let the average man who has served the tourists in the parks for thirty years try it, and he is not permitted to do so.[69]

> Canada (sic) power is allowed to go in and build Sunshine. It is a wonderful venture. But if it is right for Canada power, and if it is right for the Canadian Pacific Railway, then surely it is right for the average man who has served the tourist trade for 20 to 30 years in the Banff national park to do the same thing.[70]

Skiing was big business — squeezing out the smaller businesses of the early years.

Skiing also began in 1930 at Lake Louise, when private groups, including the Ski Club of the Canadian Rockies, proposed an alpine resort. Accommodation was added but the depression and the war intervened. By the 1960s Lake Louise Lifts was operating on Whitehorn and Temple. In 1970 Village Lake Louise, owned 50 per cent by Imperial Oil of New Jersey and 50 per cent by Lake Louise Lifts, took over. The new company proposed a huge ski resort which, more than any other proposal, finally stirred the environmental groups to action. The public debate over Village Lake Louise involved more people than any other debate over the future of the parks.

The initiative for development at Lake Louise began within government. In the late 1950s the government became interested in year-round use of the parks. A 1963 report led to announcement of the winter-use policy in 1965. Downhill skiing was consistent with natural parks values, and Marmott, Norquay, Sunshine and

Lake Louise would expand.[71] In 1967 Parks Canada received development proposals for Lake Louise. A businessman in the area wanted to expand but was turned down, and his land expropriated for the new "Lake Louise Visitors Centre", ultimately costing $10 million.[72] Lake Louise Ski Lodge Limited, was then given notice of expropriation of sixty acres in Lake Louise. Only five acres were needed for the Trans-Canada Highway. Existing businesses would evidently make way for larger development. An initial offer of $13,000 was increased by the courts to $96,000.[73]

But in 1967 security of tenure in the parks was still insufficient for new private development. The government tried three times to sell one motel site in Lake Louise.[74] By 1969 the only applicant was Imperial Oil of New Jersey. Asked why the franchise was given to a foreign owned group, Jean Chrétien admitted, "They were the only tenderers."[75] The opposition complained: "We are handing over the national parks to big international conglomerates. . . . [the government will] drive out the little man."[76]

But without a perpetual lease, no one would offer to develop anything.[77] The opposition asked if Imperial Oil would get the standard forty-two year lease. The government confirmed they would.[78] However, the words "on a long term basis" were included in the agreement as eventually published. The project's life span would be more than forty-two years, and sponsors would get lease renewals without difficulty. The corporations studied the ultimate capacity of Whitehorn and Temple, including Eagle Valley, Richardson Ridge, Purple Bowl and Larch Peak. Ten thousand skiers a day could be accommodated. Access to the Trans-Canada Highway and the railway was easy, and the scenery exceptional.[78] Lake Louise could be a world-class ski resort.

The plan for Village Lake Louise was extremely ambitious. The international resorts in the United States and Europe, which created "whole new towns" and transformed "many older villages", were taken as models. A world-class ski resort run by an oil company would become the 1980 equivalent of a world-class health spa controlled by the railroad monopoly in 1885. Lake Louise would include two developments — a redevelopment and extension of existing facilities on the valley floor (the "lower village") and an "upper village" on the slopes of the mountain above pipestone creek.[79]

The lower village would provide the basic infrastructure for tourists — automobile service stations, restaurants and picnic facilities, tourist information and shopping, and park facilities. One thousand beds would be added in the lower village. But on the valley floor businesses already existed to compete with new developments by Village Lake Louise. A development was needed in which Village Lake Louise could prevent (or at least control) competition. They proposed a new upper village on the mountain slopes with direct access to their own ski lifts.

The upper village really attracted opposition. The development would have 3,000 overnight visitors and 2,500 staff employees and dependents, 3,000 parking spaces, and twelve-storey buildings. Gourmet restaurants, discotheques, movie theatres, a health spa, concert space and tennis courts would be built. Leading architect Arthur Erikson's drawings showed massive development on both the valley floor and the mountain slopes. His designs were in the tradition of monuments in a beautiful setting (as were the CPR's hotels at Banff and Lake Louise), rather than for more modest and tactful development with minimum impact on the natural landscape. In 1971 the Parks Branch had already held hearings on the mountain parks, and rumours about Lake Louise had stimulated opposition. The government promised more public hearings before final approval. The proposal was released in December 1971, and hearings set for Calgary in March 1972. The government was overwhelmed with briefs, letters and petitions.

The Federation of Alberta Naturalists and the Federation of Canadian Naturalists said the proposals were "irreconcilable" with national parks policy. The Bow Valley Naturalists wrote of "excessive development".[80] High school students from Edmonton opposed Village Lake Louise. The National and Provincial Parks Association was opposed, and the Canadian Parks and Recreation Association called for recreation facilities outside the parks. The Committee for an Independent Canada objected to development controlled outside Canada. The New Democratic party objected to any private development.[81]

Village Lake Louise, though, had captive supporters — the skiers using their existing facilities. In February 1972 they gave skiers notice of the public hearings and brochures describing the proposals. Those opposing the development, they suggested, were "radicals": "The company is concerned that the hearings do reflect public opinion as a whole and not just the voice of a radical minority. . . . Remember it is not just Village Lake Louise that the radical groups oppose. The majority within these groups oppose any expansion of downhill ski facilities in National Parks."[82]

An information meeting was sponsored by Village Lake Louise, and skiers were asked to send for more information, to write letters or briefs to the Public Hearings Office, to write to their local newspapers or to attend the public hearings. The Canadian Ski Association sent similar material to members. The ski associations appeared at the hearings, predictably supporting development. They quoted the Canadian Government Tourist Bureau, which predicted 100,000 American skiers in Canada: "It's a whole new ball game in skiing. The Banff resort has not been promoted sufficiently in the past. Stepped up promotion and introduction of special fares for skiing holidays are the major factors behind this increase in the number of skiers that will come to Canada."[83]

The government received 2,118 briefs and 500 letters, heard 191 speakers and collected 5,500 pages of documentation.[84] Analysis revealed opposition outnumbering support by over 3 to 1. Over a thousand form letters, prepared and circulated by Village Lake Louise supported development. Dome Petroleum was in support. Together with other letters and petitions, 1,544 signatures supported development. Opponents also sent 1,630 form letters, from an advertisement placed by the NPPAC. A petition by the NPPAC had 2,350 signatures. In total 5,804 presented statements opposing development.[85]

Jean Chrétien admits that he liked the plan for the lower village. He remembers public support extensive on both sides, and was ready to give his approval. The province of Alberta also favoured development, but knowing Chrétien was supportive they decided to gain popularity with environmental groups by publicly stating their opposition. Chrétien was not prepared to take the blame for approving the scheme, and warned the Alberta Minister of Intergovernmental Affairs, Don Getty: "I hope you are a good quarterback, Don. I will be in the left field. Throw the ball there. If you throw the ball the other way I won't be there."[86]

But the Alberta government decided to publicly oppose the Village Lake Louise proposal.[87] Chrétien phoned Don Getty to tell him he had thrown the ball the "wrong way", and took the next plane to Calgary to announce there would be no development: "The proposal was rejected because, in my view, it was too large and could possibly have resulted in environmentally unacceptable concentrations of visitors to the Lake Louise area".

However, the issue did not stop there. Chrétien continued:

"There still exists, however, the problem of meeting the essential needs of an increasing number of visitors to this area both in summer and in winter, and of through traffic on the Trans-Canada Highway".[88]

His department began a planning process based on a claimed consensus on the need "for a more limited development and to clean up and improve the service at the existing visitor centre on the valley floor". A new plan for 1,900 beds in a "visitor service centre" on the valley floor, was developed. Extensive public participation and environmental impact studies began in 1974 and extended to the end of the decade.

In 1979 the government selected a "low growth option" for Lake Louise, with visitor services but no private homes. Only people who worked in Lake Louise would live there, and businesses had to house their employees. In 1981 the actual dimension of "low growth" became clear, when the minister (John Roberts) approved a $35 million development for the valley floor. Up to 1,900 new beds will be provided. Although this is less than 40 per cent of the ultimate capacity of the original Village Lake Louise proposal,[89] it almost exactly equals the 1878 new beds included in phase I of the 1971 proposal.

This approval was followed by approval for three new ski lifts, on the condition that Village Lake Louise provide employee housing.[90] However, there is no upper village, and the monopoly sought by Imperial Oil and Lake Louise Lifts has not been granted. After Chrétien's rejection of the original proposal, Imperial Oil lost interest in Lake Louise, which is now controlled by local entrepreneur, Charles Locke.

Development at Sunshine has followed a similar pattern. Calgary Power was involved in the expansions of the 1960s, and in 1975 another resource-sector company in the Thomcor group (Warnock Hersey International) applied to expand Sunshine from a capacity of 2,500 to 6,500. Eleven new lifts were proposed, a new hotel and a second day lodge.[91] The NPPAC, and other groups, complained about inadequate participation, and dangers to fragile alpine ecosystems. Although "intensive recreational activities such as downhill skiing" is against national parks policy, they complained the "four areas continue to operate and expand".[92] But officials recognize downhill skiing as "a fact of life", and in 1978 approved most new lifts proposed for Sunshine, with minor realignments. The ski resort would expand, but within existing boundaries. Parks Canada turned down the application for a second hotel. Thomcor has since lost interest in Sunshine, and the resort is controlled by local entrepreneur, Ralph Scurfield.

The resource-sector industries withdrew from the ski resorts in the mountain parks. Parks Canada policy would have protected them from competition, and preserved their monopoly control of the ski resorts — that would have been good for business. But, at the same time those policies prevented expansion of the resorts to take full advantage of their monopoly. The proposal for an upper village at Lake Louise and for a second hotel at Sunshine had both been rejected. The ultimate size of the ski areas in the national parks was set. Resorts would not be profitable enough in the long term to interest large resource companies. The ski areas have returned to the control of smaller local individually held companies.[94]

Two Conservation Movements

In the 1920s Canada's first conservation movement produced a National Parks Association that lead the struggle to prevent the damming of the Spray Lakes by Calgary Power Company. They failed in one way, for the Spray Lakes were dammed. However, in another sense they won, for hydroelectric developments were accepted as inconsistent with national park principles. The national park boundaries were redrawn to exclude the Spray Lakes, and the other areas of exploitable resources then within the parks: the cement plant at Exshaw, and the active coal mines outside Jasper. National parks legislation explicitly prevented resource exploitation within the parks.

Over the last twenty years conservation groups like the NPPAC, the bureaucrats, and some of the politicians responsible for the national parks have again tried to save the national parks, this time *from* the tourist industry. At best they have achieved a delay. Ultimately, the interests of the small business people in Banff, and the other townsites, have been primary. Those involved in the second conservation movement tried to save the parks *from* commercial tourism, but only prevented the development of large monopolistic ski resorts controlled by resource-sector giants. They saved the national parks *for* small business, rather than from it.

CHAPTER SEVEN

※ ※

The New
National Parks

D URING THE TRUDEAU YEARS Canada's national parks were dou-
bled in size and number. In 1968 Jean Chrétien was given
responsibility for national parks, and told Allan Frame of the NPPAC
that he would create ten new parks. Frame bet Chrétien five dollars that he couldn't. Frame lost the bet, and the cheque hangs
framed in Chrétien's office, surrounded by photographs of the ten
parks created during his ministry. More parks have been added
since. They were added in the Atlantic provinces, in British
Columbia, Saskatchewan and Ontario, and in the North, in the
Yukon and the Northwest Territories.

THE NATIONAL PARKS OF ATLANTIC CANADA

Every one of the national parks in Atlantic Canada, from Cape
Breton Highlands created in Nova Scotia in 1936, to Gros Morne
created in Newfoundland in 1970, was a park for profit. The
Maritimes were economically depressed, with low income levels
and high unemployment. The provincial governments, knowing
their provinces lacked natural resources, wanted to use fully all
they had.[1] National parks were not for wilderness preservation or
wildlife conservation, but to stimulate tourism and economic development. The parks were federal public works projects creating

permanent jobs in provinces dependent on the central government. The first Maritime national parks were created in the 1930s. In Nova Scotia civic leaders had pressured since 1914 for a national park, and Cape Breton Highlands was created in 1936. Public support for a national park in Prince Edward Island was mobilized in 1923, and culminated in 1936 in Prince Edward Island National Park. A New Brunswick politician also sought a park for his province. But after extensive surveys and correspondence, the two governments could not agree on a site. Member of Parliament A. J. Brooks complained that his province had missed out: "It was unfortunate that so many years had passed before it took place, and that we lost a great opportunity of tourist trade over those years."[2]

The province could have had a park if clear title to the land had been handed over to the federal government.[3] Fundy National Park was created in 1947, named after a competition among the province's school children,[4] on land lumbered throughout the nineteenth century to build wooden ships. The area had become depressed with the advent of steel ships.[5] Without reforestation, a part had been abandoned. This wasteland was sufficiently useless to be acquired cheaply for a park.

Newfoundland asked for a national park as a condition for joining Canada. Premier Smallwood wanted Terra Nova to be on the Trans-Canada Highway, so Ottawa would pay road construction costs. He also retained timber rights (though they have not yet been used) and a right of way for a future power line.[6] A promise of a new golf course was exacted. The rivers were assessed for power potential, and the park boundary redrawn to "delete areas with hydro potential".[7] Smallwood made sure that the area had no potential for any other form of exploitation. Terra Nova National Park was to be "a blessing to Newfoundland as a source of employment and for the amenities it . . . provided", but not a sacrifice.[8]

By 1960 Nova Scotia MPs wanted a second national park.[9] Cape Breton Highlands "attracted many visitors", and an area in one MPs constituency would "lend itself to this type of development".[10] In 1963 Arthur Laing wrote to the province's Premier Stanfield about a second park, recognizing that the first was "making a tremendous contribution to tourism".[11] They jointly announced Kejimkujik, which would bring economic (and political) benefits. "This will be a great addition to the tourist industry of Nova Scotia. The selection is one which, sited as it is in an area in the south-western part of the province, will have a great impact on various constituencies represented here, and one which the government of Nova Scotia have fully approved and recommended."[12]

Members of Parliament from New Brunswick and Prince Edward Island now asked for second parks for their provinces too.[13] The minister was looking for new parks all over Canada, not just in the Maritimes. Kejimkujik might be expanded.[14] The minister planned a parks bonanza in the Maritimes. The government might even change its policy, and help pay for acquisition:

> We have vast coastlines on the Atlantic and on the Pacific, much of which we are losing at the present time to individuals who are not citizens of Canada. It is imperative that we step in. We have funds for development, but not for acquisition. I do not want, in this speech at least, to predict the necessity of altering our policy, but I may be doing that in the coming year.
>
> The Atlantic parks are within two days driving for over 100 million people. This accounts for the fantastic rise in traffic in those parts. In the case of Cape Breton Highlands there has been an increase of 16.75 per cent, Prince Edward Island, 15.56 per cent, and Terra Nova, 65.21 per cent over the year before.[15]

Parks were discussed for the Bonne Bay area of Newfoundland; in Ship Harbour, Nova Scotia; for Kouchibouguac Bay in New Brunswick and the East Point area of Prince Edward Island. However, no further agreements were reached, and Laing was accused of lip service.[16] He promised to create forty to fifty new national parks by the Centennial in 1985.

In 1968 the Liberal party gained a new leader — Trudeau. Jean Chrétien, his minister responsible for parks, wanted to create sixty new national parks by 1985.[17] It would be difficult, for the provinces hesitated to surrender their rights to natural resources in potential parks. In the words of one MP: "Provincial governments in the past have been very jealous of their rights and hesitant about surrendering land under these absolute conditions, their reluctance stemming from the fact that they may one day decide that the development of mineral finds with timber stands is more lucrative than any benefit to be derived from an outdoor recreational facility and the concomitant revenue generated by increased tourist traffic".[18]

But Chrétien persisted. He negotiated with Newfoundland for a second park. The province again drove a hard bargain. A federal government ecologist proposed a park of 1,500 square miles. The province offered 480 square miles. Ottawa said no, and the province counter-offered, but still excluding the caribou range favoured by the federal government. The province wanted to keep the forest, then leased to Bowater for a pulp mill at Cornerbrook. Ottawa said that since Bowater controlled 30 per cent of Newfoundland the forest needed for a park was insignificant.[19] In 1969 negotiations stopped abruptly when a silica deposit was discovered. Mining exploration would have to be completed before boundaries were confirmed.[20] The forests were too valuable: "A proposed second national park in the Bonne Bay area of Newfoundland, where the cloak-and-dagger tactics of various levels of government and departments, and a complete lack of sincerity, will destroy a potential Mecca of forest development not equalled in the whole of the nation. . . . [a park] considered to be of fantastic value by everyone other than those who can do some good for the Canadians they represent".[21]

Newfoundland proposed integration of tourism and resource extraction, supported by a $60 million federal investment.[22] Chrétien was not interested. He only wanted a national park, not mining and oil exploitation.[23] Eventually new boundaries were drawn around a 775-square-mile park, excluding the silica deposit. Smallwood also demanded recreational facilities in the park, like those in the older western parks, even though national parks policy now discouraged such developments. In particular, he wanted a golf course, which the federal government had promised but not built in Terra Nova. The course was eventually built — just outside park boundaries.

A proposal for a third park in Nova Scotia, at Ship Harbour, failed. Rumours of park development began in 1965, but publicity had been restricted to prevent land speculation. A senator familiar with Ship Harbour described its pretty villages and small businesses jeopardized by the park. People would have to leave their homes. A 1750-name petition gave Premier Regan cold feet.[24] Chrétien's experience in the townsites of Banff and Jasper led to his insistence that people not be allowed to live in the new national parks: "There were two or three pockets containing a small number of fishermen which it was quite important should be included in the park if we were to have a real conservation area.

We decided to move the people. . . . Perhaps we were a bit tough. Perhaps we stuck to our guns too much, if you like. We are quite preoccupied because you know the kind of problems we have when there are too many people [living in] the parks."[25]

Chrétien tried to allow the fishermen to stay as long as they were fishing,[25] but local residents wanted to be able to pass land on to their children.[26] The province "caved in" and cancelled the Ship Harbour park proposal.[27]

The Maritime National Parks

Province	National Park	Date	Km²
Prince Edward Island	Prince Edward Island	1937	18
Nova Scotia	Cape Breton Island	1936	367
New Brunswick	Fundy	1948	206
Newfoundland	Terra Nova	1957	153
Nova Scotia	Kenjimkujik	1968	145
New Brunswick	Kouchibouguac	1969	225
Newfoundland	Gros Morne	1970	775

By the end of Trudeau's period in power, in 1984, there were seven Atlantic national parks, two in each province except Prince Edward Island, which contained a single larger national park. Others had been proposed, but without success. A proposal for Cape La Have in Nova Scotia was "blocked by vested interests", and one for the East Point of Prince Edward Island was withdrawn in the early 1970s after local protest.[28]

Federal government spending in these parks was significant to the Maritime provinces — or significant to their politicians. Atlantic MPs asked continually in the House of Commons about public works expenditures, job creation, wage rates and development plans in these parks. They asked about tenders for road construction in Cape Breton; about low wage rates for casual labour in Fundy; about winter works for this park or that, to relieve seasonal unemployment, and about job losses following completion.[29]

Tourism generated by the parks also promised to be significant. In Nova Scotia, for example, tourism was second in importance only to the fisheries.[30] Commenting on increased numbers of visitors to Cape Breton National Park in 1960, one MP enthused:

The great percentage of these people were tourists from the United States and they spent a great deal of money in Nova Scotia. The tourist industry itself in Cape Breton Island increased by 17% in 1959 and 39% the year before. . . . Tourism is unlimited and is one of the great present and potential industries not only of Nova Scotia but indeed of Canada. Money spent by the government to provide better facilities and make tourists welcome is an investment that will pay us well in the years ahead.[31]

Gros Morne park was also welcomed:

The ancilliary tourist industry of a national park would be very beneficial. The secondary industry and commercial enterprises that would flow from a national park would do much to uplift the economy by the creation of additional employment.[32]

and:

Anyone can see that the creation of a national park would have the effect of creating a tourist centre outside the immediate area and would necessitate the development of tourist hotels and motels, service stations, gift shops, restaurants as well as golf courses, boating marinas, sports shops, and would lead to the employment of many hundred of the citizens in the area who today cannot find jobs.[33]

In Prince Edward Island tourism was second only to agriculture:

Our province, with its somewhat restricted tax base and its narrow range of industrial capacity, has as its most expansive and most expandable industry, the tourist industry. The Dominion Government could do a great deal by developing a second national park there, to provide facilities comparable to those provided for nearly a million visitors who come [to Prince Edward Island National Park]. . . . I urge [the minister] to exercise a little alacrity in discussions with the province of Prince Edward Island in respect of one of the few areas in which we can expand our economic base, namely tourism.[34]

The golf course exacted by premier Smallwood would attract tourists.[35] Ski developments were sought for Cape Breton and Fundy, to increase tourist value in the winter — when the only visitors were "the moose that walk up and down the main street".[36] A golf clubhouse was sought for Cape Breton Park in 1963, to employ people and to attract tourists.[37]

To a limited extent the maritime national parks did fulfill their economic promise. Gros Morne reduced the number of unemployed in the immediate area by 6 per cent, with a 15 per cent reduction possible after further development.[38] Kejimkujik Park was "important" to the regional economy, but "not a major generator of growth".[39] Tourism would not be the engine of new economic development. Tourism developed, but not to the extent anticipated by the Atlantic premiers and MPs.

Because Maritime national parks are about profit, rather than conservation, they have been particularly vulnerable to erosion when other uses appeared more profitable. Part of Cape Breton National Park was given back to Nova Scotia in 1956 because of mineral potential.[40] In 1958 a section from the same park was returned to the province because of hydro potential. In 1975 conservation groups were horrified to find the government had approved hydro development just outside the park.[41] In Newfoundland the boundaries of Gros Morne and Terra Nova National parks were manipulated to exclude areas with resource potential.

Natural resources were allowed to stop national parks (or to determine their boundaries), but other interests were not. Local users were often ignored. For example, fishermen and small landholders were displaced. Fishermen, deprived of their homes and harbours, were bitter: "There is a long history of national parks being established in a way that does not take into account the interests of the local people. For instance, a national park was established in Newfoundland and the interests of the fishermen in the outports was not taken into account. Sometimes local people are bitter when young people from other parts of the country come to their national park in the summer and get employment."[42]

The people of Fundy had to move their houses, or have them destroyed.[43] Terra Nova Park in Newfoundland also displaced fishmermen, many with shacks near the shore. Some were allowed to remain for a while, but new shacks were taken down.[44] Five communities were relocated at Gros Morne, with four small enclaves allowed to remain to serve tourists. For them the park brought better conditions and municipal services. However, traditional occupations associated with subsistence living were curtailed. Rabbit snaring became illegal and park officials were "unpopular" (in their own words) when the RCMP laid charges against those caught. Also, cutting firewood was forbidden, although officials allowed it to continue until the legislation creating the park had been passed.[45]

The residents of Kouchibouguac, New Brunswick, were affected even more seriously. The area had looked to outsiders like a slum. The land was "recovering from" fire, logging and farming. People had little education, and some were on welfare. The houses were in poor condition, and junk lay around. A door-to-door survey revealed a "belligerent" attitude, and a need for community development. A small fishing village was allowed to stay, but the rest would have to go. Timber cutting was immediately prohibited.[46]

The residents were poor, but also proud and stubborn. About 200 families marched in protest, occupying the administration building. They protested poor communication, lack of jobs, unproductive retraining programs, unfair property assessments and loss of fishing rights. Over thirty legal appeals were lodged.[47] In 1975 the federal government agreed to share in relocation costs and moved the boundary inshore to restore fishing rights.[48] By 1980, over ten years after the park's creation there was still no solution. Residents had exhausted every legal means open to them, and squatted in the park. The minister described the situation as "tense, difficult and delicate", and was negotiating means of relief.[49] Comments in the House showed little sympathy for the people of Kouchibouguac:

Wear an armoured vest!
John Crosbie: Take Romeo (Leblanc) with you.
Ray Hnatyshn: Bring in the British commandos.
Move it to Peterborough or Cornwall.

A commission recommended increased compensation, but at least one appeal from the Kouchibouguac case still remained before the courts in 1985.[50]

NATIONAL PARKS FOR QUEBEC

A national park for Quebec had been suggested in 1937, again by the Conservative government in 1961.[51] But the Quebec government would not take the initiative to survey the land and hand it over free of encumbrances.[52] By 1967 the province had not acted,[53] but with Chrétien's appointment this pattern changed. The Quebec government was just like that of Newfoundland — still unwilling to hand over clear title. Chrétien accepted the land on a ninety-nine-year lease, rather than freehold as in earlier national parks.

> Under the terms of the agreement reached between the two governments, the province of Quebec will place the site of the Gaspé park at the disposal of the Government of Canada for a period of 99 years. The agreement states, as well, that the province of Quebec will have the right to regain possession at the end of 60 years on repayment of all federal capital expenditures incurred by the federal government during the 60-year period.
>
> In either case, the government of Quebec agrees that the land would be used for the purposes of a park and conservation in perpetuity. This arrangement is renewable by agreement of the two parties.[54]

The park also included an $8.3 million public works program, funded under a federal regional economic development program.[55] The agreement, announced while lease arrangements in Banff and Jasper were still being disputed, increased uncertainty as to the federal government's position. The Napoleonic Code, Chrétien explained, required a lease arrangement. Could a similar arrangment be arrived at in the other provinces asked opposition MPs? Only, replied Chrétien, if they adopted Quebec's Napoleonic Code.[56] Did this mean special status for Quebec — a policy Trudeau had rejected — asked Stanfield, the leader of the opposition? No, Chrétien replied: "Mr. Speaker, there always were particular agreements on parks under certain circumstances. Special arrangements were made with Alberta, British Columbia, Quebec and Nova Scotia. . . ."[57]

A second national park in La Mauricie was Chrétien's own initiative: "When I first mentioned the idea of a park in the St. Maurice valley, one of my bureaucrats said, 'You need a beautiful area for a park. You don't build national parks in swamps.' 'You come with me,' I said. He didn't come but he sent an assistant. We climbed to a natural lookout on the top of a hill near Shawinigan, and I pointed to the beautiful lakes, the untouched forests, and the ancient rocks of the Laurentians. 'Look at my swamps,' I said."[58]

Parks Canada studied La Mauricie in the summer of 1969. Within easy reach of Quebec and Montreal, the valley was "fairly well developed" for tourism, with adequate motels and camping sites. Logging had taken place for many years, but cutting had been selective. Mixed uses existed, but were "quite pleasing", and there were no known mineral desposits. Just over 200 square miles was relatively unimpaired,[59] with "no important forest development" foreseen for sixty years.[60]

One politician claimed the park had nothing to do with politics! "The federal government will have to consider objectively all the projects that will be presented. The St. Maurice valley will reject every biased argument, for instance, avoid choosing the eastern shore of the St. Maurice on the ground that it is part of the constituency of a Creditiste or the western shore because it is part of the constituency of the minister in charge of national parks, the Minister of Indian Affairs and Northern Development [Mr. Chrétien], or because the Quebec Minister of Labour owns a cottage there. No. Let us be serious and realistic."[61]

Convincing his bureaucrats, and his colleagues in Cabinet and in the House was relatively easy. Convincing the Quebec provincial government was more difficult. Chrétien organized a local movement in favour of the park: "To put pressure on the provincial politicians. Everyone — from the chamber of commerce to the trade unions — got involved. There were citizens' committees, slogans, petitions, and every politician was put on the spot in public: 'Are you for the national park? Yes or no?' The issue became a local factor in the 1970 provincial election; the Liberals supported the park and the nationalists opposed it as federal interference. The Liberals won, and Bourassa allowed us to go ahead shortly after he came to power."[62]

National parks were sought in Quebec for economic development through public works and tourism. Since Confederation the federal government had spent $355 million in the national parks. None had been spent in Quebec.[63] Chrétien explicitly talked about economic development when he created the two Quebec national parks. One MP agreed that Forillon would promote the Gaspé, from both "the touristic and the economic point of view".[64] Another welcomed: "A national park in the Gaspé peninsula which is an underdeveloped area where tourism alone guarantees a certain income, admittedly quite modest, to its people".

A third Quebec MP described the advantages associated with road construction in Quebec's second national park: "Our fellow citizens of Maurice valley are very happy to have obtained one of

Quebec's first two parks, and the consequences are already being felt. In addition to creating hundreds of direct jobs, this project has led to the implementation of the TransQuebec Highway between Trois Rivières and the national park. . . . [marking] the beginning of the new touristic calling of the area."[65]

But these promises were not fulfilled. The Gaspé was promised 1,000 jobs from the park, but only 200 resulted. In La Mauricie 500 jobs were promised, and only 200 developed over five years.[66] The tourism industry in Quebec expanded little following the creation of national parks. Only one more national park has since been added in Quebec. The Parti Québécois in power provincially was less interested in "national projects", preferring provincially initiated programs. Only the small Mingan Islands National Park in the Gulf of St. Lawrence was added in 1984 in a frantic rush, before the general election brought Mulroney and the Conservatives to power.[67] The islands included dumps which the public helped to clear up, and were acquired from Dome Petroleum in 1983.[68] A social impact study and public hearings were part of the planning process for the park.[69]

NEW PARKS FOR ONTARIO AND THE WEST: PARKS OF PRINCIPLE

National parks were even more difficult to create in the other Canadian provinces. Federal government public works projects were less important, and politicians had fewer illusions about the economic development resulting from tourism. Parks were not expected to be profitable, for existing land uses were usually reasonably lucrative. Ontario had several tiny national parks, some heavily used for recreation. The province preferred to develop provincial parks for multiple use (forestry and mining, as well as recreation). The Prairie provinces, particularly Alberta, already had the parks created prior to 1930, and did not need or want any more. In British Columbia the forest industry was crucial, and the province hesitated to contribute land to national parks.

But Parks Canada planners were not interested in more parks for profit. They were interested in preservation. Officials sought national parks in each region, to preserve examples of Canada's climate, wildlife, geology and plant life. By 1968 certain regions were still not represented in the system. There was none on the West Coast, and no example of West Coast forest. There was no

example of prairie grassland, of northern tundra or of arctic islands. A politician might want a recreation or tourist park for his
own constituency, but park planners were concerned about principle, not politics.

The new national parks created in these other provinces in the
Trudeau years included Pacific Rim on the west coast of Vancouver Island, Grasslands National Park in southern Saskatchewan
and Pukaskwa on the shore of Lake Superior in Ontario. The federal minister had to negotiate skillfully, though, for the provinces
and the resource sector did not give up land easily. A national park
clearly for principle rather than profit, and potentially sacrificing
other resources, would be more costly. Grasslands and Pacific Rim
show the problems of creating a national park of principle, not
profit.

Interest in Pacific Rim dates from 1930, when land was reserved
pending approval of a national park. The federal government
decided the park was not "feasible",[70] and the reserves were
cancelled. Private ownership and logging continued in the late
1940s.[71] In 1965 the province created a small provincial park. The
federal government again considered the potential for a national
park. In 1967 Dinsdale, responsible for parks under Diefenbaker's
Conservatives, praised the government for considering a national
park that would include the Long Beach area: "In my view when
we talk about a west coast park on Vancouver Island we are not
talking about a little postage stamp park somewhere on the fringes
of the Long Beach area. . . . I hope there will be growing recognition that in this area there should be put together all the necessary
elements for a west coast marine park of major proportions. Such a
park could very well become a major park in the Island. An area of
this sort carefully segregated from the conflicting resource claims
of mining or forestry interests could be something which, as the
minister said, our children, our grandchildren and their descen-
dants could treasure for all time. If steps are not taken quickly the
possibility of this ever happening will be greatly reduced."[72]

Arthur Laing, following as minister, also wanted a park on Vancouver Island. Premier W. A. C. Bennett was persistently hostile
because Laing was the former leader of the Liberal party in BC. No
co-operation was possible between them.[73] After Jean Chrétien replaced Laing in 1968, Pacific Rim again became a priority. Chrétien
avoided the impasse that had trapped Laing, and "persuaded" the
provincial premier:

The period around 1970 was the beginning of the conservation and ecology movement, and that became useful to us. In British Columbia we wanted to create the Pacific Rim National Park, to preserve the beaches and forests on the western coast of Vancouver Island. We rallied the support of the people of Victoria and of the ecologists at the universities; then I went to see the premier, W. A. C. Bennett, in his office. I always liked Bennett, even though he wasn't a Liberal and ran rather a single handed government. He was the kind of jolly, rural, populist politician I was familiar with in Quebec. . . .

"Mr. Bennett", I said, "I have two speeches prepared for tonight. If you say no to helping us build the Pacific Rim National Park, I will say you're a son of a gun. If you say yes, I will say you're a hell of a good guy. Which speech do you want me to use?"

He laughed and said, "Okay, let's have a national park".[74]

So one populist politician persuaded another to create a new national park. The agreement included several concessions. The federal government would pay half the costs of acquisition. Also, the province's Centennial gift would contribute to its own share of the cost. The agreement provided for a national park — but not for its boundaries. In 1969 BC passed legislation "to facilitate the development of a national park along the west coast of Vancouver Island". Boundaries were still not specific, but Phase I would include Long Beach, the existing provincial park, and up to 15,000 acres of forest. Phase II would include some islands at the entrance to Barkley sound, and Phase III the old West Coast "life saving trail".[75]

A year passed before regulations were approved — and those with timber leases rushed to log the area.[76] Today, inshore from the road along Long Beach, beyond a narrow band of standing trees is a clear cut. When I visited Pacific Rim the fireweed was the tallest plant life around.

But W. A. C. Bennett had not finished negotiating — and neither had the conservation groups. The West Coast trail passed through coastal forest with lucrative stands of mature timber. The forestry industry, and the provincial Minister of Lands Forests and Water Resources, Ray Williston, wanted only a narrow strip of forest either side of the trail put into the national park. The

Victoria Fish and Game Club and the Amalgamated Conservation Society forced a confrontation, and Chrétien worked out an agreement on a "sight and sound" boundary varying from a few hundred yards to as much as one or two miles.[77]

The next area in dispute was the Nitinat (or Nitimat) triangle. Virgin coastal forest had not been included, but Canada's national parks contained no other example. In 1970, at a closed meeting, the federal government told industry and the BC government that the triangle should be included in the park. The original agreement protected water quality in the park and logging the Nitinat would cause siltation and pollution. The forest industry suggested the Nitinat triangle would add 64,000 acres to the park, sacrificing 750 jobs.[78] The triangle contained "decadent over-mature forest", and logging would assist "nature in a meaningful way" creating a new "vibrant, open and healthy" forest.[79] The NPPAC and the Sierra clubs feared the Nitinat triangle would be lost altogether, and the latter proposed a compromise. Then Bennett's Social Credit government was defeated by the New Democratic Party under Dave Barrett. The new government, less tied to the resource sector, was more willing to secure virgin forests in perpetuity in a national park. Agreement was eventually reached in principle in 1973, based on the Sierra Club compromise. Detailed studies led to signed agreement in 1981.[80] However, even in 1982 the park was still incomplete, largely because of "the complexities involved in relinquishing tree farm licenses". Logging continued in areas intended for the park, but not yet acquired.[81] To bring Pacific Rim to completion will require more money, and more political will than Ottawa or BC has shown since the mid-seventies.

The large forestry companies were not the only interests displaced by Pacific Rim Park. But others were less powerful and less successful. The park displaced about 1,000 young people who had lived on Long Beach and around fifty families. Twenty-one Indian reserves with a total area of 1,818 acres were affected. Their land was provincially owned and held in reserve, and the province held oil and gas rights and could take land for public works. The federal government purchased land from the Indians, and the oil and gas rights to that land from the province. Around 1,670 registered Indians initially refused to relocate, because of their historical ties to the area.

A similar political debate occurred in the Queen Charlotte Islands. Conservative Parks minister Tom McMillan wished to create a national park. The forestry companies had permission to log. The Haida claimed aboriginal rights to the land and resisted logging. The Social Credit provincial governments generally supported the logging companies, while the opposition New Democrats supported the native people. The Western Canada Wilderness Committee, the Islands Protection Society, the NPPAC and others mobilized to defend the islands.[82] After months of bargaining, BC Premier William Vander Zalm announced a deal with Ottawa, on July 6, 1987, to create a national park the size of Prince Edward Island in the South Moresby region.[83]

Grasslands National Park in Saskatchewan, like Pacific Rim, is unfinished — and for much the same reasons. In British Columbia forestry companies resisted the park because of lost profits. Ranchers in southern Saskatchewan who relied on the grassland as cattle range resisted a park that would limit their livelihood.

Interest in a second national park for Saskatchewan dates to 1960, when an MP wanted Moose Mountain (in his constituency) created a national park.[84] By 1965 Laing was considering the Cypress Hills Provincial Park.[85] The Natural History Society of Saskatchewan proposed natural grassland be preserved instead.[86] Cypress Hills and Moose Mountain were both surveyed, but grassland near Val Marie was chosen. The proposal was opposed because it would: "Eliminate many acres of much needed grazing land required if Canada is to maintain cattle production to meet demands".[87]

Laing still anticipated provincial agreement within a year.[88] But Chrétien, not Laing, would claim credit for the new Saskatchewan national park. In 1968 he announced: "I was happy with the talk I had the other day with the Premier of Saskatchewan, who is now ready to permit the government to go ahead with the establishment of another national park in that province. I hope that in the weeks and months ahead we will find agreement on other national parks in Saskatchewan."[89]

But the new Grasslands Park was to be difficult enough to complete. No third park could be considered for Saskatchewan while Grasslands was incomplete.[90] Local ranchers were opposed. Chrétien told residents: "A new national park in this or any other part of Canada must not be established to the disadvantage of local residents whose way of life depends on their traditional use of the land". In the case of Grasslands: "There will be no compulsion on ranch owners within the ultimate boundary to move. The right of the owner to pass on his land, or the right to his land to his heirs would be undisturbed, and if and when a rancher chose to sell his property, the government would be prepared to buy it at a fair market price and to offer its services to assist the rancher to relocate."[91]

This helped to meet some concerns of both ranchers and the provincial government, and a memorandum of agreement was signed in March 1975. Two core park areas totalling seventy-two square miles would be exchanged for federally owned land near Willow Creek. The rest of the future park, eventually 360 square miles, would be gradually acquired. No one would be expropriated. The federal government would spend $20 million over five years, with 149 full-time jobs added by the fifth year.[92] A series of public hearings followed, so those affected could be respresented.

Environmental groups, such as the Saskatoon Natural History Society and national groups like the NPPAC, other interests such as local municipal officials and hunters, and of course the ranchers, all attended.[93] The park was recommended by the board conducting the hearings, with controlled grazing by range cattle as a management tool.[94] The NPPAC suggested reintroduction of plains bison would be more "traditional" than continued use by cattle.[95] The Joint Federal–Provincial Committee reached a compromise — grazing would be phased out slowly, allowing ranchers to pass property on to their heirs.[96] Studies might show ranching could be part of long-term management. The ranchers, in sum, had won.

Chrétien found the New Democratic governments of Saskatchewan and Manitoba the most difficult of all provincial governments: "That was Blakeney. It was complicated and very serious. Bureaucratic. I could not succeed, though I tried and tried. I went back again and again. I don't blame my successor. They tried too. You know who are the most difficult guys to deal with? I wanted to have a park in Manitoba, on the east side of a great lake there, where Howard Pawley lead another socialist government. I could not succeed there either. The citizens were not opposed, it was the government.

"I don't give a damn! I tell you the truth, these were the two most difficult governments to deal with. They said they were socialist, but never signed a deal for a national park."[97]

However, even this did not produce a final conclusion. In 1977 negotiations continued. "Reconciliation" was reported in 1978,[98] but no final agreement until 1980. The federal government offered another concession — and would pay for roads and tourist facilities outside the park.[99] Ranchers would not have to sell at all — if they wanted to keep their land it would be left out of the park.[100]

In 1981 the agreement was finally signed.[101] But the park still seems a long way away. The two governments will share the cost of an oil and gas exploration program. Within thirty years of the completion of this exploration the province will identify 350 square miles for the park. The federal government will pay half the cost of acquisition within proposed boundaries, and all costs of any additional land outside park boundaries. And, as a final concession to the province, the land can revert to the province of Saskatchewan upon request.[102]

National parks for Saskatchewan, like those of eastern Canada, were sought for their economic value. One MP described the new park as giving "our people an added incentive and another boost up the economic ladder".[103] But in Saskatchewan and British Columbia, unlike the Maritimes and Quebec, little economic benefit was apparent. Existing land uses were too lucrative for additional tourism resulting from a national park to appear very attractive. Parks of principle, preserving Canadian landscape from economic use, were extraordinarily difficult to create in any Canadian province. Parks for profit, for economic development and for tourism, were somewhat easier.

NATIONAL PARKS NORTH OF 60°

In the Canadian North the situation was different. Here no provincial governments owned and controlled the land and natural resources. Territorial governments lacked many of the powers that come with provincehood. Here, also, existing land use was less intensive. More areas were untouched by mining companies, without known oil or gas deposits, and devoid of urban settlement. Fewer local interests challenged creation of national parks.

Some were opposed. The native people, with many land claims unsettled, opposed national parks in areas they considered part of their aboriginal entitlement. Only an accident of minority government brought them concessions. The resource industries of the North, and the territorial governments both opposed the northern parks, and succeded in paring down some proposals. Through persistent lobbying, the territorial governments eventually gained the right to consultation, and to final approval over new parks. This right was only gained, however, after major northern parks had already been created.

The idea of national parks for the North dates from 1957, when the Parks Branch identified Kluane (a game sanctuary since the 1940s), the wild Nahanni River and Artillery Lake as possible national parks.[103] The Conservative government consulted with the territorial council about a national park for the Yukon. The minister left the decision with the council itself.[104] Mining companies opposed the parks before the territorial council and none was created. In 1963, with the Liberals back in power, Erik Nielsen, Conservative MP for the Yukon, reviewed the case: "One point of view is that we should have a park because tourism is essential to the growth of any economy, and certainly it is an important segment of the economy of the Yukon. In opposition to this view is that of the mining community, which is against the establishment of a national park because of existing restrictions which would prevent geological exploration and development within any park boundaries which might be established."[105]

The proposed park was near Hudson Bay Mining and Smelting Company holdings, where low-grade nickel deposits had been found. What, Nielsen asked, was the new minister responsible for parks going to do? Laing again left the decision with the territorial government. "I assume we would be forced to regard the territorial government in the same light as we would a provincial government. Therefore I would very much hesitate to announce that we were going to place a national park in the Yukon without an agreement with or request from the territorial council of the Yukon."[106] He would wait until the Yukon council and the mining companies had identified an area not worth mining, and turn that into a park. The territorial councils were "divided", and none were created during Laing's ministry.

Jean Chrétien was more determined than Laing.[107] He deliberately mobilized public support for the parks, openly urging the conservation groups to promote national parks. One speech to the International Association of Fish and Game Commissioners in New York was quoted in an NPPAC information brochure: "We will need even more public support than we have had if our parkland is to meet the needs of the future. It won't be enough for those concerned to be content with telling *each other* how they feel. Politicians must *know* what the public wants, more parks. Those in government who control the allocation of funds must be persuaded that parks needs are a real, vital and first priority."

The response was almost immediate. The Canadian Society of Wildlife and Fisheries Biologists found that a major French mining company, Pennaroya Canada, wanted to develop a mineral property in the South Nahanni. The society telegraphed Chrétien asking that Nahanni River be set aside as a park. The area had historic interest, included a magnificent waterfall, impressive gorges, and a stretch of wild river that delighted white-water canoeists. The society also alerted the NPPAC, which had heard of plans to harness the Nahanni for electricity. They wrote to Trudeau, describing the beauty of the Nahanni, and asking for a park.[108]

In 1971 the NPPAC sent their own expedition through the Nahanni, with Steve Hume from the *Edmonton Journal*. Ethusiastic newspaper articles resulted.[109] The NPPAC announced they would press for major northern parks, "before potential areas are taken up for resource exploitation".[110] Their campaign involved cooperation with other environmental groups in sponsoring public meetings across the country. Wildlife biologist George Scotter, returning from a government expedition in the North, was a speaker. He was a government employee, and his involvement in this pressure-group activity shows the covert government support given to the parks lobby. In Toronto parks enthusiasts packed the Eaton auditorium, providing Chrétien with needed evidence of public support.[111] The NPPAC published glossy testimonials to the natural and unique beauty of the North.[112] The Toronto *Globe and Mail* featured Nahanni on their editorial page, and articles followed in popular Canadian periodicals.[113]

Internal government discussions of northern parks were comparatively straightforward. Chrétien controlled all the departments responsible for the North. "Northern parks were easy. They were easy because it was my idea. I had to consult with myself. I had to consult with the minister of Indian Affairs; the minister of Northern Affairs; the minister of Parks Canada — and they were all me. It was easy to do. And Trudeau, who always loved the North, was happy when I came up with this idea."[114]

Chrétien had to get support from cabinet too. He encouraged his colleagues to visit the proposed northern national parks. Bud Orange, MP for the Northwest Territories, and John Turner, then minister of justice, visited the Nahanni together. Orange described Nahanni as: "One of the most spectacular sights I have seen in my lifetime. . . . we agreed that it was worthy protection."[115]

Trudeau visited the Nahanni himself, insisting his trip was "purely recreational". But environmental groups hoped for his approval once he had seen the river.[116]

Chrétien broke with his predecessor's precedents, and did not wait for territorial approval. He announced three parks, Kluane (8,500 square miles) and Nahanni (1,840 square miles) as expected, and a third 8,200-square-mile-park on Baffin Island, later called Auyittuq. No more staking or filing of mining claims would be allowed. The announcement was "almost unilateral" (according to one northern MP). Territorial councils and the mining industry were not consulted. Native people, whose traditional lands were involved, were ignored.[117] Chrétien, though, assured the House that their traditional rights would not be affected.

The throne speech of 1972 committed the government to preserving "immense areas of Canada", so that "some of the grandeur and the wilderness that is Canada's north will be guaranteed perpetual preservation".[118] The legislation first passed through the Senate (always possible for a non-money bill). The previous Liberal minister responsible for parks, Arthur Laing, shepherded the bill through the Upper House. His spoke of the profitability of the new parks, rather than preservation: "I have told the minister there is going to be a great deal of tourism in the Canadian arctic. . . . I am prepared to argue there is more money in all the national parks so far established than in the development of any resources so far established within those parks."

Laing reported opposition to the parks, but suggested most had been dealt with. Kluane had been reduced because of opposition from the mining industry: "There was representation made by the Yukon Chamber of Mines, and I am aware of this. They were the people who said, "There's gold in them thar hills, and you had better stay out of it. Happily I have a letter dated March 27 from the Commissioner of the Yukon Territory, Mr. James Smith, telling me that in the discussion with the executive of the Yukon Chamber of Mines they agree to the boundaries of the national parks as set out, but they succeeded in reducing the original intent of the National Parks Branch by some 2,000 square miles. There is an area of 8,500 square miles, to which the Chamber is agreeable." Hydro-electric potential had been of some concern: "The Nahanni and Kluane areas are the prime power potentials in these two territories (but there are other possibilities) so there is a reconciliation on the part of the mining companies and the National Parks Branch".[119]

The House of Commons also supported the northern parks. One MP raised cheers by quoting earlier Chrétien speeches about parks, and asked if "the lobbies of the powerful mining industry" were to "take precedence over what could and should be a national reserve for all time".[120]

Others were less enthusiastic. Wally Firth said all of the North should be a park, but native people feared no land would be left for them.[121] His concerns were shared by other NDP members of parliament. Nielsen, and a number of other Conservatives, deplored the government's unilateral action, and called for a careful assessment of resource potential before boundaries were set.[122] Objections relating to native claims and to mineral resources were particularly significant because from 1972 to 1974 the Liberal government was in a minority position. Support of another party was needed for legislation to be passed.

The objections came into clearer focus during the committee stage. The Standing Committee on Indian Affairs and Northern Development held hearings in Yellowknife in December 1973, so that "conservationists and industry might be heard with respect to boundaries and other park problems".[123] The committee heard from northern business groups who "did not want a park to be located in any area where there might be the slightest possibility that at some time in the future a mineral deposit of some value might be found".[124] The committee, though, did not visit Baffin Island, where they would have heard Inuit opposition to a park on "their" land.[125] National park supporters also sought a survey of resources.[126] If minerals were found subsequently, there would be pressure to change park boundaries or allow exploitation within the park.

The committee, with government members in a minority, ammended the legislation. Some changes met native concerns, preventing their expropriation. They could continue "traditional hunting, fishing and trapping activities" in the parks, which would still be subject to land-claim settlements. Amendments initiated by the New Democratic party were accepted by the government.[127] Others requiring public hearings or territorial consent (rather than consultation) were put forward by the Conservatives but defeated. The minority Liberal government's coalition with the New Democratic party was intact, and the first three national parks north of sixty were created.

The environmental groups pressed for increased land for these new parks, and for more parks in the North. The first concern was the Burwash Uplands left out of Kluane National Park because of conflicts with the mining industry. The Uplands, according to the NPPAC, were crucial sheep range. Parks Canada reviewed the NPPAC proposal,[128] and suggested other wildlife habitat be added. The Uplands, though, would be left out.[129]

Parks Canada wanted to expand Auyittuq. Initially the Inuit had been opposed, but parks officials had "succeeded in having the people understand the advantages of the creation of the park".[130] They could supply visitors with accommodation, tour guides, fishing trips and tackle. Residents could be employees, or independent entrepreneurs. The Inuit were still officially opposed to the park, but remained silent on proposed boundary changes as long as local people were hired by Parks Canada.[131]

In 1972 Jean Chrétien had been able to create national parks in the North because he had ignored the precedent set by Arthur Laing. He had not waited for territorial consent. If he had, few national parks would exist north of the sixtieth parallel. However, the territorial governments pressed for increased self-government, and ultimately for provincial status. The federal government supported increased powers for the territories, but unilateral creation of national parks countered any intent to increase territorial autonomy.

In 1972 the Yukon Council tried, through their Conservative MP Erik Nielsen, to ammend the National Parks Act to ensure they had the right to refuse future national parks. The legislation passed with a clause merely assuring consultation. When the new national parks policy was under review, the territorial councils again tried to obtain control over the national parks. All they received was the right to "consultation".[132] The councils demanded details of the process of "consultation". They wanted no repetition of the Chrétien unilateral initiatives.

In 1981 the federal government provided details of their interpretation of "consultation". The territorial governments had the right to be "kept informed", and their comments would be "solicited". Planning would no longer be secret. The territories could "participate fully", reviewing interest-group support and non-renewable resource inventories. An agreement in principle would be required, as for parks created in southern Canada. The Council would also be asked for final agreement; by implication, new national parks would require territorial consent.[133]

This agreement in principle, and the negotiations leading up to it, make it more difficult to create new national parks in the North. In 1978 the minister responsible for national parks, James Faulkner, was negotiating six new wilderness areas in the North as the "only rational way" to deal with migrating caribou. The State of Alaska asked for a park adjoining their own, and the Berger Commission had recommended more northern parks.[134] But now it is almost as difficult to create new parks in the North as in the South. Several areas were studied by Parks Canada: Pingo Park near Tuktoyaktuk;[135] the Horton–Anderson River area of the Northwest Territories,[136] and an area of Bathurst Inlet.[137] By 1984, when John Turner became prime minister for a few brief months, no new park had been confirmed.

Then, in the last days of the Liberal government, two new parks were rushed through. One was the tiny Mingan Archipelago in the Quebec St. Lawrence. The other was Northern Yukon National Park, created on the Alaska border to protect traditional migration routes of the caribou. The park had been under study since 1977,[138] and a boundary proposal developed in 1983. The park, like the earlier northern ones, is subject to native land claims. Also, native people continue their traditional way of life.

In 1984 the Liberal dynasty was replaced by the Mulroney Conservatives, advocates of increased tourism.[139] In their brief period in power in 1979 the Conservatives had talked of expanding commercial tourism in the parks. According to Gordon Taylor, Conservative MP for Bow River, tourism could now "become a great industry in this country. We have a $2 billion deficit. We have beautiful scenery and wonderful hospitality" but "because we have become so bound in red tape in parts of this country we have not provided accomodation. . . . Let us encourage entrepreneurs to build accomodation and protect the environment in our national parks. We should encourage thousands of these international people from other countries, to come and enjoy our scenery. Such a policy will bring new dollars and help our balance of trade as well as provide for jobs for people. . . . Capital is waiting to be used if we turn out the red light and turn on the green."[140]

Such a government, concerned about business development rather than preservation, did not promise new national parks, particularly in places where they offered little promise of tourist revenue. The first year of the Mulroney government, with Suzanne

Blais-Grenier as the minister responsible for parks, was not promising. The minister talked of allowing mining and timber cutting in the parks; she cut back positions in the wildlife service,[141] and presided over other cuts in her department,[142] leading to her flagellation in a non-confidence debate on the environment.[143] Parks Canada's centennial was celebrated with fifty-four layoffs, the loss of eighty full-time jobs and 148 part-time jobs, and a second non-confidence motion.[144]

Blais-Grenier created no new national parks in the North or anywhere else. However, her successor has been somewhat more successful. Tom McMillan came to the environment portfolio from a spell as minister of state for tourism. He had told a tourism conference that: "The national parks are a major tourist attraction and parks policy is tourism policy. . . . Too often parks policy proceeds in the ends of conservation and the environment."[145]

Not promising for preservation! However, the new minister quickly recovered the support of the environmentalists who had deserted his predecessor. At a meeting of environmental groups in September 1985 he received a standing ovation for his announcement of the new park on Ellesmere Island, and for his commitment to work towards a new park on South Moresby. The new northern park, though, was created for sovereignty rather than preservation. Agreement in principle had been reached in 1982, under Trudeau,[146] but without final agreement. In 1985 an American ship, the *Polar Sea,* sailed the Northwest Passage without Canadian permission. The final agreement was signed by McMillan with the council of the Northwest Territories *before* the ship went through the passage. Both Ellesmere Island National Park and the older arctic park on Baffin Island asserted "the integrity of Canadian sovereignty".[147] Canada had a new northern park, but not for the usual reasons of tourist profit or preservation.

CHAPTER EIGHT

The
Future of Profit
and Preservation

T HIS CONCLUSION is for the men and women of Canada's second national parks movement (and if necessary, the third). I draw on the experience of the first century of Canada's national parks, to make suggestions for the future. The national parks experienced a number of threats during that first century — boundary erosion, multiple resource exploitation, disestablishment and budget cuts. Tourism has been both a threat to the environmental integrity of the parks, and at the same time their source of security. These threats are still very real, and there is also a new threat: aboriginal land claims could be settled by transferring the national parks as part of the settlement. The future of preservation will be determined by the ability of environmentalists, native peoples, Parks Canada bureaucrats and politicians to withstand these threats, and to negotiate a compromise in face of the reality that Canadian national parks have been parks for profit.

The first threat to the national parks is internal to the federal government: the threat of budget cuts. Although the funding for national parks has been increased over the years, at times of national emergency such as depression or war, funding has been significantly reduced. In the 1920s parks expenditure rose to nearly $90 per square kilometer of parkland (in 1971 dollars). Regular expenditures on the parks fell in the 1930s to around half the pre-depression level, sinking again during the Second World War to $38 per square kilometer of parkland. A variety of make-work programs compensated for the reductions in regular budgetary expensitures, but involved loss of many civil liberties.

After the war expenditures rose again, reaching $400 per square kilometer of parkland in 1961. After 1968 under the Liberals new parks were created and additional funding was made available, reaching a peak of $630 per square kilometer (again in 1971 dollars).[1] However, experience since the election of the Conservatives in 1984 indicates that the Department of the Environment, and Parks Canada in particular, are considered to be areas where budget cuts are acceptable. Suzanne Blais-Grenier "celebrated" the Parks Canada centennial with a variety of budget cuts. When this was raised in the House, she eliminated more staff.[2] She was demoted in a Cabinet shuffle, much to the relief of environmentalists. The next minister, Tom McMillan, as we have seen, added another park in 1985, and introduced new parks legislation in 1986, but has not restored the budget cuts instituted by his predecessor.

Budget restrictions threaten the parks in two ways. First, inadequate staffing leads to lax supervision, so that policies controlling park use are not implemented. Poaching, timber cutting and various forms of vandalism are unchecked. Second, inadequate funding has at times justified reductions in park size. The boundary reductions of 1930 and in the 1950s were in part justified by the argument that smaller parks would be cheaper to manage. An active national parks movement can help minimize the effects of budget cuts on the national parks. Parks lobby groups need a close relationship with senior Parks Branch officials. Environmental groups must be forewarned of potential cuts, so they can alert the minister and prime minister to their concerns. If cuts become a reality, groups such as NPPAC can present material to both sides of the house. The rapid removal of Blais-Grenier from the environment portfolio was due, at least in part, to the public reaction to cuts she had instituted in a number of sensitive areas, including areas affecting the national parks.

"Privatization" to the commercial sector is currently popular with some politicians as a way of reducing government costs, and of restoring profitable business opportunities. Privatization of services and maintenance has already been proposed in national and provincial parks.[3] However, while government costs may be cut in the short term, the overall results of privatization may be totally unsatisfactory. For example, standards may be loosened, with fewer and less skilled employees doing the work. Also, those workers will be paid less, having lost the backing of a powerful public-sector union. The individual consumer may have to pay more, to ensure that the company has the profit to which it is entitled. This may limit access to park facilities by those with less income. Also, in the case of national parks, privatization has the undesirable effect of involving more commercial enterprises in the operation of parks, further strengthening the commercial-sector pressure groups who advocate more tourism and heavier park use. Those interested in park preservation should use every opportunity to prevent privatization to the commercial sector.

In some instances non-profit groups may be asked to operate a "privatized" service. Parks Canada, for example, has encouraged the development of non-profit "co-operating associations" to assist in the administration of each park, providing services, raising funds and stimulating public support for the park. This may be preferable to privatization to the commercial sector. However, here also there are negative side effects. A non-profit group directly involved in providing a service loses its effectiveness as a pressure group. If the NPPAC, for example, were to operate a gift shop at a national park the group would find time and energy absorbed in administrivia. Fewer resources would be available for the more significant role of national park watch-dog. Also, if the organization depended on gift-shop income to support its activities, it would hesitate to criticize government initiatives which threatened the parks. Those interested in park preservation should be careful not to become absorbed by the opportunities for involvement in "co-operating associations", as these detract from a more important advocacy role.

Another possible strategy is the use of government make-work programs in the national parks. The parks benefited substantially from the programs of the depression and the two world wars, but at great personal cost to those doing the work. In most instances their civil liberties were sacrificed, and they did not earn market wages. I am not proposing any repetition of work-for-relief or of the youth training program of the 1930s. However, the government is still involved in a variety of seasonal works programs, some requiring initiatives by local community groups. The organizations who care about parks could create such projects, and apply for funding. Trails could be built, and interpretation and guided hikes could continue without allocations from the regular Parks Canada budget. However, new organizations are needed for development of these programs, separate from those involved in environmental advocacy. If the same organization were to become involved in both activities, social action might be sacrified to protect project funding.

The second threat to preservation in Canada's national parks is erosion of park boundaries. The experience of 1930 and of the 1950s give clear precedents for moving park boundaries when a potentially profitable resource is found within a national park. Whether the resource is a watershed with hydroelectric potential, a promising coal seam or a gypsum deposit, national parks have been carved up to release the resource. We know that the older mountain parks still contain a great deal of coal, have extensive timber, and watersheds with hydroelectric potential. Resource inventories were conducted before the newer parks were created, to ensure valuable minerals were not locked away. However, those parks still contain much of value. They may contain minerals inaccessible by today's technology, hydroelectric potential not needed this century, or forests surplus today. Another drive towards economic development, like that after the Second World War, could be powerful enough to propel politicians into raiding the parks. Boundary erosion is not just a possible threat. In the next century there will be many attempts to change national park boundaries to release exportable resources. If this drift into boundary erosion is to be prevented then groups like the NPPAC (recently renamed the Canadian Parks and Wilderness Society), the Alpine Club and the Sierra Club must keep informed about government initiatives affecting the parks, and be ready to protest. A visible group, whose active objections can be anticipated, will make governments hesitate before they try to reduce the parks.

A third threat, also related to economic development, is the pressure for multiple use of the resources within the national parks. All the provincial governments have prefered multiple-resource use in their own parks, permitting commercial forestry, hydro development and other forms of exploitation. A shortage of merchantable timber is imminent in Canada, and provincial governments and the lumber industry may conceivably ask for access to the timber in the parks. Timber berths were leased in the early 1960s, and the federal government might find it economically and politically convenient to do so again, without actually changing any park boundaries. Also, in an extreme energy shortage governments might agree that the best solution would be to harness the coal or hydroelectric resources in the parks.

Multiple-use would have an impact different from (and in some ways less drastic than) erosion of the park boundaries. If the boundaries are moved the park is forever reduced in size, and the aesthetic and environmental concerns related to national park status are not considered when the resource is developed. In multiple-use, on the other hand, the Parks Branch still controls the aesthetic and environmental impact of the resource exploitation. Trees could be selectively felled, rather than clear cut, retaining the character of a climax forest. Restoration of lakeshores after hydro developments could be enforced, as they were at Lake Minnewanka earlier this century. Mining developments could be located and developed to minimize their impact, and with anticipation of the necessity of returning the landscape to its original state after the mine is closed. National park status gives governments more powers to ensure environmental standards than any other provincial or federal legislation.

This form of commercial multiple-resource exploitation is at present only a "potential use" of most national parks. However, what Parks Canada euphemistically describes as "traditional use" continues today in many national parks. Ranchers continue to range cattle in Grasslands National Park. Commercial fishing continues at Gros Morne. Berry picking, technically against park policies, continues in many parks. Wood Buffalo's bison were the basis of subsistence livelihood of local people, and native people are still allowed to hunt, trap, fish and cut lumber in the park. In the new northern parks local people continue their traditional way of life: hunting, fishing and trapping.[4] Decisions to permit traditional use have been political decisions. The decision in the northern parks was a compromise necessary for a minority Liberal government to retain the support of the New Democratic party in the House of Commons. The decision related to Grasslands was necessary to provincial approval.

The resulting policy, though, has the curious (and dangerous) result of treating local people as if they were part of the wildlife. They are entitled to take the resources from the land necessary for "subsistence".[5] Human beings, clearly, are not wildlife. Human beings living in a democratic society with a capitalist economy have the right to profit, to use the most effective tools, to acquire material goods and to live in comfort, and to live in larger communities with services typical of an urban centre. Other Canadians have these rights, but native groups using the national parks are entitled merely to "subsistence". If traditional users are to have their rights as Canadians then they are entitled to pursue their livelihood in more profitable ways; they have the right to exploit the land in ways that are not very different from the commercial exploitation sought by outside companies. National park policy forbids this. If traditional users accept the restrictions implied by "subsistence", then they are also accepting exclusion from the economy. The ambivalence that aboriginal groups have shown to national parks policy reflects their recognition of this dilemma.

The problems associated with "traditional" use will increase as the northern parks are subjected to further control by the National Parks Branch. As frustration mounts over conflicts stemming from the limitations implied by "traditional" use, the national parks could easily become an element in the bargaining over land claims. Canada's aboriginal people are asking for self-government and for settlement of land claims. The new northern national parks belong to the federal government. Resource surveys have been conducted to ensure that the parks contain no valuable mineral deposits. Mining claims and urban settlement have been prevented within park boundaries. The wildlife has been protected, and limited tourism has begun. The federal government might find it easy to offer the northern national parks as part of a land-claim settlement, particularly if those accepting the land agreed to manage the parks as game reserves, much as Wood Buffalo has been managed since its inception. The parks would not be sanctuaries for preservation of a wilderness untouched by man or woman (as implied by the United Nations definition of a national park), but would be managed for the conservation of wildlife for perpetual support of aboriginal people. These northern parks would become the game reserves of the north, where wildlife management provided more than a subsistence livelihood. Aboriginal people would be able to profit from both tourism and harvesting the wildlife. The northern parks alone are unlikely to be sufficient for a total land-claims settlement. They contain little mineral value. Certain northern parks, however, might be acceptable as part of a land-claims package including other lands or a cash settlement.

The future of the northern parks may well be determined by the nature of the alliance that can be created between those who wish to preserve land in national parks and those whose livelihood is tied to "subsistence" use of that land. The future of the northern parks, and of Pukaskwa and South Moresby are inextricably tied to the future of Canada's native people. Groups concerned about the national parks should be concerned about the future of aboriginal peoples, both in the parks and out. A contest between the native people and those who would preserve the parks, would probably result in reducing the area available for parks. Governments and large industries could play one side against the other, preventing creation of new parks.

A better option would be for a conscious attempt by the groups (such as the NPPAC and the Sierra Club) who are concerned about national parks, to find out about and understand the situation facing aboriginal peoples. This means fewer monthly programs about whooping cranes and beaver dams, and more about the trap-line and the seal-skin economy. Similarly, the parks groups should seek opportunities to discuss with native groups the various meanings of "conservation" and "preservation", and to hear from them about the significance of Parks Canada bureaucratese such as "traditional use" and "subsistence". An alliance between the parks lobby and the native groups is essential for preservation of the northern parks, but can only be built on a mutual understanding of the significance of those parks to both groups.

Commercial tourism is the last major threat to the national parks. In a state such as Canada, with a liberal democratic political system and a capitalist economy, government policy has to ensure both that entreprenueurs make a profit and that the government retains public support. "Parks for Profit" has described the way national parks policy in Canada has both impeded and stimulated capital accumulation. Certain forms of resource exploitation have been limited, but only so that another form of resource exploitation, tourism, can continue.

Commercial tourism is the last major threat to the national parks. All parks have to deal with the tension between the need to preserve a landscape with as little human impact as possible and the need to make that landscape accessible so people may enjoy and benefit from the natural environment. That tension is exacerbated by economic imperatives. Services to park visitors are provided by private entrepreneurs, who try to increase profit by stimulating the tourist industry and expanding their own enterprises. Also, when potentially profitable natural resources are found within national parks, resource industries pressure to disestablish the national parks. These tensions were present when the first park was created at Banff, have been evident throughout the national park system's first hundred years, and are still a factor in discussions over the future of the Queen Charlotte Islands in British Columbia.

In the older mountain parks small business has become entrenched in townsites within park boundaries. These businesses are both frustrated by and benefit from national park status. Their expansion plans are thwarted by park policies which limit urban growth, but these policies also protect local business from competition. Representatives of this small business sector have noisily challenged Parks Canada's attempts to limit the expansion of tourism, and are likely to continue to do so. They have learned how to use their access to Ottawa, to their MP, to provincial governments, to the opposition and to the minister and cabinet. They have support within governments. The ministers with tourism or small business portfolios want to promote the national parks as a means of enhancing tourism. The pressure for increased tourism is inexorable.

This pressure could be even more difficult to resist while the Conservative government is in power. The party has an explicit commitment to small business, and while in opposition had consistently supported the business people of Banff and Jasper in their struggles to roll back Parks Canada policies. The current minister, Tom McMillan, when responsible for the tourism portfolio, commented in the House on the need to ensure that parks were managed for profit. Since then he has announced a new plan for the mountain parks that will permit increased tourist development, though within clearly defined limits. This plan is embodied in the new National Parks Act introduced in the House of Commons in December 1986. McMillan has attempted a plan that is: "Sensible, sensitive and a reasonable balance between the need for visitors and the need for preservation".[6] Although resources that are significant, unique, endangered, or vulnerable will be given "special protection", the overall impact of the plan will be to increase use, both within and outside existing urban areas.

This challenge of increased commercial tourism and heavier use can not be met merely by continuing the watch-dog role, by meetings with senior Parks officials and continued contact with the minister. This will not be enough, for tourism continued to expand in the parks even during the parks lobby's most active period in the 1970s. Resistance to the expansion of tourism will require a broader base of support than the parks groups have at present. Social scientists have shown that environmentally concerned individuals such as those who join the NPPAC or the Sierra Club tend to be predominantly white, younger, more educated, and richer than their less concerned counterparts.[7] The NPPAC executive at one point reflected a similar composition: 13 per cent lawyers, 26 per cent educators and 35 per cent other professionals. The remainder were businessmen, and one homemaker.[8] Environmentalists have never risen to more than 15 per cent of the population, and even at the peak of the environmental movement in 1972 the environment was considered a poor third behind unemployment and inflation among the major concerns of Canadians.[9]

The purist environmentalist position until recently was not shared beyond this privileged minority of the population, although a recent Canadian poll seems to reflect some change in this regard. Sixty-nine per cent of Canadians polled in June of 1986 "were willing to back moves to protect the environment even if those measures affected employment". And, "most Canadians believe the risks of pollution are not worth the benefits to society or the economy".[10] Environmentalists favour government intervention (whether in pollution control, wildlife management, or the creation of recreational parks), while business will only support intervention when environmental damage patently threatens the economy. In the national parks the conflict between the resource industries and the parks enthusiasts dates from the 1920s. Also, the environmental groups tend to wish to minimize environmental damage by minimizing human access. This also brings them into opposition with both park visitors and those business interests that serve park visitors. The promoters of down-hill skiing had only to ask, and thousands of patrons wrote to ask that skiing be expanded.

Environmental groups face the challenge of organizing support for the parks that extends beyond the middle-class professionals that currently form the backbone of the environmental movement. Progressive members of the business community must be recruited. This will require acknowledgement that in a capitalist society individuals are entitled to engage in profitable enterprise, even within or near a national park, as long as that enterprise does not threaten the natural environment of the park. Working people need to be recruited. This will require two concessions. First, the primary need for access to the parks must be acknowledged, for popular support is most likely to be generated as a result of successful visits to the parks. And as Mackenzie King knew when he visited Prince Albert National Park, and Chrétien knew when he created La Mauricie, people enthusiastic about government projects (including parks) also become loyal constituents. Second, the reality that parks generate economic development, and produce jobs, must also be recognised as legitimate.

In short, the generation of popular and political support for the parks requires recognition of the Canadian reality that our national parks have always been parks for profit. The reality that Canadian national parks are parks for profit in turn secures their future. The parks are planned and operated in ways that encourage tourists but leave the park unimpaired for future generations. Successful tourism, if allowed to expand uncontrolled, would damage and eventually destroy the environment that had proved so attractive to tourists. Hence, environmental protection within the parks has an economic value, and has become part of government policy. In the first century of Canada's national parks, preservation has been both a means to an economic end, and an end in itself.

The pressure for exploitation of the natural resources contained in the parks will continue in the second century of national parks development. Parks may be seriously threatened by boundary erosion, or by proposals for commercial forestry, mining or hydroelectric dams. The reality that our national parks have been also parks for profit may again be crucial to their protection. Because of the commercial value of the parks to the Canadian tourist industry, business groups will put forward economic arguments for their preservation. These arguments were used a century ago by the CPR; by Parks Commissioner James Harkin when he attempted to protect the western parks from the resource hungry western provinces in 1930; and by Jean Chrétien as he struggled to create the first national park in Quebec. Suzanne Blais-Greiner heard these arguments when she mused about resource exploitation in the parks. We will need these arguments again, if Canada's national parks are to be protected and preserved unimpaired for future generations. Canada's parks have survived and expanded over their first century because they are parks for profit.

But it would be perverse if the profit motive were the only force securing the future of Canada's national parks. Preservation implies values that are more fundamental and significant than those involved in economic development. We will need to ensure that there is a broader basis of popular support for and understanding of the non-economic purposes of national parks in Canada. The first century of Canada's national parks was one in which parks were for profit, and we still deal with the political results of that history. But in the second century of our national park system we will need to build an alternate vision of national parks which recognizes the natural environment as worthy of preservation, independent of economic factors. In 1987 Parks Canada captured this in their own vision of parks in the twenty-first century.

National parks and other protected places are our lifeline to an ecologically stable future. They are places where the forces that animate our planet and make it unique are allowed to operate with minimal interference by man; places where we can wonder and pay respect to other living things and the intricacies of ecosystems; places that produce oxygen, stabilize the hydrological cycle, grow abundant fish and wildlife, stay erosion, pour out no man-made toxicants into air or water. They are places where people can study the vital functions of nature, to understand better the potentially threatening human impacts elsewhere. They do not impede our future. They anchor it. They are not a repudiation of economic development. They balance it.[11]

For a century Canada's national parks have been parks for profit. Now for the next century we need to move towards a broader and more popular vision of our parks as a lifeline that stabilizes and anchors our future. Parks for preservation rather than profit symbolize our commitment to that future. Here we are preserving part of the natural heritage of this planet, protected from the impact of resource exploitation and pollution. In these parks future generations will find a lifeline to their own past, and a heritage to leave to their own children. These parks were created for profit, but their future purpose must be to preserve.

Appendix 1

Banff National Park
Date of Creation: 1885
Province: Alberta
Size: 6,641 km²

A ten-square-mile park reserve was established around a hot spring in the Bow Valley of the Rocky Mountains, so that the CPR could ensure suitably prestigious surroundings for tourists visiting the mountains by train. Coal was mined within the park until the 1920s. The park was enlarged at various times, to further protect the railroad monopoly of tourist services. In 1930 the park was reduced in size, to exclude a river to be used for hydro development. The Trans-Canada Highway was also built through Banff National Park in the 1950s. As a result this is still one of Canada's best known national parks, attracting many international tourists each year. Today most visitors arrive by car or coach, rather than by rail, and scenic highways thread through the park. The town of Banff, which serves visitors to the park, is urban in character and scale. There is also pressure for other urban development in the park, which contains a number of world-class ski resorts. These are questionable uses under the UN standards for national parks.

Yoho
Date of Creation: 1886
Province: British Columbia
Size: 1,313 km²

Banff park was extended west along the Canadian Pacific Railway (CPR) right-of-way into British Columbia, further protecting the CPR monopoly of tourist services. After 1930 the western portion of the park was renamed "Yoho". The park straddles the "great divide", and includes the Kicking Horse Pass which challenged the railroad builders. Today the park is accessible from the Trans-Canada Highway, and contains both government campsites and commercial motel developments.

Glacier
Date of Creation: 1886
Province: British Columbia
Size: 1,349 km²

The CPR crossed the "mighty" Selkirks at Rogers Pass. Glacier National Park was created in the Rogers Pass, to provide another site for a prestigious CPR tourist lodge. The dangers of avalanches in the Rogers Pass led the CPR to build spiral tunnels under the pass, and the CPR lodge fell into disuse. The beauties of Glacier Park were not rediscovered untill the construction of the Trans-Canada Highway through the Rogers Pass in the 1950s. Today most travellers stop for a few minutes at the top of the pass, to admire the glaciers hanging above them.

Jasper
Date of Creation: 1907
Province: Alberta
Size: 10,878 km²

The company building a railroad through the northern Yellowhead Pass through the Rocky Mountains wanted privileges similar to those given the CPR in the Bow Valley and the Rogers Pass. Jasper Park was created as a result. Like Banff, Jasper Park contained working coal mines until the 1920s. The park also contains hot springs similar to those in Banff, a large ski resort, a railway hotel called "Jasper Park Lodge", and an urban townsite with commercial tourist services. The railway company subsequently collapsed, and is now part of the crown corporation, Canadian National Railway. Canada's second major transcontinental highway, the Yellowhead Highway, goes through Jasper National Park. Jasper and Banff national parks have contiguous boundaries, and are joined by a scenic highway called the "Icefields Highway".

Waterton
Date of Creation: 1910
Province: Alberta
Size: 526 km²

Waterton was the first of Canada's national parks to be built as a result of popular pressure rather than pressure from railway interests, and was the first park without a railway line through the middle. This area of southwestern Alberta, adjoining the US border, had been a forest reserve since 1895. There was an oil boom in the area in the 1890s, but by 1907 this had died out. People in south-western Alberta liked the camping and fishing in the area. Also, the lake was accessible from the United States, and American tourists were visiting Canada by boat. Park status allowed roads to be built, and a hotel provided for visitors. This park is adjacent to Glacier Park in the United States, and the area has been renamed "The Waterton Glacier International Peace Park". Never served by rail, and not on a major highway, Waterton is less commercially developed than the parks on the CPR or CNR railoads.

Elk Island Park
Date of Creation: 1913
Province: Alberta
Size: 194 km²

The first national park to be created for preservation rather than profit, this park was established to preserve buffalo and elk. In 1922 the park was extended south to highway 16, which brought day visitors from Edmonton. For many years the park had heavy recreational use. However, although the trails are still used for hiking and cross-country skiing, the lakes are no longer good for swimming. A number of commercial activities in the park have closed, and the park is returning to its original preservational purpose.

Mount Revelstoke
Date of Creation: 1914
Province: British Columbia
Size: 263 km²

Like Waterton, the national park at Revelstoke was created as a result of pressure from local civic leaders. They began to lobby in 1912 for a road to the top of the mountain. During the First World War German prisoners-of-war worked on the road, but it was not completed until the late 1920s. Revelstoke National Park was sought by local leaders because they believed that the government would then build them a road, and they would have access to the top of their mountain. The park was for purposes of access, rather than preservation.

St. Lawrence Islands
Date of Creation: 1914
Province: Ontario
Size: 14 km²

This park consists of coastline and seventeen islands in the St. Lawrence River. This first national park in Ontario is very small in comparison with those in western Canada. Many of the other islands had been sold to private individuals, and the park was created to ensure that some remained in the public domain and available for camping and picnicking. The land was purchased from land held in trust by the government for the Indians. The primary concern for this park was, and continues to be, access for recreational purposes.

Point Pelee
Date of Creation: 1918
Province: Ontario
Size: 16 km²

This peninsula is the southernmost point of Canada, and has unique plant life. It is also on a significant bird migration route. The park was created when Canada's concern about preservation of wildlife was at a peak, and is the second park (Elk Island was the first) created primarily for that purpose. Much of the land had belonged to the admiralty, and so was already within federal government jurisdiction. Other land had to be purchased from private individuals. The park is within easy reach of urban centres in southern Ontario, and has been heavily used by weekend visitors. There have been a variety of studies and programs to reduce the impact of human use in the park. Since the 1960s zoning has been introduced, and the permitted number of campers reduced.

Kootenay
Date of Creation: 1920
Province: British Columbia
Size: 1,378 km²

Kootenay Park consists of strips of land either side of a highway in the interior of British Columbia. It was created because the BC government wanted financial help for the construction of a road that would allow mineral development in the interior. The federal government agreed to build the portion of the road within the national parks, if the province would build the rest. British Columbia agreed to the creation of Kootenay Park, because then the Canadian government would build more road. Kootenay also contained mining claims which remained active for a number of years. Like several other mountain parks, Kootenay Park contains hot springs. Until the park was created these were commercially operated, and rather sleazy. Now standards are comparable to those in the other mountain parks.

Wood Buffalo
Date of Creation: 1922
Province: Alberta and Northwest Territories
Size: 44,787 km²

Buffalo Park was created primarily to preserve the buffalo, providing them with a large range where they would be protected from hunting.

There was no access to the park by rail or by road, and the area is still remote. The park was not managed like the other parks, for native Canadians were allowed to continue their traditional use of the land. This has lead to aboriginal land claims related to asbestos deposits in the park.

Prince Albert
Date of Creation: 1927
Province: Saskatchewan
Size: 3,875 km^2

Prime Minister Mackenzie King created Prince Albert National Park to thank his constituents in the town of Prince Albert, who had elected him to the House of Commons. He had been defeated in a general election in central Canada, and needed success in a by-election to retain his position as prime minister. King built a cabin in the park, and used it when he was in his constituency. One of the lakes was named "Kingsmere" in his memory.

Riding Mountain
Date of Creation: 1929
Province: Manitoba
Size: 22,976 km^2

The provincial politicians of Manitoba wanted a national park, like those that had been created for Saskatchewan and Alberta. The federal government proposed that one be created in Whiteshell, shield country on the eastern border of Manitoba. This would have been accessible to people from Ontario. However, leading Manitoba politicians, with constituents in Dauphin and Brandon, recommended that the park be in the forestry reserve north of Dauphin. A popular resort was created at Clear Lake, and a downhill ski area has also developed.

Georgian Bay Islands
Date of Creation: 1929
Province: Ontario
Size: 14 km^2

In the Georgian Bay of Lake Huron, this park consists of seventy-seven small islands, accessible by water taxi and by boat. This park was created primarily for recreation purposes, to ensure that some islands remained in the public domain and accessible for camping. The land was purchased from land held in trust for the Indians.

Cape Breton Islands
Date of Creation: 1936
Province: Nova Scotia
Size: 367 km^2

This is the first of the Maritime parks, most of which were supported by local leaders because of the promise of provincial economic development through expanded tourism in the area. The emphasis in most of these parks has been on providing access and facilities for visitors. Civic leaders in Cape Breton had requested a national park for the province since 1914, pointing to the social and economic benefits such a park had brought in other provinces. The park contains a golf course, at that point an almost mandatory addition to the recreational resources of any national park. The historic Cabot Trail threads through the park, which is promoted for good hiking and fishing.

Prince Edward Island
Date of Creation: 1937
Province: Prince Edward Island
Size: 18 km²

Public support for a national park in Prince Edward Island began to mobilize in 1923. As in the other Maritime parks, this national park was intended to stimulate the tourist industry in an otherwise depressed region of Canada. The park includes a fine bathing beach, tennis courts, and (again) a golf course. The latter is called "Green Gables", after one of Canada's best known novels — *Anne of Green Gables* —which was set in this part of Prince Edward Island.

Fundy
Date of Creation: 1948
Province: New Brunswick
Size: 206 km²

The leaders of New Brunswick lobbied for nearly twenty years before this park was finally created in 1948. Part of the delay was due to disagreements on a proposed location for the park, since many possible areas were either already used for summer cottages, or had forestry potential. As in the other Maritime parks, tourist development was a priority. Campsites, a golf course a heated swimming pool, tennis courts and a bowling green were built in the park.

Terra Nova
Date of Creation: 1957
Province: Newfoundland
Size: 153 km²

Premier Joey Smallwood negotiated Newfoundland's entry into the Canadian confederation in 1949. Part of the "deal" was the gift of a national park in the province. By this time parks officials felt national parks should not contain recreation facilities such as golf courses. However, Smallwood demanded that Newfoundland's national park should have all the recreation facilities available in the national parks in the other Canadian provinces — such as golf courses, tennis courts and swimming pools. He also wanted the Canadian government to provide access to the park, by building a new road up to and through the park. The federal government finally agreed. Even then, formal creation of the park was delayed nearly ten years while the two governments tried to find an area that had no potential value for mineral, timber or hydro development.

Kejimkujik
Date of Creation: 1968
Province: Nova Scotia
Size: 145 km²

This interior woodland of Nova Scotia had been popular for hunting and fishing since 1908. Leading Nova Scotians had lobbied for a national park in the area since 1945. With the election of the Trudeau government in 1968, the national parks portfolio received increased attention. Trudeau appointed Jean Chrétien as the minister responsible for Indian Affairs and Northern Development — a portfolio that included the national parks. Both Trudeau and Chrétien enjoy exploring the Canadian outdoors, and Chrétien moved quickly to confirm some proposals for national parks, and to develop new ones. These proposals all received support from environmentalists, who were active in Canada in the late sixties and the seventies.

Kouchibouguac
Date of Creation: 1969
Province: New Brunswick
Size: 225 km²

The people of Kouchibouguac opposed the creation of a park, since it would displace them from homes they had lived in for several generations. However, they had little money, and their houses were substandard. They were forced to sell or be expropriated. A number protested through the courts, and one case is still being heard. Sandy beaches and warm lagoons provide good swimming in this national park. The area also includes unique peat bogs. Typical of the newer national parks, Kouchibouguac does not contain a townsite with commercial accommodation or cottages. Also, there are none of the more urbanized recreation facilities, such as tennis courts or golf courses. There are, however, provisions for camping, canoeing, boating, bicycling, fishing, cross-country skiing and surfing — activities that are today considered to be reasonably compatible with wilderness preservation. Most of the national parks created after 1968 have reached this form of compromise between access and preservation.

Pacific Rim

Date of Creation: 1970
Province: British Columbia
Size: 389 km²

The west coast of Vancouver Island has an extensive sand beach, fringed by the remnants of coastal forest. Jean Chrétien persuaded the Social Credit government of British Columbia to hand over the beach as a national park, but the lumber industry claimed the forest was too valuable. Bennett agreed to the park, but then delayed the legislation so that the area could be logged. The park now includes eleven km of Long Beach, a coastal trail, a series of islands, and a portion of coastal rain forest added when the New Democrats were in power. The Social Credit government has since returned to power in British Columbia.

Forillon

Date of Creation: 1970
Province: Quebec
Size: 90 km²

Forillon was the first national park in Quebec. Located in the depressed Gaspé region of the province, the park was part of a regional economic development agreement signed between the federal and provincial governments, involving an exenditure pf $8.3 million by the federal government. Quebec refused to hand over permanent title to the land to the federal government, and the Canadian government agreed to accept a ninety-nine year lease. After this time the land will revert to provincial control, although the province is committed to retaining it as parkland. The rationale for this exception is the different legal system in place in Quebec (the Civil Code). New jobs were created in the park, which also increased economic activity from tourism in nearby villages.

La Mauricie

Date of Creation: 1970
Province: Quebec
Size: 160 km²

Jean Chrétien had admired the St. Maurice Valley, and created a park there when he became minister. He organized local support for the park, to obtain provincial agreement. Chrétien's own constituents (his riding was "St. Maurice") have easy access to the park.

Gros Morne

Date of Creation: 1970
Province: Newfoundland
Size: 775 km²

People dependent on the local fishing industry in the coastal villages of Newfoundland objected to the creation of a national park that would displace families. However, the park was expected to increase year round income from tourism. The Gros Morne area also has potential as a world heritage site.

Kluane
Date of Creation: 1972
Territory: Yukon
Size: 22,015 km²

The provincial governments of southern Canada were reluctant to hand over large areas to the federal government for park purposes. But the Canadian government could unilaterally create national parks in the Yukon and the Northwest Territories. These parks north of 60° are far larger than the southern parks, and are inaccessible to most Canadians. However, even here preservation required concessions to various interests. The boundaries of Kluane were drawn to exclude areas with mineral potential. Also, the Canadian Liberal government was in a minority position after the 1972 election. The New Democratic party required, as the price of its support, a concession that would make the status of the park subject to the settlement of native land claims.

Nahanni
Date of Creation: 1972
Territory: Northwest Territories
Size: 4,766 km²

This park contains a spectacular wild river, and the Virginia Falls which have been recognized as a world heritage site. The confirmation of park status for this river followed an intensive lobby by environmentalists, and a canoe trip down the river by Prime Minister Trudeau. A small industry has now developed, flying visitors in and guiding them down the river. As with Kluane, the status of this park is subject to the settlement of native land claims.

Auyittuq
Date of Creation: 1972
Territory: Northwest Territories
Size: 21,471 km²

Access to this remote park on Baffin Island is difficult. The Inuit continue their traditional lifestyles within the park reserve, as they are considered to live in harmony with the environment. The Inuit also serve as guides in a park where travel is difficult, and dangerous to both the visitor and the delicate ecological balance of the arctic environment. The status of this park will be confirmed following the settlement of native land claims.

Pukaskwa
Date of Creation: 1978
Province: Ontario
Size: 1,879 km²

Pukaskwa is the largest national park in central or eastern Canada, and is comparatively wild. Logging took place in the area untill the 1930s, but ceased when the price of lumber collapsed. None has taken place since, although there are both timber berths and mineral claims in the area. Pukaskwa National Park is not directly on the Trans-Canada Highway, and the impression on approaching the area is that this was a forgotten corner of Ontario.

Grasslands
Date of Creation: 1981
Province: Saskatchewan
Size: 900 km²

The intention of Grasslands Park is to preserve unique areas of prairie grassland. However, ranchers use the land at present, and have objected strenuously to being displaced by a park. They suggest that they are part of the natural environment, like the Inuit in the Arctic, or the farmers in the national parks of the United Kingdom. As a result land acquisition for this park has been slow, and the park is unfinished.

Mingan Archipelago
Date of Creation: 1984
Province: Quebec
Size: 87 km²

In the Gulf of St Lawrence, these forty islands will be developed as a national park. This park, and the Northern Yukon park (see below), were created in the final days of the Liberal regime in Ottawa, and gave the impression of being hurried decisions to earn votes in an upcoming general election. This national park is subject to the settlement of native land claims.

Northern Yukon
Date of Creation: 1984
Size: 6,050 km²

The native peoples co-operated with the federal government to create a park that would preserve the traditional migration routes of the caribou.

The agreement was signed between the Committee for Original People's Entitlement (cope) and the Government of Canada, after concern developed about the damage that could result from pipeline and other resource development in the area.

Ellesmere Island
Date of Creation: 1985
Size: Under consideration

An American ship had used the North West passage without Canadian permission. This park had already been under negotiation by the Liberal government. The Conservative government quickly signed the agreement creating this arctic park, as a way of enforcing Canadian sovereignty over the arctic islands.

Appendix 2

Banff
Stony Squaw Mountain Road; secondary road improvements; cement sidewalks for Banff; new bathhouse; clear and survey park boundaries; Banff–Jasper Highway; cutting and hauling logs; 5 culverts; brushing campgrounds; construct camp building; burning slash; build ice slide and toboggan slide for carnival, etc.

Jasper
Jasper–Yellowhead Highway; rock excavation, Miette Hot Springs Road; road improvements; clearing and burning brush; improve bridge approaches; Banff–Jasper Highway; load and haul rock; build retaining wall; snow removal; clear right-of-way for new entrance; hauling fill, etc.

Kootenay
Asphalt on bridge; road widenings and improvements; bunkhouse at Radium Hot Springs; new bridge over Sinclar Creek, etc.

Yoho
Two bridges on boundary road; road improvements; snow clearing; extend and improve campsite, etc.

Waterton
Sidewalk construction and drainage improvement in townsite; comfort stations and septic tank at campsite; clear right-of-way on Alberta/BC border; road improvements; surveying cutlines; cut logs and haul to mill for sawing, etc.

Elk Island
Road improvements; brushing out and clearing park areas and buffalo meadows; two bathhouses; build storehouses, etc.

*Canada, Department of the Interior, Reports of the Commissioner of Dominion Parks, 1930–35.

Prince Albert

Rabbit Meridian Road located and right-of-way cleared; highway improved; campground enlarged and improved; park boundary located and cleared; tote road built to airfield; camp kitchen, dining hall and bunkhouse built; foundation laid for tennis courts; snow fence; golf course, etc.

Riding Mountain

Road improvements and construction; park boundaries located and cleared; town site surveyed; superintendent's cabin built; fireguard cleared; lakeshore brushed out; bandstand built; parking area laid; muskeg drained; landscaping; extend telephone system; laid foundation for museum; logging, etc.

PARKS CONSTRUCTION UNDER THE PUBLIC WORKS CONSTRUCTION ACTS, 1934–36 *

Banff

Banff–Jasper Highway; Stoney Squaw Road; Banff Castle Road grading; Spray Avenue improvements; bridges on Lake Louise Road and Banff–Calgary Road; sewer for Tunnell Mountain campground; caretaker's cottage for upper hot spring; forest telephone lines; warden's cabins; golf course improvement; administration building; post office; bath houses at cave and basin and upper hot springs; eastern entrance building; forest trails; landscape grounds of administration building, etc.

Jasper

Banff–Jasper Highway; Jasper Yellowhead Highway; Miette Hot Springs Road widening; Edith Cavell Road widening; Patricia Lake Campground; Connaught Drive improvement; airfield; sewer extension for Jasper; Portal Creek Bridge; Cemetery Road; telephone system for Jasper Townsite; forest trails, etc.

Waterton

Belly River Road; public campgrounds; addition to general stores building; entrance and registration building; second nine-hole golf course; water supply; rest room for recreation building, etc.

Yoho

Stephen–West Boundary Road; road widening; Kicking Horse Campgrounds; blacksmith's shop, etc.

Elk Island Park

Maintain Sandy Beach Road; improve South Gate Road; clear beach and

*Canada, Department of the Interior, Reports of the Commissioner of Dominion Parks, 1934–37.

construct facilities at Sandy Beach; construct golf course; build government garage, etc.

Prince Albert

Road improvement; construct recreation area and golf course; improve tennis, swimming and camping facilities; construct golf club house and staff quarters; museum building, etc.

Riding Mountain

Complete second nine holes of golf course; improve lakeshore drive; improve campground drainage; improve townsite; road construction and maintenance; staff quarters; firehall; garage; horsebarn; repair breakwater; complete bandstand, etc.

Glacier

Construct warden's cabin, etc.

WORK COMPLETED BY ALTERNATIVE SERVICE WORKERS, 1941–46*

1941–42

Built 1.7 miles highway, 28.25 miles secondary road, 2,000 rods fencing; Rebuilt 50 miles highway, 120 miles secondary road, 8.6 miles pony trail and 10 miles telephone line; improved campgrounds; built permanent buildings; dams and flumes constructed; began large breakwater in Prince Albert park.

1942–43

Built 28.4 miles of fire trails, 10.7 miles telephone lines, 3 bridges and 147 rods fencing, 210 feet guard rail and completed the breakwater in Prince Albert; improved 34 miles fire trails, 13 miles pony trails, 37 miles of telephone lines. Worked on insect control, salvaging 67,712 linear feet of mine props; improved camp grounds and built some small buildings; worked in fire protection and conservation.

1943–44

Built 10.5 miles of fire trails and 2.25 miles of telephone lines; improved 6 miles secondary road, 108 miles of fire trails, 176 miles of telephone lines; prepared 1,930 logs for guard rails and 471 fence posts; tourist and campground facilities were improved and several buildings constructed; control of forest infestation produced 800,000 board feet of sawn timber, 1,610,822 linear feet of mine props and 3,851 cords of fire wood.

1944–45

Produced 305,912 linear feet of mine props, 455,000 feet board measure of saw timber, 268,260 feet board measure of saw logs, 2,732 cords of fuel

*Canada, Department of Mines and Resources, Annual Reports, 1940–46.

wood and 92 poles. Built one steel bridge and 7 wooden bridges, 14 culverts, one cabin, 7½ miles of trail, telephone lines, buildings, bridges and culverts, as well as many other small projects.

1945–46

Forest protection, fire suppression, construction and maintenance of fire trails, buildings, telephone lines, roads, bridges, and culverts. Salvaged 570,000 board feet of sawn lumber, 9,302 linear feet of mine props, 9,655 board feet of saw logs, 439 cords of fuel wood, 100 telephone posts, 260 hub rails, and 2,000 fence posts. Hauled and spread 3,112 cubic yards of gravel, built 1,400 feet of secondary road, 175 feet of hub rail and 17 culverts.

Notes

Introduction

1. Following the 1982 World National Parks Congress, sponsored by the International Union for the Conservation of Nature and Natural Resources, and other agencies associated with the United Nations, the magazine of the United States National Parks and Conservation Association devoted a special issue to national parks around the world. *National Parks,* vol. 57, no. 5–6 (May/June 1983).

2. International Union for Conservation of Nature and Natural Resources, "United Nations List of National Parks and Equivalent Reserves" (Geneva, 1975), 35.

CHAPTER 1

1. D. McCowan, *Hill Top Tales* (Toronto: Macmillan, 1948), 25–37.

2. Esther Fraser, *The Canadian Rockies: Early Travels and Explorations* (Edmonton: Hurtig, 1969), 21.

3. William McCardell, "Reminiscences of a Pioneer", Glenbow Archives, D920 M123A.

4. A. P. Coleman, *The Canadian Rockies* (Toronto: Frowde, 1911), 20.

5. A. R. Byrne, *Man and Landscape Change in the Banff National Park Area Before 1914* (University of Calgary, 1968), 92–94.

6. A. P. Coleman, op. cit., 53–54.

7. E. A. Mitchener, "William Pearce and Federal Government Activity in Western Canada 1882–1904" (Ph.D. diss., University of Alberta, 1971), 181.

8. William Pearce, "Establishment of National Parks in the Rockies", *Alberta Historical Review,* vol. 10 (1962), 8–17.

9. McCardell, op. cit, 271.

10. K. A. Stotyn, "The Development of the Bow River Irrigation Project, 1906–1950" (M.A. thesis, University of Alberta, 1982).

11. Pearce, op. cit.

12. W. F.(Ferg) Lothian, *A History of Canada's National Parks* vol. 1 (Ottawa: Parks Canada, 1976), 18–21.

13. *The Daily Manitoban,* August 26th, 1886. Public Archives of Canada, Macdonald Papers, vol. 113, #46060. Quoted in R. Craig Brown, "The Doctrine of Usefulness: Natural Resources and National Park Policy in Canada, 1887–1914", J. G. Nelson and R. C. Scace, eds., *Conference on the National Parks Today and Tomorrow: Proceedings* (University of Calgary, 1968), 94–110.

14. James Parker, "Medical Pioneering in Alberta: Dr. Robert George Brett, 1851–1929", Calgary Associate Clinic, *Historical Bulletin,* vol. 4, no. 1 (May 1939): 5–12.

15. M. B. Williams, *Through the Heart of the Rockies and Selkirks* (Ottawa: Department of the Interior, 1929).

16. E. J. Hart, *The Brewster Story: from Pack Train to Tour Bus* (Banff: Brewster, 1981).

17. "Report Made for the CPR on Banff by Dr. J. S. Lynch, Winnipeg, 1887, for William Van Horne, Vice President, CPR", Rocky Mountain Archives, M305.

18. Robert G. Brett Papers, Rocky Mountain Archives.

19. W. F. Lothian, op. cit., vol. 2, 30–31; vol 1, 27.

20. Judy Root, "The History of Radium Hot Springs, British Columbia", 1971, Rocky Mountain Archives, M285.

21. Rupert Brook, L. H. Thomas, "British Visitors Perceptions of the West, 1885–1914", Western Canadian Studies Conference, University of Calgary, 1971.

22. Glenbow Archives, CB7M679.

23. John Marsh, Untitled Manuscript Prepared in Conjunction with Ph.D. thesis, University of Calgary. Glenbow Archives, M676, Box 2, f. 55.

24. Tom Wilson to J. B. Harkin, 28 June 1922. Glenbow Archives, AP359.

25. Sylvia Vankirk, "The Development of National Park Policy in Canada's Mountain National Parks, 1885–1930" (M.A. thesis, University of Alberta, 1969), 23.

26. Gordon Brinley, *Away to the Rockies and British Columbia* (New York: Dodd, Mead and Co., 1938), 51.

27. Ibid., p. 103.

Chapter 2

1. Harold Innis, *A History of the Canadian Pacific Railroad* (Toronto: University of Toronto Press, 1971), 212, 221.

2. A. R. Byrne, *Man and Landscape Change in the Banff National Park Area Before 1911,* National Park Series no. 1, University of Calgary, 1968, 102.

3. W. F. (Ferg) Lothian, *A History of Canada's National Parks,* vol. 3, Environment Canada (1981), 72–74.

4. Lothian, *A History of Canada's National Parks,* vol. 4, 97.

5. E. J. (Ted) Hart, *The Brewster Story* (Banff: Brewster, 1981), 14.

6. Glenbow Archives Calgary, CPR Papers, Box 201, f.1980.

7. John Ise, *Our National Park Policy: A Critical History* (Baltimore: John Hopkins University Press, 1961), 18.

8. Canada. House of Commons. *Debates,* May 3, 1887, 233.

9. Robert Craig Brown, "A Doctrine of Usefulness: Natural Resource and National Park Policy in Canada, 1887–1914", Conference on the Canadian National Parks Today and Tomorrow, 1968, vol. 1, 94–110.

10. P. Lewis, "The Development of the Bow Corridor, 1880–1930", Rocky Mountain Archives, Banff, M467.

11. Alice Fulmer, Rocky Mountain Archives, Banff, M 70, f.5.

12. N. K. Luxton, Rocky Mountain Archives, Banff, M705, f.25.

13. Canada. Department of Interior. *Annual Report,* 1903–04.

14. F. Wheatley, Rocky Mountain Archives, Banff, M117, f3.

15. Michael Weiss, Glenbow Archives, Calgary, D970.6 W431. Lothian, vol. 4, 97.

16. Ibid., 98.

17. Alberta Transportation, Rocky Mountain Archives, Banff, M335.

18. Stephen Jones, "Mining and Tourist Towns in the Canadian Rockies", *Economic Geography,* vol. 9 (1933), 368–378.

19. Rocky Mountain Archives, Banff, M467, f.1.

20. Canada. *Labour Gazette,* vol. 7, June 1907, 1388–1405.

21. Western Coal Operators Association, Glenbow Archives, Calgary, BL652, Box 6, f. 35.

22. Canada. *Labour Gazette,* vol. 9, August 1909, 227.

23. Glenbow Archives, Calgary, BL652, Box 7, f.42.

24. Canada. *Labour Gazette,* vol. 18, 1918, 309.

25. Ibid., vol. 20, February 1922, 138.

26. Glenbow Archives, Calgary, CPR Papers, BNC212G, Box 49, f.538.

27. Lothian, op. cit., vol. 4, 104.

28. P. Lewis. Rocky Mountain Archives, M467, f.1.

29. Ibid.

30. E. G. Luxton, *Banff: Canada's First National Park* (Banff: Summer-thought, 1978).

31. Lothian, op. cit., vol. 4, 103.

32. Parks Canada, "Gravel Extraction Activities: Background Paper 5, Four Mountain Parks Planning Program", R63–1183/2, v. 1.

33. Lothian, op. cit., vol. 4, 104–104; vol. 1, 42.

34. Lothian, ibid., vol. 4, 106–107.

35. Glenbow Archives, Calgary, BB2C151 c f.738.

36. Lothian, op. cit., vol. 3, 43.

37. Robert C. Scace, *Banff: A Cultural-Historical Study of Land Use and Management in a National Park Community to 1945* (University of Calgary, Department of Geography, 1968).

38. A. R. Byrne, op. cit., chapter 7.
39. Lothian, ibid., vol. 1, 73.
40. Lothian, ibid., vol. 4, 116.
41. Lothian, ibid., vol. 4, 127.

CHAPTER 3

1. E. A. Mitchener, "William Pearce and Federal Government Activity in Western Canada 1882–1904" (Ph.D. diss., University of Alberta, 1971).
2. Esther Fraser, *Wheeler* (Banff: Summerthought, 1979).
3. A. O. Wheeler, *The Selkirk Range* (Ottawa: Government Printing Bureau, 1905).
4. A. O. Wheeler, Banff, 30 November 1905. Canadian Archives, MG26, vol. 396.
5. Sir Wilfred Laurier to Mrs Parker, 11 January 1906. Canadian Archives. MG26. vol. 396, p. 105183.
6. NPPAC, *Park News*, vol. 19, no.1.
7. The Alpine Club and the Dominion Government, Canadian Archives, MG26, vol. 606, 164432–164435.
8. The Alpine Club to Sir Wilfred Laurier, 1 December 1909. Canadian Archives. MG26. vol. 601. 163003–163012.
9. Fraser, op. cit., 81.
10. Alpine Club, Canadian Archives. RG84. vol. 102, u36-1-1.
11. Fraser, op. cit., 36.
12. F. O. (Pat) Brewster, *Weathered Wood* (Banff: Cragg and Canyon, 1977), 45.
13. Paul A. Wallace, Glenbow Archives, Calgary, AW193, f.1,2.
14. K. A. Stotyn, "The Development of the Bow River Irrigation Project: 1906–1950" (M.A. thesis, University of Alberta, 1982).
15. Canada. House of Commons. *Debates,* 12 May 1909, 6367.
16. Canada. Commission of Conservation, Department of Interior. *Annual Reports,* 1910–1918.
17. Commission of Conservation. *Annual Report,* 1912, 64–75.
18. Canada. House of Commons. *Debates,* 28 April 1911, 8084.
19. W. F.(Ferg) Lothian, "The Parks of Yesteryear", *Intercom,* vol. 9, no. 2 (Ottawa: Parks Canada, 1966), 13–15.
20. R. Scace, *Elk Island National Park: A Cultural History* (Ottawa: Parks Canada, 1976).
21. P. A. Taverner, "Recommendations for the Creation of Three New National Parks in Canada", Commission of Conservation. *Annual Report,* 1915, 304.
22. W. F.(Ferg) Lothian, *A History of Canada's National Parks,* vol. 1 (Environment Canada, 1976), 81.
23. E. A. Mitchener "William Pearce and Federal Government Activity in

the West, 1974–1904", *Canadian Public Administration,* vol. 10, June 1967: 235–243.

24. Canada, *Labour Gazette,* vol. 8, 1907–08, 124.
25. Pearce to White, 20 June 1920. Glenbow Archives, Calgary. BNC212G. Box 20. f.239.
26. Walker to Coleman, 17 June 1921. Glenbow Archives, Calgary. BNC212G. Box 20, f.237.
27. Agreement, 12 February 1912. Glenbow Archives, Calgary. BB2C151F. Box 6, f.47.
28. Canada. House of Commons. *Debates,* 14 June 1923, 3490.
29. Canada. House of Commons. *Debates,* 14 June 1923, 3939.
30. Sibbald to Minister of the Interior, 18 August 1923, Canadian Archives. RG84. vol. 107, f.u25.
31. Pearce to Bennett, 12 May 1923. Pearce Papers, University of Alberta, Special Collections. f.421.
32. Pearce to Wheeler, 7 May 1923. Op. cit.
33. Wheeler to Pearce, 24 May 1923. Op. cit.
34. Alan Mason, "William Pearce and the Spray Lakes Controversy", unpublished paper, Recreation and Leisure Studies, University of Alberta, 1984.
35. Sibbald to Harkin, 9 August 1923. Canadian Archives. RG84. vol. 107. f. u25.
36. A. P. Pross, "Pressure Groups: Adaptive Instruments of Political Communication", *Pressure Group Behaviour in Canadian Politics* (Toronto: McGraw-Hill Ryerson, 1975), 1–26.
37. Memorandum to Gibson, 11 December 1936. Canadian Archives. RG84. vol. 107. f.u25.
38. Lett to Field, 15 February 1924. Canadian Archives. RG84. vol. 107. f. u25.
38. Bulletin No. 1, 1 January 1924. Canadian National Parks Association. Canadian Archives. RG84. vol. 107. F. u25.
39. Leslie Bella and Susan Markham, "Parks First: Patriotic Canadians from Coast to Coast in Support of National Parks", *Recreation Canada,* vol. 42, no. 5, December 1984.
40. Walker to R. M. Young, 10 March 1924. Glenbow Archives. BLC652. f.110.
41. Pearce to Coleman, 23 June 1923. University of Alberta, Pearce Papers, f.421.
42. Pearce to Black, 22 December 1923. Op. cit.
43. Canada. House of Commons. *Debates,* 4 May 1925, 2779.
44. Canada. House of Commons. *Debates,* 10 June 1925, 4118.
45. Canada. House of Commons. *Debates,* 3 June 1924, 1261.
46. Pearce. 31 March 1926. Canadian Archives.
47. Canada. Department of the Interior. *Annual Report* 1930, 92–116. "National Parks of Canada: Report of the Commissioner".

48. Op. cit., p. 93.
49. Canada. House of Commons. *Debates,* 10 April 1930, 1454.

CHAPTER 4

1. W. F. (Ferg) Lothian, *A History of Canada's National Parks,* vol. 2 (Ottawa: Parks Canada, 1977), p. 31.
2. Lucy Alderson and John Marsh, "J. B. Harkin, National Parks and Good Roads", *Park News* (Summer, 1979): 9–16.
3. Lothian, op. cit., 13.
4. J. B. Harkin, *The History and Meaning of the National Parks of Canada* (Saskatoon: H. R. Larson, 1975), 5.
5. W. F. (Ferg) Lothian, "James Bernard Harkin: A Brief Biographical Sketch," 31 Oct. 1972. Rocky Mountain Archives. M113. f.6..
6. Ibid.
7. Harkin, op. cit., 7
8. Lothian., *Canada's National Parks,* vol. 2, 31.
9. Memorandum re Dominion Parks, 24 January 1914, 9. University of Alberta Archives. Pearce Papers. f.479.1.
10. Op. cit., p. 10.
11. J. B. Harkin, Speech to the Good Roads Association, Victoria, BC 1922.
12. Alderson and Marsh, Op. cit..
13. Lewis, Canada. House of Commons. *Debates,* 14 June 1923, 3942.
14. Canada. Department of Interior. *Annual Report,* 1918, 6.
15. Stewart, Canada. House of Commons. *Debates,* 14 June 1923, 3942.
16. *Calgary Albertan,* 12 April 1911.
17. Canadian Archives. 21 May 1914. RG84. vol. 191-1.
18. Superintendent to Harkin, 24 April 1914. Canadian Archives. RG84. vol. 190. 577708-2.
19. Bennett to Harkin, 25 Sep. 1914. Canadian Archives. RG84. Bennett.
20. Clarke to Harkin, 19 June 1917. RG84. Canadian Archives. vol.191-1.
21. Clarke to Harkin, 20 June 1917. RG84. Canadian Archives. vol. 191-1.
22. Pearce to Davidson, Good Roads Association, 4 June 1920. University of Alberta Archives, Pearce Papers. f.479.3.
23. Ommaney to Pearce, 10 August 1922, University of Alberta Archives, Pearce Papers, f. 479.3.
24. Pearce Papers, University of Alberta Archives, f. 479.1.
25. *Calgary Herald,* 20 March 1927.
26. Canadian Archives. RG84. vol. 212. f. G605.
27. Harkin to Cory, 6 Dec. 1926. RG84. vol 212. G60-5.
28. John Marsh, Untitled Manuscript Prepared in Conjunction with Ph.D. thesis on Glacier, University of Calgary. Glenbow Archives. M676. Box 2. f.55. p.12.
29. E. J. Hart, *The Brewster Story* (Banff: Brewster, 1981), 54.
30. Hart, ibid., p. 50.

31. RG84. vol. 5. B155-6. 1938.
32. Banff Board of Trade. Minute Book. 1912–34. Rocky Mountain Archives. M212.
33. Canadian Archives. RG84. vol. 102. f. u36-1. vol. 2.5
34. Bennett to Harkin, 31 May 1913. Canadian Archives. RG84. Bennett.
35. Harkin to Bennett, 15 July 1914. Canadian Archives. RG84. Bennett.
36. McAllister to Stewart, 20 August 1927. Canadian Archives. RG84. vol. 212. f. G605.
37. L. Bella, "Explaining Parks and Outdoor Resources Policy: Transportation Technology and National Parks Development", Canadian Congress on Leisure Research, University of Alberta. 1981.
38. C. H. Grant, "A Record of Progress", *Good Roads,* vol. 2, 1923. Alberta Provincial Archives.
39. Gordon to Harkin, 5 July 1916. Canadian Archives. RG84. vol. 190. MR176.
40. *Revelstoke Mail and Herald,* 15 July 1915.
41. Dale Zieroth,"A Road for Windermere", *Conservation Canada,* vol. 4, no. 4 (1979).
42. Dale Zieroth, *Nipika: A Story of Radium Hot Springs* (Ottawa: Canada Supply and Services, 1978), 16–17.
43. Dominion Parks Branch. Report of the Commissioner. Sessional Paper No. 25, 1920, 9.
44. R. Scace, *Elk Island National Park: A Cultural History* (Ottawa: Parks Canada, 1976).
45. *The Morning Leader,* Regina, 16 Feb. 1926.
46. Blair Neatby, *The Lonely Heights: William Lyon Mackenzie King,* vol. 2 (Toronto: University of Toronto Press, 1958), 263.
47. Lothian, *Canada's National Parks,* vol. 1, 71.
48. Canada. House of Commons. *Debates,* 29 May 1929, 2717.
49. Canada. National Parks Branch. *Annual Report,* 1930, 106.
50. Lothian, *Canada's National Parks,* vol. 1, 81.
51. Harkin to Deputy Minister, 2 December 1918. Canadian Archives. RG84. vol. 194. P60-1.
52. Cornover to Harkin, 26 August 1924. Canadian Archives. RG84. vol. 194. P60-1.
53. Canadian Archives. 6 March 1931. RG84. vol. 194. P60-2.
54. In 1911 there had been 37 million railway passengers, and 80 million tonnes of freight. By 1931 there were 26 million passengers and 74 million tonnes of freight. The relative significance of passenger services continued to decline so that in 1961 there were 19 million passengers earning the railways $3.32 a passenger train mile, and 153 million tonnes of freight earning $16.72 a freight train mile (*Canada Year Book,* 1911 to 1965).
55. Canadian Archives. MG28 I25. vol. 70.
56. Canadian Archives. RG84. vol. 162. U125.

CHAPTER 5

1. Canada. House of Commons. *Debates,* 17 April 1916, 2922.
2. Canada. House of Commons. *Debates,* 30 April 1919, 1946.
3. E. W. Bradwin, *The Bunkhouse Man* (New York: Columbia University Press, 1928).
4. Canada. House of Commons. *Debates,* 15 February 1916, 849–851.
5. Russell to Harkin, 30 December 1915. Canadian Archives. RG84. Y176.
6. Russell to Harkin, 17 January 1916. Canadian Archives. RG84. Y176.
7. Stinson to Harkin, 7 February 1916. Canadian Archives. RG84. Y176.
8. "The Interned Aliens Try to Tunnel out of Stockade: Timely Discovery Balks Plot for a Wholesale Delivery", *The Golden Star,* 5 October 1916.
9. Canada. Commissioner of Dominion Parks. *Annual Reports,* 1916–1917, 54.
10. Ibid., 1917–18, 8.
11. Harkin to Rogers, 24 March 1924. Canadian Archives. RG84. vol. 212. J121-K3-1.
12. Rogers to Harkin, 27 March 1924. Canadian Archives. RG84. vol. 212. J121-30-1.
13. Statistics Canada, *Labour Force Bulletin* (71–001).
14. Canada. Department of the Interior. *Report of the Commissioner of Dominion Parks,* 1930–31, 95. Gross relief calculated on basis of $2.40 per day. Harkin to Wardle, 14 Nov. 1931. Canadian Archives. RG84. vol. 213, J121-3.
15. Canada. Department of the Interior. *Report of the Commissioner of Dominion Parks,* 1931–32.
16. M. Horn, *The Dirty Thirties* (Toronto: Copp Clark, 1972), 125.
17. Snape to Superintendent, 30 March 1931. Canadian Archives. RG84. vol. 212. J121-3-1.
18. Bury to Hon. T. G. Murphy, 18 November 1931. Canadian Archives. RG84. vol. 213, J121-3-3.
19. J. B. Hartstone to Hereford, 27 November 1931. Canadian Archives. RG84. vol. 213. J121-3-3.
20. Wardle to Harkin, 4 January 1932. Canadian Archives. RG84. vol. 213. J121-3-3.
21. December 24 1931. Canadian Archives. RG84. vol. 213. J121-3-3.
22. Wardle to Harkin, 19 February 1932. Canadian Archives. RG84. vol. 213. J121-3-3.
23. Harkin to Rowatt, 6 November 1931. Canadian Archives. RG84. vol. 218. U315.
24. Harkin to Rowatt, 2 June 1933. Canadian Archives. RG84. vol. 212. B60-23. vol. 11.
25. 12 July 1933. RG84. vol. 212. B69-23, vol. 11.

26. I. Abella, *On Strike* (Toronto: James, Lewis and Samuel, 1974).
27. J. A. Gray, *The Winter Years* (New York: Macmillan, 1966), 38–47.
28. J. A. Gray, *The Troublemaker* (New York: Macmillan, 1978), 8–9.
29. M. Horne, *The Dirty Thirties* (Toronto: Copp Clark, 1972), 325–328.
30. R. Liversedge, *Recollections of the On-to-Ottawa Trek* (Toronto: McClelland and Stewart, 1973).
31. Canada. Department of the Interior. *Reports of the Commissioner of Dominion Parks* 1930–1935.
32. Ibid., 1934–37.
33. The idea of work for relief re-emerged in Alberta in 1982, and was enthusiastically welcomed by leaders in the rural south of the province. L. Bella, "Work for Welfare: Examples of Western Canadian Experience", Western Association of Sociologists and Anthropologists, Brandon, 1983.
34. Canadian Archives, RG84. vol. 32. U182-3.
35. J. C. Veness, "Report Covering Inspections of the National Forestry Program: Dominion Section Summer 1939", Canadian Archives. RG84. vol. 32. U182-3.
36. 6 July 1939. Canadian Archives. RG84. vol. 5. B182-3-1.
37. "Alternative Service Work Camps: Summer Operations, 1941", Canadian Archives. RG84. vol. 3, U165-2-3.
38. Rattray to Smart, 8 September 1941. Canadian Archives. vol. 110. U165-2-2.
39. Op. cit.
40. "Alternative Service Work Camps: Summer Operations, 1941", op. cit.
41. Tunstell to Smart, 31 July 1941. Canadian Archives. RG84. vol. 194. RM165-2-4.
42. "Alternative Service Work Camps: Summer Operations, 1941", op. cit.
43. Canada. Department of Mines and Resources. *Annual Reports,* 1940–46.
44. K. Adachi, "A History of Japanese Canadians in British Columbia: 1877–1958", R. Daniels, ed., *Two Monographs on Japanese Canadians* (National Japanese Canadians Citizens Association, 1958), 3.
45. R. Knight and M. Koizumi, *A Man of Our Times* (Vancourver: New Star Books, 1976), 38–57.
46. K. Adachi, *The Enemy that Never Was* (Toronto: McClelland and Stewart, 1976), 182.
47. Canada. House of Commons. *Debates,* 3 February 1942, 280–281; 9 February 1942, 433; 16 February 1942, 560–610; 19 February 1942, 706, 708, 715–717; 29 February 1942, 156–158.
48. B. Broadfoot, *Years of Sorrow, Years of Shame* (Toronto: Paperjacks, 1979), 79–99.
49. P. Elliott, "No Guard Kept on Japanese Building Roads in Mountains", *Edmonton Journal,* 7 April 1942.

50. P. Elliott, "Rich Men, Poor Men in Camps Set up for Coastal Japanese", *Edmonton Journal,* 11 April, 1942.
51. C. M. Walker, "Report: Yellowhead/Blue River Project". Canadian Archives. RG84. vol. 211. EC7-27-2.
52. Mills to Wardle, 8 June, 1942. Canadian Archives. RG84. vol. 211. EC7-27-1.
53. Wood to Gibson, 24 June 1942. RG84. vol. 148. J165.
54. Canada. House of Commons. *Debates,* 29 January 1942, 154.
55. Mills to Wardle, 18 June 1942. Canadian Archives. RG84. vol. 211. EC7-27-1.
56. 10 August 1942 and 13 August 1942; Canadian Archives. RG84. vol. ENG20-3.
57. Knight and Koizumi, op. cit., 122–123.
58. Eastwood to Walker, 10 March 1943. Canadian Archives. RG84. ENG20-3.
59. Gibson to Macnamara, 18 May 1943. Canadian Archives. RG84. vol. 165. U165-7.
60. To Gibson, 20 March 1944. Canadian Archives. RG84. vol. 167. RM165-7.
61. "A Narrative of the Human History of Riding Mountain National Park and Area", Parks Canada, Undated, Wasagaming, 281–288; Teresa Tabulenas, "Whitewater Lake Prisoner of War Camp", unpublished manuscript, Parks Canada, Wasagaming, 1978.

CHAPTER 6

1. Canada. Dominion Provincial Conference on Reconstruction, 1945. "Public Investment", 22.
2. Canada. Dominion Provincial Conference on Reconstruction, 1945, "Proceedings", 81.
3. Canada. Second Dominion Provincial Tourism Conference, 30 September, 1 and 2 October, 1947. "Proceedings", 25.
4. Hal Burton, *Saturday Evening Post,* 8 June 1957, 38.
5. Canada. House of Commons. *Debates,* 4 July 1947, 5145.
6. W. F. Lothian, "The Parks of Yesteryear", *Intercom,* vol. 9, no. 2 (National Parks Branch, 1966), 13–17. Rocky Mountain Archives, M676, Box 3, f.82.
7. Canada. House of Commons. *Debates,* 23 March 1949, 1911.
8. Ibid., 30 July 1956, 6693.
9. Ibid., 9 July 1958, 2064.
10. Ibid., 29 May 1950, 2957.
11. Ibid., 28 April 1959, 3145.
12. W. F. Lothian, *A History of Canada's National Parks,* vol. 4 (Ottawa: Parks Canada, 1981), 96–130.
13. Canada. House of Commons. *Debates,* 1957–58, p. 1396.

14. Ibid., 23 July 1960, 6852.
15. Canadian Archives, RG84. TC60. vol. 2.
16. Glenbow Archives, BE22 A333.
17. Canada. House of Commons. *Debates,* 15 July 1960, 6394–5.
18. Ibid., 23 July 1960, 6859.
19. Ibid., 20 January 1960, 254–5.
20. Ibid., 23 July 1960, 6852.
21. Ibid., 23 July 1960, 6857–8.
22. Ibid., 23 July 1960, 6858.
23. Director to Smart, 13 February 1947. Canadian Archives. RG84, vol. 164, U125-20.
24. Canada, Resources for Tommorrow Conference, 23–28 October 1961, 177.
25. Ibid., vol. 3, 455.
26. Ibid., 177.
27. United States Parks Service, *Parks for America* (1964).
28. Parks Canada Document Centre. SB481 W6 1962.
29. J. Black, "They are Rehoning Teeth in Mining Ways and Means", *Financial Post,* 8 September 1962, 38.
30. Canada. House of Commons. *Debates,* 4 May 1964, 2880.
31. Ibid., 24 July 1964, 5964.
32. National and Provincial Parks Association of Canada, "NPPAC — A Summary of Main Activities and Accomplishments, 1965–73".
33. J. G. Nelson, "The Canadian National Parks: Today and Tomorrow", vols. 1 and 2 (University of Calgary, 1968). The papers of North American interest were also gathered into a single volume. *Canadian Parks in Perspective,* J. G. Nelson, ed., (Montreal: Harvest House, 1969). It remained for some time the major source on Canadian national parks.
34. Op. cit.
35. Canada. House of Commons. *Debates,* 29 May 1950, 2956.
36. Grant Crawford, "National Parks Townsites Study" (National Parks Branch, 1959). Parks Canada Document Centre. (9b) JS 1703 C85 (s)
37. Peter Oberlander, "Urban Development Plan: Banff, Alberta" (Ottawa: National Parks Branch, 1961).
38. Canada. National Parks Branch, Planning Section, "Recommended National Parks Policy Revised by Planning Section", 15 January 1962. Parks Canada Document Centre. SB 481. P6 C16r(f).
39. When previously in power the Liberals had been absorbed by concerns with economic development. However, they had shown some concern for limiting the growth of townsites in the National Parks. Canada. House of Commons. *Debates,* 2 August 1956, 6886.
40. Ibid., 26 June 1963, 1618.
41. "Statement on National Parks Policy by the Honorable Arthur Laing, Minister of Northern Affairs and National Resources", Ottawa, 10

August 1965. Parks Canada Document Centre A #88.

42. Canada. House of Commons. *Debates,* 24 July 1964, 5940.

43. Banff Lake Louise Chamber of Commerce, 1964. Rocky Mountain Archives M132 f.7.

44. Rocky Mountain Archives. M132, f.7.

45. Canada. House of Commons. *Debates,* 15 September 1964, 8021.

46. Ibid., 18 September 1964, 8290.

47. Ibid., 17 November 1964, 11418.

48. Ibid., 1 February 1966, 543.

49. Ibid., 21 January 1966, 109–110.

50. Ibid., 3 March 1966, 2175–6.

51. "National Park Policies", no. 2, December 1967 and no. 3, 1 January 1968. Rocky Mountain Archives. M132, f.7.

52. Canada. House of Commons. *Debates,* 3 March 1966, 2156–60.

53. Alberta. "The Detrimental Effect of the National Parks Policy on the Tourist Industry of Alberta", January, 1966. Rocky Mountain Archives. M132, f.7.

54. Canada. National Parks Branch, "Comments by the Honourable Arthur Laing on the Detrimental Effects of the National Parks Policy on the Tourist Industry of Alberta", Parks Canada Documentation Centre, SB 481, Pb L14.

55. Rocky Mountain Archives, M132, f.7.

56. Canada. House of Commons. *Debates,* 24 September 1968, 430.

57. Ibid., 21 May 1969, 8888.

58. "Banff Park Town", Banff Park Citizens Association, 18 January 1968. Rocky Mountain Archives. M132.f.9.

59. Canada. Parks Canada. "National Parks Policy", 1969. Parks Canada Documentation Centre. CA1 IA71 69N16.

60. Canada. House of Commons Debates. 24 February 1970, 4032.

61. Ibid., 21 March 1970, 527; 12 July 1970, 8047; 20 March 1970, 5396–7; 1 May 1970, 6467; 21 October 1970, 425.

62. Ibid., 6 November 1970, 955–6.

63. Canada. Parks Canada. "The Banff Provisional Administration Board Report to the Minister Responsible for National Parks", September 1976. Parks Canada Documentation Centre. HD1265 B22(5)

64. Canada. Parks Canada. Banff Urban Development Plan. Parks Canada Documentation Centre. (9B) SB 481 D4 P236.

65. Canada. Parks Canada. Program Policy Group. "Parks Canada Policy", February 1978.

66. Canada. Parks Canada. *Parks Canada Policy,* 1979.

67. Parks Canada, "Program Update: Four Mountain Parks Management Planning Program", *Participation,* November 1984.

68. E. J. Hart, *The Brewster Story: From Pack Train to Tour Bus* (Banff: Brewster, 1981).

69. Canada. House of Commons. *Debates,* 14 October 1966, 8710.

70. Ibid., 18 November 1966, 10078.
71. "Proceedings of the Public Hearings: Banff, Jasper, Yoho and Kootenay National Parks". 19 to 26 April 1971. Parks Canada Documentation Centre. SB 481 H4 C16t. vol. 1, 78–82. Presentation by R. Scace.
72. Canada. House of Commons. *Debates,* 31 January 1967, 12508.
73. Ibid., 15 May 1967, 219–220.
74. Ibid., 4 July 1967, 2241.
75. Ibid., 15 January 1971, 2443.
76. Ibid., 10 February 1970, 3430–31.
77. Ibid., 3 March 1970, 4350.
78. Ibid., 11 May 1970, 6788.
79. Development Plan, Village Lake Louise, December 1971. Parks Canada Documentation Centre. SB 481. D4 P13e(s).
80. Bow Valley Naturalists. Rocky Mountain Archives. M186 f.8.
81. Canada. Parks Canada. "Transcripts of the Proceedings of Public Hearngs on the Lake Louise Area of Banff National Park", 9 to 11 March 1972, Calgary. vols. 1, 2 and 3. Parks Canada Documentation Centre. SB481 H4 C16tr (s).
82. "Dear Skier", February 1972. Rocky Mountain Archives. M186. f29.
83. "Transcripts. . . .", 1972, op. cit.
84. Canada. House of Commons Debates. 12 June 1972, 3074–5.
85. J. G. Rouse, "Numerical Analysis of Written Briefs and Oral Testimony for Public Hearings on Lake Louise Proposals", June 1972. Parks Canada Documentation Centre. SB 481. GH4 R79(s).
86. Jean Chrétien, in interview with Leslie Bella, December 1985.
87. Canada. House of Commons. *Debates,* 13 May 1972, 2726.
88. Parks Canada, "Public Hearings Report Mountain Parks and Lake Louise Area", 1974.
89. Parks Canada, "Lake Louise Planning Study: Interim Planning Report", 1979. Parks Canada Documentation Centre. SB481. V5 1b4a(f).
90. Parks Canada, *PARKSCAN,* vol. 1, no. 2, Dec/Jan 1970; vol. 2, no. 5, Oct/Nov 1981; vol. 3, no. 4, Sep/Oct 1982.
91. Parks Canada, "Sunshine Ski Area Expansion Recommendations: Prepared by Western Region", 1976. Parks Canada Documentation Centre. (9B) GV854. D4. P23s(f)
92. National and Provincial Parks Association, "Brief Regarding the Proposed Expansion of Sunshine Village Ski Facilities in Banff National Park", 1976. Parks Canada Documentation Centre. GV854 D4 N21 (f).
93. Details on ownership obtained from Statistics Canada, Intercorporate Ownership, 61–517, 1975 and 1982, and for most recent information a telephone interview with Bruce Wilson, Travel Alberta, conducted by L. L. Lanier, 1985.
94. Marmott in Jasper is the exception, and is controlled by a group of physicians.

95. The National Parks Policy of 1979 and the documents associated with the Four Mountain Parks Planning Program all ignore the presence of downhill ski resorts in the mountain national parks.

CHAPTER 7

1. J. B. McClelland and G. W. Raymond, "The Development and Use of Public Land in the Maritimes", *Canadian Public Land Use in Perspective* (Ottawa: National Research Council, 1973), 69–92.
2. Canada. House of Commons. *Debates,* 8 June 1951, 3865.
3. Ibid., 27 August 1946, 5470.
4. Ibid., 23 March 1949, 1911.
5. D. E. E. Day, "Fundy National Park: Small but Impressive", *Canadian Geographical Journal,* vol. 92 (1977): 28–35.
6. Don Cayo, "The Lloyds and Terra Nova: Power or Protection", *Park News,* vol. 12 (1975): 24–26.
7. Canada. "Terra Nova National Park: Background", 1969. Parks Canada Documentation Centre. QH9J27(f).
8. Canada. House of Commons. *Debates,* 8 July 1961, 7730–31.
9. Ibid., 4 May 1961, 4373.
10. Ibid., 21 April 1961, 3890.
11. Ibid., 22 May 1963, 140.
12. Ibid., 24 July 1963, 2562.
13. Ibid., 8 April 1965, 99; 3 June 1965, 1930; 24 April 1967, 15232.
14. Ibid., 8 April 1965, 99; 7 May 1965, 1035; 16 June 1965, 2491; 16 February 1966, 1309.
15. Ibid., 12 December 1966, 11039.
16. Ibid., 9 June 1967, 1350.
17. Ibid., 19 June 1969, 10442.
18. Op. cit.
19. Cal Holloway, "Conflict at Bonne Bay", *Atlantic Advocate,* vol. 59 (June, 1969), 241–43.
20. Canada. House of Commons. *Debates,* 30 January 1969, 4940.
21. Ibid., 27 February 1969, 6047–8.
22. Ibid., 27 May 1970, 7388–89.
23. Ibid., 12 June 1970, 8051.
24. Canada. Senate. *Debates,* 25 January 1973, 157–8. 11 April 1973, 495–97.
25. Canada. House of Commons. *Debates,* 26 June 1973, 5072.
26. Ibid., 25 May 1977, 5933.
27. Ibid., 4 April 1975, 1152.
28. Rosemary Nation, "Canadian National Parks: A Critical Analysis of the Processes of their Acquisition and Management" (M.A. thesis, Dalhousie University, 1979), 44.
29. Canada. House of Commons. *Debates,* 1 June 1950, 3098; 8 June 1951,

3867; 18 August 1958, 3528; 22 January 1960, 254–5; 23 February 1967, 13426; 9 June 1967, 6754; 9 July 1969, 11012; 23 July 1969, 11524; 17 April 1978, 4553; 16 November 1984, 301; 29 November 1984, 756–7.

30. Ibid., 4 July 1967, 2237–8.
31. Ibid., 22 January 1960, 254–5.
32. Ibid., 25 June 1969, 10661.
33. Ibid., 2 June 1969, 9376.
34. Ibid., 19 June 1969, 10447; 14 April 1983, 24467.
35. Ibid., 21 April 1961, 3895; 25 May 1977, 5934.
36. Ibid., 4 May 1961, 4375; 9 June 1967, 1372; 10 Feburary 1970, 3445; 14 April 1983, 24501.
37. Ibid., 9 July 1963, 2011.
38. Canada. Parks Canada. Parks Planning System Division. "Gros Morne Park Area Development: Subsidiary Agreement: An Interim Evaluation", 1975. Parks Canada Documentation Centre. (5G) SB 481. D4 C16g(f).
39. M. S. Foster and A. S. Harvey, "The Regional Socio-Economic Impact of a National Park: Before and After Kejimkujik" (Institute of Public Affairs, Dalhousie University, Halifax, 1976).
40. Canada. House of Commons. *Debates,* 30 July 1956, 6693; ibid., 1955, p. 6754.
41. NPPAC. *Parks For Tomorrow,* vol. 3, no.1, 1975, 2.
42. Canada. House of Commons. *Debates,* 4 April 1974, 5072.
43. D. E. E. Day, Op. cit.
44. Canada. Parks Canada. "Terra Nova National Park: Background", 1969, Parks Canada Documentation Centre. QH 9J27 (f)
45. Canada. Parks Canada. Parks Planning System Division. "Gros Morne Parks Area Subsidiary Agreement: An Interim Evaluation", 1975. Parks Canada Documentation Centre. (5G) SB 481. D4 C16g(f).
46. Canada. Parks Canada. "Proposed Kouchibouguac National Park: Boundary Adjustments". Parks Canada Documentation Centre, SB481B6 C16p(f)
47. Nation, op. cit, 34, 45. and "Campers Raid in the Park", *Ottawa Citizen,* 22 August 1979.
48. G. D. Boggs, "Observations on Land Exchange Priorities in South-western Nova Scotia", Parks Canada Documentation Centre. SB 481 P76 B63 (f). NPPAC, *Parks for Tomorrow,* vol. 3, no. 1, (1975), 2.
49. Canada. House of Commons. *Debates,* 6 May 1980, 745–6.
50. "Vautour Pleased Supreme Court of Canada to Hear Case", *Moncton Times Transcipt,* 21 September 1985, 21.
51. Canada. House of Commons. *Debates,* 13 April 1961, 3611.
52. Ibid., 5 August 1964, 6415.
53. Ibid., 25 September 1867, 2416.
54. Ibid., 21 May 1969, 8883.

55. Ibid., 21 May 1969, 8902.
56. Ibid., 18 April 1969, 7689.
57. Ibid., 30 May 1969, 9270.
58. Jean Chrétien, *Straight from the Heart* (Toronto: Key Porter, 1985), 69.
59. Canada. Parks Canada. "The National Parks Potential of St. Maurice Area, Quebec", July 1969. Parks Canada Documentation Centre. 6L QH9 C16 (f).
60. Canada. House of Commons. *Debates,* 17 February 1970, 3689.
61. Op. cit.
62. Chrétien, ibid., 69–70.
63. Canada. House of Commons. *Debates,* 10 February 1970, 3457; 13 February 1969, 5508–9.
64. Ibid., 21 May 1969, 8885.
65. Ibid., 17 February 1972, 14.
66. Nation, ibid., 56.
67. Canada. House of Commons. *Debates,* 29 June 1984, 5322–4, 5341, 5345.
68. Canada. Parks Canada. "Reserve de Parc National de L'Archipel de Mingan", May 1984. Parks Canada Documentation Centre. 6M SB481. M2 P23l(f). Canada. House of Commons. *Debates,* 13 March 1984, 2056.
69. Canada. Parks Canada. *Mingan Archipelago: Information Bulletin,* no. 3, no. 4, and no. 5. Parks Canada Documentation Centre. SB481 P7 P23m.
70. Melanie Miller, "The Origins of Pacific Rim National Park", J. G. Nelson and L. D. Cordes, eds., *Pacific Rim: An Ecological Approach to a New Canadian National Park* (University of Calgary, 1972).
71. Robert A. Beatty, "Pacific Rim National Park", *Canadian Geographical Journal,* vol. 92, no. 1 (January/February 1976): 14–21.
72. Canada. House of Commons. *Debates,* 9 June 1967, 1358.
73. Miller, op. cit., 8.
74. Chrétien, op. cit., 68.
75. Miller, op. cit., 11.
76. R. Robinson, "Legal Problems in the Protection of Recreation Values", *UBC Law Review,* vol. 6, (1971): 236.
77. *Victoria Colonist,* 28 February 1970.
78. *Vancouver Sun,* 28 January 1971.
79. *Vancouver Sun,* 23 April 1971.
80. Canada. Parks Canada. Frances Rennie, "An Assessment of the Park Values of the Nitimat Triangle Portion of Pacific Rim National Park", 1982. Parks Canada Documentation Cantre. SB 481 E8 R29(f)
81. Op. cit.
82. Canada. Parks Canada. P. Matrosovs, "Cursory Assessment of the Indian Lands in Pacific Rim National Park", 1973. Parks Canada Documentation Centre. (01)SB481. A8. M42(f)

83. *The Globe and Mail,* 7 July 1987.
84. Canada. House of Commons. *Debates,* 22 July 1960, 6787.
85. Ibid., 26 April 1965, 403–404.
86. *Blue Jay,* Saskatchewan Natural History Society, vol. 39, no. 3 (September 1981): 131.
87. Canada. House of Commons. *Debates,* 11 July 1966, 7465.
88. Ibid., 28 October 1966, 9272.
89. Ibid., 19 June 1969, 10445–6.
90. W. C. Holmes and S. E. Markham, "Outline of Alternatives for the Preservation of Examples of Short Grass Prairie and Associated Unique Natural Features of Southern Saskatchewan". Parks and Recreation Branch. Department of Natural Resources. Saskatchewan, 1973. Markham collection.
91. Canada. House of Commons. *Debates,* 4 April 1974, 1169.
92. J. A. MacMillan, S. Lyon and N. Brown, "Analysis of Socio-Economic Impacts of the Proposed Grasslands National Park". Department of Agricultural Economics. University of Manitoba 1976. Markham collection.
93. Joint Federal Provincial Committee on the Proposed Grasslands National Parks, Proceedings of the Public Hearings on the Proposed Grasslands National Parks, vols. 1, 2, 3, 4 and 5. See also "Report of the Public Hearings Board on the Proposed Grasslands National Park", 9 August 1976. Markham collection.
94. "Grasslands Committee Favours Park Plan if Ranchers get Sympathetic Treatment", *Western Producer,* August 26, 1976.
95. NPPAC, *Parks for Tomorrow,* vol. 4, no. 4, (1976).
96. Joint Federal-Provincial Committee on the Proposed Grasslands National Park, "Supplementary Information on a Proposed Grasslands National Park", April 1976.
97. Jean Chrétien, in interview with Leslie Bella, December 1985.
98. Canada. House of Commons. *Debates,* 14 March 1977, 3933. Ibid., 28 November 1978, 1269.
99. Larry Kusch, "Some Movement seen in Park Plan", *Western Producer,* 9 October 1980.
100. Lorraine Froelich, "Answers Wanted on Status of Grasslands Park", *Western Producer,* 25 September 1980.
101. *Blue Jay,* Saskatchewan Natural History Society, vol. 39, no. 3 (1981): 131.
102. Canada, Parks Canada, "Agreements for the Establishment of a New National Park in the Val Marie–Old Post Rural Municipalities, Province of Saskatchewan", signed by Rt. Hon. John Roberts, 19 June, 1981. Parks Canada Documentation Centre. (8g) FC 3514 G7C15 (f)
103. W. M. Baker, "Extract from Prospects for National Park Development in Parts of the Yukon and Northwest Territories", May 1963. Parks Canada Documentation Centre. QH9 B17e(f).

104. Canada. House of Commons. *Debates,* 4 May 1961, 4388.
105. Ibid., 13 December 1963, 5823–4.
106. Op. cit.
107. Ibid., 19 June 1969, 10446.
108. NPPAC files, Edmonton chapter.
109. *Edmonton Journal,* 21 August 1971, 22; 26 August 1971; 27 August 1971, 8.
110. NPPAC Press Release, 13 November 1971. (NPPAC Files, Edmonton chapter).
111. Scotter, in interview, October 1978; Robin Fraser, President, NPPAC, in interview, 1978.
112. J. B. Theberge, "Kluane National Park: A Perpsective from National and Provincial Parks Association", (NPPAC, circa 1971); "Heritage Saved". NPPAC, circa 1972.
113. W. D. Addison, "Parks or Power in Canada's North", *Toronto Globe and Mail,* 13 January 1972; and "Indecisions on the Nahanni", ibid., 5. N. M. Simmons and George Scotter, "Nahanni: A Magnificent National Park in the North", *Nature Canada,* vol. 1, no. 1 (Jan/March 1972): 21; D. Graham, "Land and Legends of the Nahanni", *Canadian Geographical Journal* (June 1972): 188–195; Paul Grescoe, "The Northern Teasures we Almost Lost", *Canadian Magazine* (25 March 1972).
114. Jean Chrétien, in interview with Leslie Bella, December 1985.
115. Canada. House of Commons. *Debates,* 19 October 1970, 360.
116. John Burns, "Background on the Nahanni Controversy", *The Globe and Mail,* 1 August 1970.
117. Canada. House of Commons. *Debates,* 17 February 1970, 3707.
118. Ibid., 17 February 1972, 3.
119. Canada. Senate. *Debates,* 10 April 1973, 481–4.
120. Canada. House of Commons. *Debates,* 21 October 1971, 8920–21.
121. Ibid., 2 November 1973, 7494.
122. Ibid., 26 November 1973, 8133–4.
123. Ibid., 1 March 1972, 427.
124. Ibid., 17 February 1970, 3718.
125. Canada. Parks Canada, "The National Park on Baffin Island: A Preliminary Management Statement: Report 73-1". January 1973. Parks Canada Documentation Centre. SB481 M2 8A c41 (f)
126. Canada. House of Commons. *Debates,* 4 April 1974, 1152.
127. Op. cit., 1166 and 1150.
128. "Yukon's Burwash Uplands: The Need for Inclusion in Kluane National Park" (NPPAC, 1975).
129. Canada. Parks Canada, "Boundary Considerations Kluane National Park", 1976. Parks Canada Documentation Centre. SB 481. B6 C16k(f).
130. Canada. Parks Canada, "Baffin Island Park", 1973. Parks Canada Documentation Centre. SB481. B3B14 (f).

131. Canada. Parks Canada, "The National Park on Baffin Island: A Preliminary Management Statement: Report 73-1". January 1973. Parks Canada Documentation Centre. SB481 M2 8A C41 (f).

132. Canada. Parks Canada, *Parks Canada Policy,* 1979, 28, s.1.3.3.

133. Canada. Parks Canada, "National Park Selection and Establishment Process: the Involvement of the Government of the Northwest Territories", 1981. Parks Canada Documentation Centre. (50)SB481 N49 P23.

134. Canada. House of Commons. *Debates,* 7 April 1978, 4235.

135. Canada. Parks Canada, "Proposal to Establish a Pingo Park in the Tuktoyaktuk Area of the North West Territories", 1973, SB481. P7 K84 (s).

136. S. C. Zoltai, D. J. Karasiuk and G. W. Scotter, "A Natural Resource Survey of the Horton–Anderson River Area, North West Territories" (Parks Canada, 1979).

137. S. M. Roscoe, "Assessment of Mineral Resource Potential in the Bathhurst Inlet Area, including the Proposed Bathhurst Inlet National Park" (Canadian Geological Survey, 1984) Parks Canada Information Centre. TN177. N6 R71(s).

138. Canada. Parks Canada, "Northern Yukon National Park Boundary Proposal", 1983. Parks Canada Documentation Centre. SB481. B6 R29 (f).

139. Canada. House of Commons. *Debates,* 14 April 1983, 24465.

140. Ibid., 18 October 1979, 380.

141. Ibid., 19 November 1984, 359–60.

142. Ibid., 11 December 1984, 1112.

143. Ibid., 5 March 1985, 2721–2759.

144. Ibid., 1 April 1985, 3580.

145. D. Thomas, "Resist Developers — Parks Group", *Edmonton Journal,* 31 August 1985, E5.

146. Canada. Parks Canada, "Ellesmere Island National Park Reserve Proposal", 15 February 1984.

147. Kevin Cox, "New Park to Reflect Sovereignty: Environmental Groups Cheer McMillan", *The Globe and Mail,* 9 September 1985.

CHAPTER 8

1. For expenditures: Canada, *Public Accounts,* 1911 to 1981. For 1971 and after calculation of Parks Canada expenditures excludes epxenditure on the expanding National Historic Sites program. For park names and areas: *Recreation Canada* vol. 42, no.5 (December 1984): 26–27. Calculations based on the areas of national parks as they existed in 1984. Corrections to 1971 dollars using the consumer price index. F. H. Leacy (ed) *Historical Statistics of Canada,* second edition (Ottawa: Statistics Canada, 1983), K8–18. and Statistics Canada Year End Supple-

ments to Catalogue 62-010, 1981 and 1984. Canadian population statistics from Statistics Canada, *Canada Year Book,* 1911 to 1982.

2. Canada, House of Commons. *Debates,* 14 April 1983, 24465.

3. L. Bella and P. Servos, "Privatization in Recreation and Community Services: Towards Conceptual Clarification", Administrative Sciences Association of Canada, May, 1985.

4. J. Bates, "Resource Use by Local People in National Parks" (unpublished, Parks Canada, 1978), Parks Canada Documentation Centre. SB481 P6 B31.

5. "Subsistence" is used by Bates, and is contained in Parks Canada policy.

6. Ottawa: Minister Environment Canada, "Release: National Parks Master Plan Unveiled", 3 February 1986.

7. R. H. Weigel, "Ideological and Demographic Correlates of Proecology Behaviour", *Journal of Social Psychology* (October 1977): 39–47.

8. L. Bella, "The Liberal Park Renaissance", *Katimavik,* vol. 5, no. 3/4 (1978).

9. H. R. Penniman, *Canada at the Polls: the General Election of 1968* (American Enterprise Institute for Public Policy Research, 1975), 221.

10. See the Canadian Press report by Robert Plaskin in *The Globe and Mail* of 19 November 1986, citing a Decima Research Ltd. of Toronto poll.

11. *Our Parks — Vision for the 21st Century,* Report of the Minister of the Environment's Task Force on Park Establishment (Ottawa: Environment Canada, 1987), 4–5.

Select Bibliography

BOOKS AND MONOGRAPHS

Abella, Irving. *On Strike*. Toronto: James, Lewis and Samuel, 1974.

Adachi, K. *The Enemy that Never Was*. Toronto: McClelland and Stewart, 1976.

Brinly, Gordon. *Away to the Rockies and British Columbia*. Toronto: McClelland and Stewart, 1938.

Broadfoot, B. *Years of Sorrow, Years of Shame* Toronto: Paperjacks, 1979.

Byrne, A. R., *Man and Landscape Change in the Banff National Park Area Before 1914*. Calgary: University of Calgary, 1968.

Chrétien, Jean. *Straight from the Heart*. Toronto: Key Porter, 1985.

Coleman, A. P. *The Canadian Rockies*. Toronto: Frowde, 1911.

Fraser, Esther. *The Canadian Rockies: Early Travels and Explorations*. Edmonton: Hurtig, 1969.

_____. *Wheeler*. Banff: Summerthought, 1978.

Gray, J. A. *The Winter Years*. Toronto: Macmillan,1966.

_____. *The Troublemaker*. Toronto: Macmillan, 1978.

Hart, E. J. *The Brewster Story: from Packtrain to Tour Bus*. Banff: Brewster, 1981.

Horne, M. *The Dirty Thirties*. Toronto: Copp Clark, 1972.

Innis, Harold. *A History of the Canadian Pacific Railroad*. Toronto: University of Toronto Press, 1971.

Ise, John. *Our National Parks Policy: A Critical History*. Baltimore: John Hopkins Press, 1961.

Liversedge, R., *Recollections of the On-to-Ottawa Trek*. Toronto: McClelland and Stewart, 1973.

Lothian, W. F. [Ferg]. *A History of Canada's National Parks*, vols. 1, 2, 3 and 4. Ottawa: Parks Canada, 1976 to 1981.

Luxton, E. G. *Banff: Canada's First National Park*. Banff: Summerthought, 1979.

McCowan, D. *Hill Top Tales*. Toronto: Macmillan, 1948.

Nelson, J. G. and Scace, R. C. eds. *Conference on the "Canadian National Parks: Today and Tomorrow"*. Calgary: University of Calgary, 1968.

Nelson, J. G. and Cordes, L. D. eds. *Pacific Rim: An Ecological Approach to a New Canadian National Park.* Calgary: University of Calgary, 1972.

Pross, A. P. *Pressure Groups Behaviour in Canadian Politics.* Toronto: McGraw Hill Ryerson, 1975.

Scace, R. C. *Banff: A Cultural-Historical Study of Land Use and Management in a National Park Community to 1945.* Calgary: University of Calgary, Department of Geography, 1968.

Wheeler, A. O. *The Selkirk Range.* Ottawa: Government Printing Bureau, 1905.

Williams, M. B. *Through the Heart of the Rockies and Selkirks.* Ottawa: Department of Interior, 1929.

Zieroth, Dale. *Nipika: A Story of Radium Hot Springs.* Ottawa: Canada Supply and Services, 1978.

PERIODICALS

Alberta Historical Review.
Blue Jay, (Saskatchewan Natural Historical Society).
Canadian Geographical Journal.
National Parks, (National Parks and Conservation Association, Washington).
Nature Canada.
Park News (National and Provincial Parks Association, Victoria, BC)
Recreation Canada (Canadian Parks and Recreation Association, Ottawa)

ARCHIVAL SOURCES

Canadian Archives, Ottawa. Files included in RG84.

Glenbow Archives, Calgary. Files including AP359; D920 M123A; BL652.

Parks Canada Documentation Centre, Ottawa.

Rocky Mountain Archives, Peter Whyte Foundation, Banff, Alberta. Files including the Robert Brett papers; M305; M467; M335; M70; M705 and M113.

University of Alberta Special Collections, Edmonton. Pearce Papers.

Personal collections of Irene Spry, Susan Markham, Elly Dejongh, Lou Lanier and the author.

UNPUBLISHED THESES

Mitchener, E. A. "William Pearce and Federal Government Activity in Western Canada, 1882–1904" (Ph.D. diss., University of Alberta, 1971).

Nation, Rosemary. "Canadian National Parks: A Critical Analysis of the Processes of their Acquisition and Management" (M.A. thesis, Dalhousie University, 1979).

Stotyn, K. A. "The Bow River Irrigation Project, 1906–1950" (M.A. thesis, University of Alberta, 1982).

Vankirk, Sylvia. "The Development of National Park Policy in Canada's Mountain National Parks 1885–1930" (M.A. thesis, University of Alberta, 1969).

Published Government Documents

International Union for Conservation of Nature and Natural Resources. *United Nations List of National Parks and Equivalent Reserves,* Switzerland, 1975.

Canada. *Labour Gazette.*

Canada. Department of the Interior. *Annual Reports.*

Canada. House of Commons. *Debates,* 1880–1986.

Canada. Commission on Conservation. *Annual Reports,* 1910–1918.

Canada. Dominion Provincial Conference on Reconstruction, 1945.

Canada. *Resources for the Tomorrow Conference: Proceedings.* 1961.

Index

The Author

Leslie Bella was born in the United Kingdom and came to Canada at the age of twenty. Her first degree was in Architectural Studies from the University of Newcastle-upon-Tyne and was followed by a masters degree in Social Work at the University of British Columbia. In Vancouver she learned about social planning and community development. This was in the mid-sixties when university campuses were in an uproar and she learned more from practice than from her classes. Practice included broad service as a community worker in Winnipeg and Edmonton. Search for part-time teaching to combine with motherhood led to her being "appointed by accident" at the University of Alberta in Edmonton. ("They found my interdisciplinary background helpful".) The university supported her efforts to obtain a Ph.D. in Political Science and she remained there teaching Recreation and Leisure Studies for twelve years. In 1986 she was appointed dean of Social Work at the University of Regina.

Leslie Bella has become well known for her many research papers and journal articles, prizes and awards, and for an original and outspoken approach to her field, including her imaginative interpretation of the relation of voluntary organizations to government departments and ministries. The scope of her involvement in community life extends far beyond academic concerns. She was a member of the Edmonton Social Planning Council from 1972 to 1974, its chairman in 1973–74, and president of the Urban Reform Group of Edmonton from 1974–76. Active politics have claimed her attention as well. She stood for election to the Alberta Assembly as a New Democratic candidate in 1982 and served a term as president of her constituency association in 1983–84. Her interests in community welfare and the arts are reflected in her service as a board member of the Edmonton United Way, 1976–79, as president of the Philharmonic Society, 1983–85, and as vice-president of the Catalyst Theatre Society, 1984–85.

Leslie Bella is married to outdoor educator Lewis L. Lanier. She has one daughter, Mary. Together they enjoy many of Canada's national parks.